Introduction

The English Coordination Group has been set up with the aim of producing specialised revision material for National Curriculum English. This book provides concise coverage of the Key Stage Three programme of Study for English up to Level 7 with particular emphasis on essential Grammar, Spelling and Punctuation.

Our Guides have *three features* which set them apart from the rest:

Careful and Concise Explanations and Rules

We work hard to give accurate, concise and carefully written details on each topic. This guide places particular emphasis on learning Thirty Rules to improve Grammar, Spelling and Punctuation — areas where students frequently lose valuable marks.

Deliberate Use of Humour

We consider the humour to be an essential part of our Revision Guides. It's there to keep the reader interested and entertained, and we are certain that it greatly assists their learning. We don't expect to win any awards for it though...

Key Skills for Critical Reading and Writing

This guide introduces the key skills and techniques of reading and writing for fiction and non-fiction texts. These techniques include comprehension, critical reading, essay writing and personal writing skills. We also give practical advice on reading and writing about different styles of text — focusing on language, tone and bias.

Contents

Essential English

Section One — **How To Improve Your Marks**

Learning the Rules 1
Standard English 2
Jargon and Abbreviations 3
Using a Dictionary and a Thesaurus 4

Section Two — **Speaking and Listening**

What It All Means 5
Formal and Informal Speaking 6
Holding a Conversation 7
Having a Discussion 8
Having a Debate 9
Giving a Talk 10
Listening and Asking Questions 11
Playing a Role 12
Revision Summary for Section Two 13

Section Three — **Grammar and Punctuation**

Making Grammar Easy 14
Being able to; Shall/Will; Should/Would 17
Nouns and Pronouns 18
Describing 20
Comparing 21
Joining Words and Relationship Words 22
Mistakes with 'of', 'from' and 'to' 23
Avoiding Common Spelling Mistakes 24
More Spelling Tips 25
A Mark-Saving Page 26
Punctuation 27
Apostrophes 28
Using Quotation Marks 29
Brackets, Hyphens and Dashes 30
Negatives 31
Sentences and Word Order 32
Paragraphs 34
Revision Summary for Section Three 35

Reading Skills

Section Four — **Comprehension**

Reading for a Reason 36
Scanning and Close Reading 37
Making a Summary 38
How To Take Notes 39
Putting Comprehension Skills Together 40
Answering the Question 41
Revision Summary for Section Four 42
Revision Example for Section Four 43

Section Five — **Reading Literary Texts**

Looking at Literature 44
Looking at Style 45
Language and Meaning 46
Imagery 48
More Imagery 49
Understanding the Text 50
Where, When, How and Why 51
Extra Exam Hints 52
Revision Summary for Section Five 54
Revision Example for Section Five 55

Section Six — **Reading Non-Fiction**

Non-Fiction and Media Texts 56
Looking At Non-Fiction 57
Fiction vs Fact 58
The Media 59
Magazines 60
Adverts 61
Posters and Leaflets 62
Autobiographies, Diaries, Letters 63
Film and TV 64
Texts in the Exam 65
Revision Summary for Section Six 66
Revision Example for Section Six 67

Writing Skills

Section Seven — Essay Writing Skills

How to Write an Essay 68
Essay Style 69
Planning and Drafting 70
Introducing Your Argument 71
Your Argument 72
Examples and Quotation 73
Concluding Your Essay 74
Writing about Narrative 75
Writing about Plays 76
Writing about Poems 77
Writing Exam Essays 78
Revision Summary for Section Seven 79

Section Eight — Personal Writing Skills

Personal Writing 80
Persuasive Language 81
Writing about Experiences 82
Descriptive Writing 83
Writing Dialogue 85
Writing Stories 86
Writing Responses to Texts 88
Writing Reviews 89
Writing Reports 90
Writing Letters 91
Presenting Your Work 92
Revision Summary for Section Eight 93

Examples and Reference

Section Nine — Texts From Other Cultures

Talking About Culture 94
Cultural Context 95
Multicultural Societies 96
Revision Summary for Section Nine 97

Section Ten — Practical Examples

Looking at a Novel Extract 98
Looking at a Drama Extract 100
Looking at a Non-Fiction Extract 102
Worked Example of a Poem 104

Index 105
Commonly Misspelled Words 108

Published by Coordination Group Publications
Typesetting, layout and illustrations by The English Coordination Group
Original illustrations by: Sandy Gardner, e-mail: Zimkit@aol.com

Written and Edited by Gemma Hallam BA (Hons) and Simon Cook BA (Hons)
Illustration Editor: James Paul Wallis BEng (Hons)

Clipart Sources: CorelDRAW

Printed by Hindson Print, Newcastle upon Tyne.

Learning the Rules

This book is about how to pick up *good marks* in your Key Stage Three Exams. This first Section will tell you what you can do to *improve* your work — and *improve your marks* too.

You Need Two Skills to Improve Your Marks

1) Make sure you *don't make mistakes* in your *grammar*, *spelling* or *punctuation*.
2) Practise writing *clearly* and *accurately*, so that anyone reading your work will *understand* exactly what you mean.

You Can Do Well Even if You Find English Boring

1) The *secret* is learning the key skills of studying English. Skills are like *shortcuts* — when you know about them, they can make your life *much easier*.
2) Make sure you *read texts properly* — that means reading *carefully* for the *important points*.
3) These skills can be used with *any books* you read — all you need to do is *practise*.
4) Start by practising with *books you like*. Remember, if you like a book then you should show that you like it when you write about it. Look at Section Four, P.36, on comprehension skills.
5) In your English lessons, you may have to read and write about books you *don't like*. Don't worry — if you've practised enough, then this won't matter. You'll have the *skills* to find out the information you need and to *write* about it in an *interesting* way.

REMEMBER: even if you think a book is boring, you can still write about it in an interesting way. Learn the rules for essay writing in Section Seven, P.68.

Practise Writing Clear, Simple Personal Essays

1) Personal essays always seem much *easier* than writing about literature. Make sure you still *take the time* to do it *properly*.
2) You need to learn the different essay styles which the Examiners ask for. Look at Sections 7 and 8 to find out more.
3) *Read the question* carefully to work out what it's asking you to do.
4) If you are asked to give an *opinion* on a topic, then give a balanced argument. Give both sides of the case and then explain why you would choose one side over the other.
5) If you have to write about personal experience, make sure you write about your *feelings* as well as *what happened*. Try to make the story *come to life* for the reader. Look at P.82-87.
6) Don't forget to *vary your vocabulary* with some lively descriptive words.
7) Try using more *interesting sentence structures* to make your work *exciting* to read.

No time to lose — start improving your marks now...

There's really *no time* to lose. If you want to do well in English, then you need to start *learning* and *practising* the main skills now. Each Section in this book covers a *key area* of your course, so you must *work through* each one.

Standard English

Standard English is the *formal English* that you need to use when you speak or write in formal situations or in the *Exam*. A lot of people confuse this with "speaking posh" — but it's *not* the same thing. You really need to know *how to use it* if you want to do well.

Standard English is just Formal English

1) *Standard English* is the form of English you learn in *school*.
2) All *written English* should be standard — that means it should be clear enough for *anyone in Britain* to *understand* it.

The Four Main Features of Standard English

1) All *written English* should be standard English — any *grammar rules* you learn are for standard English, and you definitely need to *learn* them to avoid mistakes in your work.
2) Standard English means using the *correct forms* of words with the *correct spellings*.
3) When you do your *Speaking tasks*, you must use the forms of standard English grammar.
4) Your *accent* and your *pronunciation* don't have anything to do with standard English — the secret is avoiding any dialect words or phrases.

How to Use Standard English

1) Avoid *slang* words — words that your teachers or parents wouldn't understand. You'll *lose marks* if the Examiners can't understand what you say or write.
2) Don't use *dialect words*. Every region has words or phrases that are used *only* there. If you use them in your Exam, you won't be understood.
3) Revise grammar and punctuation in Section Three, and learn the list of commonly misspelled words on P.103. There's *no time to lose*, remember.

Don't Use Clichés — They're Boring

1) Clichés are *ideas or sayings* which have been used so often that they've become *boring* and unoriginal.
2) *Phrases* like, "as good as it gets"; "at the end of the day"; "in the fullness of time," are all *clichés*. So are *images* like, "as fierce as a lion"; "as cunning as a fox"; "as red as a beetroot."
3) These were all original once, but they've been *used so often* that they don't mean much any more.
4) If you use them, you will sound *boring and unimaginative* — so avoid clichés.
5) It's best to use your own *imagination*.

Clichés are boring — at the end of the day...

Some people say if you don't speak standard English, then you don't speak properly — but that's wrong. The important thing is to speak clearly. Spend some time revising *grammar*, *spelling* and *punctuation* — especially if you find them tough.

Jargon and Abbreviations

These are two more things which people make a *mess* of. Learn when to *use* them and when to *avoid* them — it could make a *big difference*.

Jargon is Technical Language — Try to Avoid it

The aforementioned plaintiff, hitherto pursuant of the claim...

1) Jargon means language used by any group of people that *can't* be understood *unless* you're part of the group.
2) Most jargon is *meaningless* to a lot of people.
3) Doctors, Lawyers, Teachers and even Poets and Actors all use their own forms of jargon — special technical words and phrases that help them to do their jobs.
4) *Sports* and *hobbies* also have jargon words — *football* has words like "*offside*," or "*indirect free kick*" which don't mean anything unless you know about football.
5) *Never use jargon* in your speaking or written work — if you give a talk, make sure that any *technical* words for a hobby or a sport are *explained* so that everyone *understands*.
6) Don't use *literary jargon* in essays unless you know *exactly* what the words mean — and you can *explain* them. Otherwise, what you're actually writing won't be what you mean. There's always a simple way to say things — make your written work clear to understand.

Abbreviations are Short Forms of Words

1) Abbreviations make writing *easier*. They are *short forms* of words and only have a *few letters*.
2) Abbreviations *don't need full stops* in between the letters — just *leave space* around them.

Common Abbreviations You Should Learn

Take a letter Charlie: "Dear Mr Wye, meeting Fri am, yours etc, PS Bring wellies."

Right away Ms Burns!

zzZZZ

eg	for example
etc	and the rest / and so on (*not* ect)
ie	that is (clarifying a point)
NB	note well
PS	for adding a note to the end of a letter

Mr	is the short form of Mister
Ms	is used to address *any woman* instead of Miss or Mrs

am	comes from the Latin ante meridian	before noon (ie the morning)
pm	comes from the Latin post meridian	after noon (ie the afternoon)
BC	means Before Christ	
AD	comes from the Latin anno domini	in the year of Our Lord (eg AD 2004)

Remember the Three Rules for Abbreviations

1) *Don't use* eg, ie or etc in *formal written work* like essays. Only use them in letters or notes.
2) Don't *confuse* eg and ie; *eg* is used to give an example — *ie* is used to *explain* something.
3) Never write ect instead of etc — it's a *careless* mistake which looks sloppy.

Don't abbreviate in essays — you'll be caught short...

Three short rules for *abbreviations* to learn — and don't forget to *avoid jargon* in your work too.

Using a Dictionary and a Thesaurus

Using a Dictionary

1) Words are listed in a dictionary in *alphabetical order*.
2) The *pronunciation* of the word in Received Pronunciation is given in the International Phonetic Alphabet. There will be a *key* to this alphabet in the front of the dictionary.

headword (the word you're looking up) in **bold**

pronunoiation in International Phonetic Alphabet

shows the word is an *adjective* (see P.18)

abbreviation for '*colloquial*' shows this usage is from *informal* spoken English

happy /'hapi/ *adj.* (happier, happiest) **1** feeling or showing pleasure or contentment. **2a** fortunate. **2b** (of words, behaviour etc.) fitting, pleasing. **3** *colloq.* slightly drunk. **4** *(in comb) colloq.* inclined to use excessively or at random (*trigger-happy*).
• *happy as a sandboy* see SANDBOY •**happily** *adv.* **happiness** *n.* [Middle English, from HAP + Y]

shows the *adverb* derived from the word (see P.18)

cross reference to another word

shows *where* the word comes from

Using a Thesaurus

1) A thesaurus is a special dictionary of *synonyms* (words which mean the same thing, see P.46)
2) Some thesauruses list words in *alphabetical order*, like a dictionary.
3) Others (like Roget's Thesaurus) classify words into *subject groups*. There is an alphabetical *index* at the back to help you find them.

synonyms are listed in alphabetical order

happy 1. blessed, blissful, blithe, cheerful, cock-a-hoop, content, contented, delighted, ecstatic, elated, floating on air, glad, gratified, jolly, joyful, jubilant, merry, on cloud nine *(informal)*, overjoyed, over the moon *(informal)*, pleased, rapt, sunny, thrilled, walking on air *(informal)*
2. advantageous, appropriate, apt, auspicious, befitting, convenient, enviable, favourable, felicitous, fortunate, lucky, opportune, promising, propitious, satisfactory, seasonable, successful, timely, well timed.
Antonyms depressed, despondent, discontented, displeased, down in the dumps *(informal)*, forlorn, gloomy, inapt, joyless, low, melancholy, miserable, mournful, sad, sombre, unfortunate, unhappy, unlucky.

Call no man happy till he dies, he is at best fortunate
Solon

These are synonyms for happy in the sense of *fortunate* or *fitting*, as sense 2 in the dictionary above.

These are *antonyms*, or words that mean the opposite of happy

Here is a *quotation* about happiness

What It All Means

Speaking and *Listening* are about expressing yourself clearly and showing you can *respond* to other people's ideas. That can only come with *practice*.

We Speak and Listen all the time

1) In your Key Stage Three tests, you're assessed on how you *speak* and *listen* in English.
2) This sounds *odd*, because it's something that you do all the time.
3) Obviously you can speak and listen to English *pretty well*. Even if it's *not* the language you speak at home, you hear it around you *all the time*.
4) You've actually been using the skills in this Section all your life.
5) The trick here is to get *better* at something you already do. You need to look at this Section *page by page* and *learn it*. Think about how you speak and listen in class.

Standard English is basic Formal Language

1) Everyone in Britain speaks *different versions* of English — sometimes with *accents* and sometimes with different *local words* that are difficult to understand.
2) Accents are cool — they're part of people's *characters* — but it's also important that everyone around the country can *communicate clearly*, whatever accent they have.
3) *Standard English* is just the formal English we use that *avoids* any local dialect words and helps people all over the country to understand each other when they speak.

Braw bricht moonlicht nicht tonicht

4) Remember — this *doesn't* mean standard English is better than other dialects. The main thing is that you use it *clearly* when you speak in class and in your Speaking tasks.

The Key Skills You Must Practise

La la la, I can't hear you!

1) Most people *speak too much* and *fail to communicate* important information. Their skills never improve because they don't *listen* to other people properly.
2) The first key skill is learning to *listen* to people — what they're *saying* to you and also what they *don't say*.
3) You need to listen to other people, to the TV or to adverts *critically* — ask yourself *why* people say certain things and *how* you should react.
4) The other key skill is *expressing yourself clearly*. That means working out the *most important* piece of information and telling other people so that they can *understand* it.
5) Talk *clearly* and *plainly* — long and fancy words are *useless* if no one understands what you're saying.
6) Take the time to *practise* your Listening and Speaking skills — then you'll find it easier to put your ideas across clearly.
7) That will help you to sound *relaxed*, and *avoid* nervousness.
8) Practising these skills will also help your *written work* too.

...overmuch verbiage can impediment understanding...

I listen all the time — except when I'm speaking...

Hmm... It looks like a lot to learn — and some people really hate speaking in public. Don't worry, though. If you're *organised* and you know *what to expect*, then you can face your Speaking tasks with a lot of confidence. The secret is being *prepared*, and *practising* as often as you can.

Formal and Informal Speaking

It's very important to be able to *change* the way you speak to suit different situations.

Three Things affect the Way we Speak

The way we speak to each other varies according to:

1) Who we're speaking to.
2) What we're saying.
3) Why we're saying it.

On closer inspection you are incorrect!

Sir, I insist that you alter your opinion!

The way you speak to your *headteacher* is *different* from the way you'd talk to one of your *mates* — that's obvious.

When you're talking to your best friend, you would use a different style of speech to *invite* him to a party, *apologise* for breaking his favourite CD, *argue* with him about football or *cheer him up* after the tragic death of his faithful pet ferret.

Speak Formally in Formal Situations

It's important to be able to recognise *formal* situations and adapt yourself by speaking in a more formal way.

1) This is because it's *polite*.
2) If the way you speak doesn't go with what you're saying, you'll end up sounding *silly*.

Formal Speaking Needs Standard English

Using standard English means following some simple rules.

1) *Avoid* saying *"OK"* or *"like"* or *"innit"* at the *end* of *every* sentence — they sound careless.
2) Don't raise the *tone* of your voice at the end of every sentence — it sounds like you're asking a question even when you're not, which is confusing.
3) Don't use *slang* words that some people might not understand. Slang words you use with your friends aren't always clear — so think before you speak.
4) Don't use *clichés* — corny phrases that people use all the time, without thinking. They will make you boring to listen to: for example, "at the end of the day"; "I'll take that on board".
5) Make sure you don't make any *grammatical mistakes* — spend some time going over the Grammar Section of this book (see P.16 onwards):

REMEMBER — Think what you're saying: "I *was* sitting..." NOT "I *were* sitting..."

6) *Avoid* using *double negatives* in a sentence — eg "I don't never want to go back." Remember, *two negatives* make a *positive*. So if you say "don't" *and* "never" together, the negatives cancel each other out, and the sentence means that you *do* want to go back.

Speak properly — like what I does, innit...

Time to think about whether *your English* is clear enough for the Speaking test. That *doesn't mean* changing the way you speak. It just means checking your *grammar*, and making sure that other people can *understand* you. Try *recording* your own voice and listening to yourself speak — it sounds horrible but it really will help you to speak more clearly.

Holding a Conversation

Conversations are the *best way* to practise the skills of *listening*, *understanding* and *responding* that will help you earn *top marks* in your Speaking tests. Make sure you revise all this carefully.

Learn to be a Good Listener

1) *Concentrate* on what the other person is saying. This means you won't miss anything and you'll make them feel more relaxed.
2) You should look them *in the eye* and seem *interested* in what they're saying — be an encouraging and sympathetic listener.
3) Listen for the speaker's *tone* — see if you can pick up their *mood*.
4) Look at their body language — do they look relaxed, tired or worried?

Make sure you Understand

Therefore... Hence...
On the other hand...
z z z z

1) If you're unsure of a point they've made, *ask* them to *repeat* it more clearly or *rephrase* it yourself, say it *back* to them and ask whether that was what they *meant*.
2) Asking *questions* to find out *more* shows that you've been listening. (See P.11 on questions)
3) *Don't interrupt* people in mid-flow; it's just plain rude. Let them *finish* before you have your say — never cut them off.

And in Response — Just be Clear and Polite

1) Respond to what the other person *actually said* and not just what you *thought* they said. Listen *carefully* and *think* before you speak.
2) Always respond *constructively* — talk about any *good things* that the other person said.
3) If you want to *criticise*, then be critical about their *opinion*. Explain *why* you think their argument is wrong. *Never* attack people personally — you'll *lose marks* in a practical task.
4) If you *criticise* then you have to be sure that *your own views* make sense. Never criticise people if they are talking about subjects you don't understand. Ask them to *explain*.

Everyone knows the moon's made of cheese, it's obvious

5) *Don't be vague* — back up anything you say with *examples*. Try to be interesting and organised in what you say. And most of all, *stick to the point*.
6) *Never generalise* — comments like "Everyone knows" or "It's obvious" *don't help* your case if you don't give evidence. Generalising makes people sound *arrogant* — so don't do it.

You talk — I'll just listen...

There's quite a lot for you to remember on this page, so look at each point carefully. Think about it — the best way to practise your speaking skills is *conversation*. Be careful, though — it's not just *talking*, but *listening* as well. In theory, if you do all these things all the time, then you'll never find yourself in a row with anybody. It'd be nice if life was so simple...

Having a Discussion

Discussions are *more formal* than conversations— but they still have to be *constructive*.

Plan the Discussion Before You Begin

1) Usually you'll be *given a topic* to discuss in class or in small groups. If the group has to choose its own topic then suggest something that will *interest everybody*, and about which there's *a lot to say*.
2) *Prepare* a few ideas for *questions* (see P.11) to get the discussion going.
3) You may need to choose a *leader* or a *secretary* to control who speaks when and to let everybody have their say.
4) If you *are chosen* then you'll have to *lead* the discussion. If you aren't, then don't worry, you will get a chance to speak.

How to Lead a Discussion

1) The leader's job is to *develop* the views of the group — not to force everyone to accept their point of view.
2) Keep the discussion *to the point*. Don't let people *sidetrack* the group into talking about irrelevant subjects.
3) *Ask questions* — it makes people think and *provokes* ideas. *Don't* ask *yes or no* questions and *avoid* asking specific individuals. It's better to ask the *whole group*.
4) Sometimes *a few members* of the group will *dominate* — they'll want to speak all the time. Let them have their say but make sure that the *other group members* have a *chance* too.
5) If some people *aren't contributing*, then *invite* them to say something — but *don't make* them take part — some people just *don't want* to. Your job is to give them the *opportunity*.
6) If there's an *awkward silence* then you can *summarise* the arguments made so far. Feel free to *contribute* your *own* thoughts but remember, you *mustn't* talk all the time.

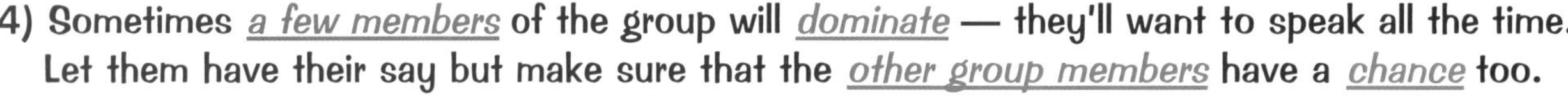

Taking Part in a Discussion — Stick to the Point

1) Be *polite* — if you *disagree* with someone, be *friendly* and give your *reasons*.
2) *Agreeing* with other people's points is an good way of moving the discussion on.
3) When you agree with someone, try to *develop* their argument further — think of reasons why their point is *valid*.
4) Give *examples* from your own *experience*, or from your *reading*, that might interest others — a story can be a *tactful* way of presenting a *sensitive point*.
5) Remember that some people are *easily offended* and discussions can become *emotional* — think *before* you speak.
6) Listen to what *other people* have to say.

Be sharp — stick to the point...

The secret of leading a discussion is *staying aware* of *what's going on*. You've got to keep the discussion going, keep it *to the point* and make sure everyone has a *chance to speak*.

Having a Debate

A debate is a *formal* discussion with firm *rules* — learn how the rules work and then you won't be caught out if you have to debate a topic.

How a Debate Works

The subject to be debated is called the *motion* — it always takes a specific form:

This House believes/demands/condemns etc + whatever the topic is

1) The Chairperson *controls* the debate. They can't take sides.
2) The Chairperson *reads out* the motion, then takes an *initial vote* from the audience and *writes down* the result. The *Proposer* is then asked to speak. The diagram shows how it works.
3) During the debate the Chairperson controls *who speaks when* and keeps the audience *quiet* by calling for *order*. The Chairperson is the *final authority* while the debate is going on.
4) *All speakers* must begin their speeches with 'Mr. Chairman' or 'Madam Chairwoman'.

THE CHAIRPERSON opens the debate

FOR

THE PROPOSER gives a speech in favour of the motion — keeping to the point and giving good reasons

THEN

AGAINST

THE OPPOSER argues against the motion — concisely and clearly, giving reasons

THE PROPOSITION SECONDER argues for the motion, supporting the proposer and arguing against the opposer

THE OPPOSITION SECONDER argues against the motion, supporting the opposer

Letting the Audience have Their Say

1) The Chairperson then lets people in the audience have their say. This is called "*Opening the Debate to the Floor*". If you want to speak, you have to put up your hand and wait until the Chairperson tells you that you may speak.
2) All speakers should address the *Chairperson* before they speak.
3) After a *few minutes* of Floor debate, the Chairperson should ask the *Opposer* to *sum up* the case *against* the motion briefly. The *Proposer* should then *sum up* quickly too.
4) The Chairperson takes a *final vote* from the audience — people can vote *for* the motion, *against* it or *abstain* (don't know).
5) If the vote is *tied* then the Chairperson has a *casting vote* — deciding who wins.

Defending Your Corner

1) *Research* your case and work with the other person on your team.
2) *Prepare* your speech in the same way that you would prepare a *talk*.
3) Use *two or three* strong arguments with your best point for a *conclusion*.
4) You're *allowed* to be *one-sided* — but use *facts* to support your ideas.
5) Try to prove your opponents are *wrong* — but *without* being rude.
6) Be ready to *answer* any criticisms they make about your arguments.

Gilbert defended his corner rather too well

This house believes that debates are a bit odd...

Debates follow some *tricky procedures* — they can seem confusing until you actually try it out. See if you can organise a debate in class.

Giving a Talk

Giving a talk is a frightening business — but you still need to learn the *key skills* to help you speak in public and speak confidently in class.

Choose a Topic You Know About

1) Don't talk about topics that you *don't understand* and *can't explain* properly — choose something you *know about*.
2) Then comes the really tricky part; you need to make it *interesting* for your listeners. The secret of this is *planning*.

Planning a Talk — the entertaining kind

1) *Don't* write out every single word you're going to say — your talk will just be boring. Make a *simple plan* that helps to relax you.
2) You must grab your *audience's attention* right from the start — tell a *brief story*, give a relevant *statistic* or use a *visual aid* to illustrate the *main point* of your talk. It must be really striking.
3) Once you have their attention, you have to *keep* it. Make sure people *follow* what you say.
4) After your opening, you'll need to *introduce* your topic, *explain* what you are going to tell them and then *present* your information in a clear and logical form.
5) Finish on a high note — *sum up* your talk and end with a story, a joke or even an appeal to people's consciences.

It's as easy as 1-2-3

1) Tell the audience what you're going to say.
2) Say it.
3) Tell them what you've said.

The Real Thing — Don't Panic

1) When you give your talk remember to *stay calm*.
2) Be *enthusiastic* and make *eye contact* with your audience.
3) Talk to *everybody* in the room, not just your teacher and not just your friends.
4) Don't be afraid to *ask* the audience if they can all *hear*.
5) Stick to the point, and after any *long sentences* pause to check everyone has understood.
6) If people laugh or make a noise, wait for them to *quieten down*.
7) *Stress* any significant words and try to *vary* your tone — loud or soft, fast and slow — this will make you sound more interesting.
8) *Try not* to er and um — just take your time and speak slowly.
9) Don't fidget about, and *don't look* at your notes the whole time.
10) Even if something goes *wrong*, just keep on going. If you lose your place then just say so — take a deep breath and start again.
11) If you make a *mistake*, you can *still* get great marks if you *react well* and *keep talking*.

Get rid of the rough edges — be a smooth talker...

Speaking in public can be terrifying — especially if you get *nervous*. Don't panic, try *speaking out loud* by yourself — this will help you get used to *hearing* your own voice. The real secret is *preparation*, but remember, *don't* just read from your notes.

Listening and Asking Questions

If you can show your teacher that you *listen intelligently in class*, you'll pick up a *top grade*.

Listening in Class and in Speaking Tasks

1) If you're listening to a talk, or to your teacher, *take notes* — it'll help you to *stay awake* if it's boring. Listen out for *important stuff*, and make a note of things you *don't* understand.
2) If you're taking part in a *discussion*, listen carefully to what *everyone* says.
3) Don't just decide what *you* want to say and *wait* until you get a chance to say it.
4) If there's a point you want to make, but *someone else* is speaking, jot down a *quick note* to help you to *remember* it.
5) If you're *interviewing* someone for one of your Speaking tasks, prepare a list of *questions* first.
6) Listen to what they say, and if they start to talk about something *really interesting* that you *didn't expect* to hear, then *adapt* your questions and ask them about that *instead*.

Just a few questions...

A Careful Question is Better than a Speech

Are you sure you actually read the book?

1) A good question is an effective way of *showing* that you've been *listening*, and that you have *understood* what the speaker is saying.
2) The secret is to *contribute* to the discussion or conversation in a *constructive* and *clear* way.
3) Don't ask questions to make other people look stupid. No one likes a smart alec — and you'll *lose marks* for distracting the class.

How to ask a Good Question

1) If you *don't listen*, you could end up asking a really stupid question that has already been answered. Listen to *other people's* questions.
2) When you get the chance, ask about the things you *didn't understand*. Make sure the speaker *explains* things clearly so that the discussion can move on.
3) *Never interrupt* — wait until whoever is speaking has *finished*. If the discussion has a *chairperson*, then wait until they let you speak. Remember to be *polite*.
4) *A constructive question* is one that *develops* the discussion — a question with a yes or no answer is *not* a good one. Ask for people's *opinions*.
5) *Avoid* being negative — if you *disagree* with the speaker then *explain why* clearly.
6) If you are going to be *critical* then try to do it as *positively* as possible.

Who was King Duncan?
He's in Macbeth
I wonder who King Duncan is...

Don't forget: Never insult people personally, even if you think their views are wrong. It'll *lose you marks* — and people will start *criticising you*.

Questions annoy me — they're always asking for it...

If you're going to talk in class, you may as well *pick up marks* for it. That's why you need to practise asking *constructive questions*. Remember to listen to other people's questions.

Playing a Role

Apart from ordinary *acting*, any *discussion* or *debate* can also involve role-playing. The secret of all three skills is *persuading* other people to *believe* you.

Role-Play is about Persuading People to Believe You

I'm not drunk,
I've just eaten
a lot of potatoes

1) *Role-playing* is about making people *believe you* — especially if you're *acting* on-stage. You must be *believable*.
2) If Macbeth turns to the audience and says "Did you see the football last night?" in the middle of Shakespeare's play, we *stop believing* that he is Macbeth straight away.
3) Role-playing is also about *arguing a point* — in a *debate* a speaker can *play a role* to exaggerate an opinion. This *involves* the audience and can also be very *funny*
4) Best of all, role-plays help you to *get inside* other people's *characters* — to pretend to be someone else. All literature is about getting inside *other people's heads* and finding out what they *think about* and what *they're like*. Role-playing helps you develop this skill.

Use Your Imagination

1) Playing a role means using your *imagination* to express the *emotions* and *reactions* of others.
2) Picture the *character* — the setting, their clothes, personal details, emotions and attitudes — until you can imagine how they *speak* and *behave*.
3) *Respond* to other people *in character* — that means *reacting* in the way that the *character would react* : eg if you're playing a nervous person, you might faint at the slightest noise.

ROLE-PLAYING **could come up as one of your Speaking Tasks, and it'll definitely improve your speaking skills. It'll also help you to write better about drama — you can act out scenes from plays and work out how they might appear on-stage.**

Get into Character

1) Your *body language* must fit your character.
2) Your *voice* and your *expressions* should reflect the *feelings* of the character.
3) If you have a *script*, it will give *stage directions* which tell you where to move and how to react.
4) If you're *improvising* then *make them up* as you go along.
5) *Respond* to the actions of any *other characters* in the role-play, so that your behaviour seems *natural*.

No, lads, I said "let's get into our roles"

Don't call us — we'll call you

1) Whether you're giving a *talk*, leading a *discussion* or playing the *French Herald* in Shakespeare's *Henry V*, you are *playing a role* and you must *focus* on it.
2) Ask for *feedback* — there's always room for *improvement*, and helpful *criticism* is essential.
3) Don't just think about your role — think about the *other characters* in the role-play and think about how the whole thing would *look* and *sound* to an audience or an assessor.

Do you like English — or are you just acting that way...

Role-play isn't just for actors — you can use it in *all* of your Speaking tasks. Sometimes it's easier to speak in public if you *pretend* to be someone else — so *learn* this page.

Revision Summary for Section Two

At Key Stage Three, you'll be assessed on speaking tasks that you do in class. Some of these will be related to the Shakespeare plays that you've been studying. Speaking in front of the class can be terrifying, but it needn't be if you're prepared for it. Go through all of these questions to make sure that you've learned the key points in this section. Don't miss any out, and don't look back for the answers until you've had a go at them all.

1) What is Standard English?
2) What are the two key skills to practise if you want to do well in Speaking Tasks?
3) What three things affect the way we speak?
4) How can you show someone that you're listening to them?
5) If you're chosen to lead a discussion, does that mean you get to do most of the talking?
6) What should you do if people don't want to join in the discussion?
7) What does the chairperson do in a debate?
8) What happens after the proposer has given their speech?
9) What do we mean by 'opening the debate to the floor'?
10) What's the 1-2-3 method of planning a talk?
11) Should you read from your notes when you give a talk?
12) What should you do if people start making a noise while you're speaking?
13) What should you do if it goes horribly wrong and you can't remember what you were saying?
14) What should you do when listening to someone else's talk?
15) What two things will this help you to do?
16) In a discussion, what should you do if you've thought of a great point that really needs to be said, but someone else is speaking?
17) Why shouldn't you try to prove how clever you are by asking questions that make someone else look stupid?
18) What is a constructive question?
19) Why is roleplaying useful in all your Speaking tasks?
20) Why is roleplaying useful when you're writing about drama?

Making Grammar Easy

Let's face it, grammar is boring. Unfortunately, every year students just like you end up *losing loads of marks* because they *can't spell* and because they make *silly grammatical mistakes*.

This Section is about Picking up the Easy Marks

1) We *already know* most of the rules of grammar *instinctively* — we use them whenever we speak or write, but perhaps no-one has ever *explained* them in grammatical terms.
2) Grammar is just the *group of rules* that help us to use words correctly in a language.
3) You only need to know the *key rules* of grammar and punctuation to help you avoid *mistakes* that could *lose you marks* in your work.
4) It'll help you write more *precisely*, more *clearly* and more *accurately* — and that will win you extra marks. You will also start to recognise the ways in which authors use language for effect.

The key to grammar is making sure you know how different words work — what their function is in a sentence and how you choose the right form to use.

The Verb is used to describe an Action

1) The *verb* tells us *what* is happening and *when*. It is the *'DOING'* word of a sentence.
2) Verbs *change* their *form* and are sometimes formed using the auxiliary verbs 'to have', 'to be', 'will' and 'shall', according to *when* the action is taking place. These changed verb forms are called *tenses*.

eg			
	I *go* to town	The action is happening now	= *present* tense
	I *went* to town	The action has already happened	= *past* tense
	I *shall go* to town	The action hasn't happened yet	= *future* tense

3) There are *several* different ways of saying that something happened in the *past*. 'I have eaten' suggests that the action is in the *recent past*. 'I have been eating' suggests that the action is in the *recent past* and was *not finished*. 'I ate' says that the action was in the *past* and was *finished*.

Read through and then scribble your own *copy* of this *timeline of tenses*:

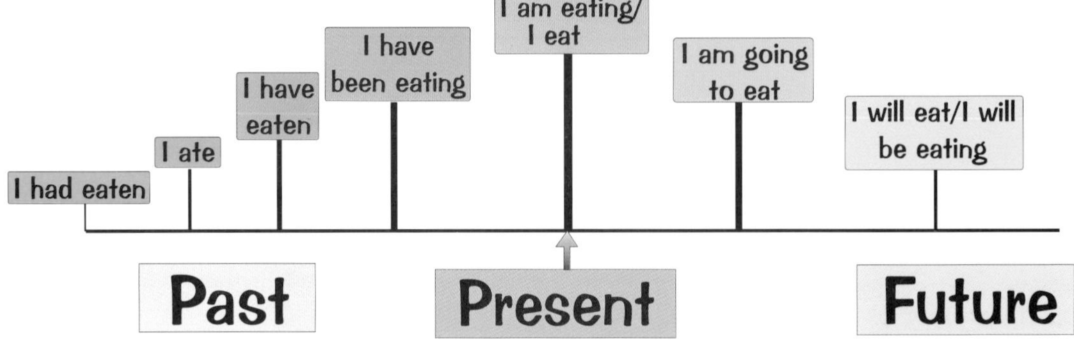

I remember what my Grammar used to tell me...

These two pages have the basics on *verb forms*. Make sure you read through it all *carefully*, though. Get the mistakes ironed out *now*, and you won't have to worry about them *later*.

To Be (or not To Be)

The verb *to be* is the most important verb in English and it's really very easy to use, as long as you avoid making a few *obvious mistakes*.

Learn the Simple Present and Past forms of 'to be'

You use this verb all the time, so if you're *writing* these forms wrongly you must be *saying* them wrongly. Make sure you know the basic forms.

Present:	Past:
I am	I was
You are	You were
He/She/It is	He/She/It was
We are	We were
You are	You were
They are	They were

I, You, He/She/It = singular

We, You, They = plural

NB: The word *'you'* has a singular and a plural form — it can mean one person or a whole group.

When to use Were and when to use Was

People often say *'I were'* instead of *'I was'*, or *'we was'* instead of *'we were'*. These forms are wrong. If you use them in an *essay* or an *Exam* you'll automatically *lose marks*. The rule is simple:

RULE 1: You must use were with all plural forms and always with you — singular and plural. Only I, he, she and it take was.

Don't confuse were with we're; were is part of the verb to be, but we're is the short form of we are (see P.28).

A Terrible Mistake — 'Been' and 'Being'

These are two words that *sound* very similar and can easily be *confused*. Fortunately there's a very practical way of *telling them apart:*

RULE 2: you can only use been with have, has or had in front of it. Being must have another part of the verb to be — is, am, are, was, or were.

eg
I had *been* to the shops — the action happened in the *past* and was *completed*.
I have *been* unwell — the action was in the *recent past* and may still be going on.
I am *being* followed — the action *is happening* right now.
I was *being* chased — the action *was still going on* at the moment described.

Don't forget — '*been*' and '*being*' are used to help form some tenses of other verbs:

eg
I have *been* eating dog food.
Heathcliff had *been* gone for years.
She has *been* seeing him since September.
They had *been* going to the same hotel for over thirty-five years.
He is *being* watched.

Mistakes with the Verb 'Have'

The verb '*to be*' and the verb '*to have*' are auxiliary verbs — this means they *combine* with other verbs to form different tenses (eg I was shopping, he has crashed). You must avoid *any mistakes*.

A Multi-talented Verb — 'to have'

1) The verb '*to have*' is used to mean *owning* something, as well as to form several *tenses*.
2) The *present* tense of 'to have' (have, has) is added to a verb to form a *past* tense where the action was quite *recent* — I *have bought* a new jacket (see P.15).
3) The *past* tense of 'to have' (had) is added to a verb to talk about action that happened before the action taking place in the past. I *had* eaten.

You must say 'I did' or 'I have done' — never 'I done'

1) There are two confusing ways to talk about actions you completed in the *past*:

You can use *'I did'* or *'I have done'*

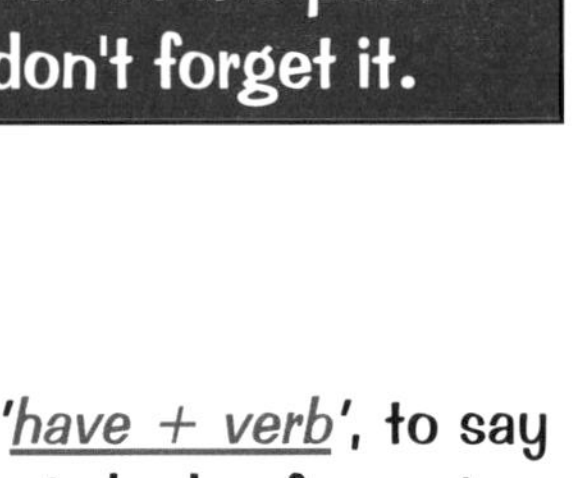

'*I did*' emphasises that the action was a *single* past event.
'*I have done*' suggests that the action was more *recent* in the past.

2) Don't confuse the two — you'll lose lots of *valuable marks*:

Some people say 'I done' — this is wrong

3) Remember — '*done*' isn't a verb form on its own: it's only *part* of a verb. Learn the forms.

I did	Or	I have done
You did		You have done
He/She/It did		He/She/It has done
We did		We have done
You (plural) did		You (plural) have done
We did		They have done

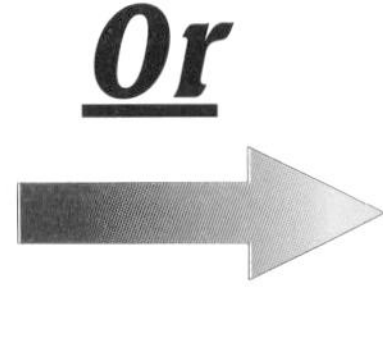

Remember that *He*, *She* and *It* use *has* instead of *have*.

4) To avoid this mistake, make sure you learn the *simple rule*:

RULE 3: Either 'has', 'have' or 'had' must always go before 'done' in the past tenses. There are NO EXCEPTIONS to this rule, so learn it and don't forget it.

eg She *did* the only thing she could. Katy *has done* her best.

The Short Form of Could Have is Could've

1) The words *could*, *should*, *would*, and *might* are used with the verb form '*have + verb*', to say that something might have been possible in the past — each has a different shade of meaning:

eg I could *have escaped* to Florida if the police hadn't arrested me in Stoke Newington.

Parts of Verb

2) Many people say '*could of*' instead of '*could have*'. This is totally wrong. The '*have*' is part of the verb form that follows (eg have escaped) — it *doesn't* go with the verb '*could*'.
3) The proper way to shorten *could have* is '*could've*' — but you should never use it in *formal* written English, only for writing *dialogue*. It sounds like could of but isn't — remember:

RULE 4: Could've is short for could have because have is part of the verb that follows — the same goes for might've, would've and should've.

4) The word '*of*' is not part of a verb, so never use it that way — see P.23.
5) For the *differences* between could, should, would, might etc, see next page.

Being able to; Shall/Will; Should/Would

Can, may, might, shall, will, could, would and should can be rather confusing so study this page carefully.

Can means 'being capable of doing'

1) The word can is used in the present tense to mean being able to do something.
   eg When I leave school I *can* travel.
2) It also means a physical ability: eg I *can* touch my toes. In Mexico the beans *can* jump.
3) The opposite of can is cannot, which has the short form can't. In your essays you must only use 'cannot'. I've used short forms in this book because I'm writing informally.

Could — the past tense and for polite questions

1) In the past tense, can becomes could — although could is also used when asking other people questions:
   eg *Could* you pass me the salt please?
2) To talk about something that was possible in the past, use 'could + have done' (see P.16).
3) The opposite of could is could not, or couldn't:
   eg He *couldn't* finish his lunch yesterday.

May is used for Possibility and to ask Permission

1) The word may is used for asking permission: eg *May* I leave the room, please?
2) May is also used to say something is possible — but only if it is likely to happen:
   eg I *may* be going to see Craig 'Rock God' Gibbons at the weekend.

Might is used for Unlikely Possibilities

Might is used with possibilities, but only when something is unlikely to happen:
eg Next year I *might* be discovered and asked to be the new member of the Stones.

Shall and Will are Used to Form the Future Tense

1) Shall and will are auxiliary verbs. Both are used with a verb to talk about events in the future.
2) If you want to stress a point, you can use will:
   eg I *will* go sailing.
3) Strictly, it's more correct to use shall with 'I' and 'we' and will with 'you', 'he' 'she' 'it' and 'they'. If you want to stress a point, use will with 'I' and shall with 'you', 'he', 'she', 'it' and 'they'. This is a bit confusing, and you won't lose marks if you forget to do it.

Should and Would are Past Tense Forms

1) Should is the past tense form of 'shall', and is used when something is necessary(a duty) or when something is very likely: eg You *should* apologise. They *should* be home soon.
2) Would is the past tense of the verb 'will'. It is used in the past tense to talk about something in the future: eg He said he *would* go. = past of 'he says he *will* go.'
   It is also used to show willingness: eg I *would* like to come. *Would* you like a drink?
   It can also show a habit: eg He always *would* complain about the weather.
3) Don't confuse would and should — remember the rule:

RULE 5: only use should when it's necessary or likely; would has lots of uses.

Nouns and Pronouns

You need to go over nouns and pronouns so that you can avoid the *big mistakes*. This *'subject'* and *'object'* business sounds confusing but if you take the time to *learn* it, it'll make things a whole lot easier.

Nouns are for Naming People and Things

1) Any word that names an *animal, person, place* or *thing* is a *noun*.

2) Words that name *kinds* of things, places or people are called *common nouns*:
eg cat, evening, woman, tree, bus.

3) The names of *people*, *organisations* or particular *places* are called *proper nouns* — remember to write them with a *capital letter*:
eg William Shakespeare, the Fire Brigade, Cumbria.

4) *Collective* nouns name a *group* or a *collection* of things or people:
eg herd(of cows), pride(of lions), team (of players)

5) *Nouns* can be used in *two ways.*

The SUBJECT of a sentence is the person or thing that does or is something
The OBJECT of a sentence is the person or thing that has something done to it

eg The *Sheriff* arrested *Juan*

SHERIFF
I was looking after it for a friend, honest.

SUBJECT

The *sheriff* is *doing something* — he's making the arrest.
He is the *subject*.

OBJECT

Juan is having something *done to him* — he's being arrested.
He is the *object*.

Pronouns Replace Nouns to Avoid Repetition

1) Pronouns are words like *he*, *she* or *it*, used to avoid repeating the noun over and over. This is because it sounds clumsy to *repeat* the noun, especially a long word or a proper name, for example:

Juan robbed the bank. *Juan* hid the money in the desert. The Sheriff came to look for *Juan*.

Juan robbed the bank. *He* hid the money in the desert. The Sheriff came to look for *him*.

Juan had spent most of the money on pies...

2) In the second sentence, the noun Juan is the *subject* so it can be replaced by the pronoun *he*.
3) In the third sentence, the noun Juan is the *object* so it can be replaced by the pronoun *him*.

Pronouns

People sometimes find pronouns difficult, but if you *learn* this page carefully, you'll be fine.

Use the Right Pronouns

1) You need to use the *right sort* of pronoun to replace the noun, or your sentence won't *make sense*.
2) You really need to *learn* the difference between *subject* and *object* — look back at the last page if you're not sure. Here is a list of some *basic pronoun forms* — don't get them confused:

SUBJECT		OBJECT	SUBJECT		OBJECT	SUBJECT		OBJECT
I	—	me	she	—	her	we	—	us
you	—	you	he	—	him	they	—	them
			it	—	it			

RULE 6: when the noun is a subject, use a subject pronoun; when it's an object, use an object pronoun. When nouns stand for things, they take it or they.

eg *They* talked to *us* more than *we* talked to *them*. *She* likes *him* and *he* likes *her*.

When to use You and I and when to use You and Me

1) This is one people always get muddled up — but it's very *easy* if you know your *pronoun table*.

Use 'you and I' when both words are the subject of the sentence.
eg *You and I* need to have a word.
Use 'you and me' when both words are the object of the sentence.
eg Dave came to look for *you and me*.

2) Many people say 'Dave came to look for you and I', which is *incorrect*. Learn the rule:

RULE 7: when you have a choice between you and I and you and me, write the sentence out twice — once using only the word I and once using only the word me. Only one form will make sense — I must always be a subject.

3) After all *prepositions* (see P.22) you must always use *'me'*:

eg *Between* you and *me*, he's going to leave his job.
The cat leapt *past me*.
He hadn't given his address *to* her or *me*.
You can come to the cinema *with* Paul and *me* if you like.

Fluffy had been eating catnip again

4) You've got to follow rule 7 for *all* pronouns that have *different* subject and object *forms* (her, us, them etc): eg *The lead singer and he* are alike. Shameer is friends with *you and her*.

Describing

Adjectives and *adverbs* are just *descriptive* words — adjectives describe nouns, while adverbs describe verbs and adjectives.

Use Adjectives to Describe Nouns

Adjectives *describe* nouns or pronouns. They give you more information about the noun, and help to make a piece of writing *clearer* and more vivid — eg 'There was a large, grey horse', is a much clearer image than just saying 'There was a horse'.

I like to stand out from the crowd

Where to put your adjective...

1) Most adjectives come *before* the noun they describe.
2) When an adjective is used with the verb '*to be*', it doesn't go next to the noun.
3) There are set phrases where adjectives *follow* the noun instead.

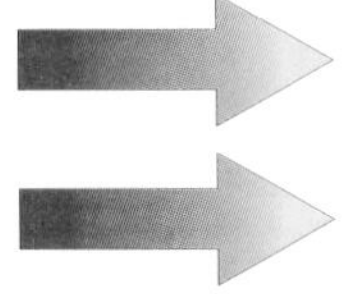

Lucy has a *second-hand* car.
The *vicious* dragon attacked them.
This box is too *small*.
That officer has been *brutal*.
court *martial*,
Mission: *Impossible*, etc.

Adverbs Describe Verbs and Adjectives

1) Adverbs describe *how* an action was performed:
   eg They danced *energetically*. (NOT 'energetic')

He ate *quickly*. (NOT 'quick')

IMPORTANT NOTE — YOU MUST REMEMBER THIS:
To describe *how* something is *done* you need an *adverb*, *not* an *adjective*.

2) They also describe *adjectives* — eg *happily* married.
3) Most adverbs *end* in the letters *-ly*.
   Be careful; some *adjectives* also end in -ly:
   eg lovely, lively, smelly, friendly.

And the penguin said, "not on your nelly!"

A ***truly witty*** man can always tell a ***jolly*** story, without being ***really rude*** to anyone.

In this example, truly and really are *adverbs* — they're describing *adjectives*. Jolly is an *adjective* — it's describing a *noun*. Also, notice how really and jolly have *two 'l's* and truly only has *one*. Remember to learn the spellings of 'ly' words if you aren't sure.

Comparing

Comparisons — using more and most or -er and -est

Sometimes people run into problems when they try to *compare* things. Don't worry, it's actually quite *simple* if you *learn* these rules.

There are Three ways to Compare Things

1) When you want to *compare things*, use *more* + adjective/adverb + *than*.

   eg He is *more charming than* his friend. She danced *more energetically* with Paul *than* with you.

2) you can add *-er* + *than* to the end of *short* words.

   eg Robert is a lot *taller* than Andrew. This question is *harder* than the last one.

Remember that you should use 'er' with short words with only *one syllable*. Watch out for irregular forms — see the table below. The word *than* is used to introduce the *second* thing you are comparing. Sometimes it is *left out* — this is because it is taken as understood already. *Don't* do this in your written work.

eg My car is now a lot *flatter*.

Her fish seems much *happier*.

Make sure you learn the *rule* for comparatives:

RULE 8: Never use more and -er together when you compare things. Use -er with shorter words and some special cases. Otherwise use more + adjective/adverb. Always use than to introduce the second thing you are comparing.

3) When you want to say something is the *best*, or highest quality, use *most* in front of the adjective, or *-est* at the end of the *short* adjective — these are called *superlative forms*:

   eg It is the *biggest* bird in the World.
   Of all the volunteers, he is the *most willing* to help.

   The *superlative* form doesn't use *'than'*. It's only used to compare *three* or *more* things.

Time to make sure that you're clear on those *comparatives* and *superlatives* — learn the table.

Table of Comparatives and Superlatives

	Comparative adj./adv.	Superlative adj./adv.
good (adjective) well (adverb)	better	best
bad (adjective) badly (adverb)	worse	worst
much (adj./adv.)	more	most
few* (adjective)	less	least

* Fewer and fewest also exist. The adverbial equivalent of few is little.

Joining Words and Relationship Words

These are really important little words — they are *linking* words, and their job is to *connect* the different parts of a sentence. If you can use these *properly*, then you'll be able to write more *complex sentences*, and that means *more marks* in the Exam. Get *learning*.

Conjunctions are the basic joining words

1) These are words like *and* or *but* which join words or phrases in a sentence. They are used to form *longer* sentences:

   eg The army tried to advance, *but* after a few yards the horses and cannon became stuck in the mud.

2) Common conjunctions are:

   and, but, although, as soon as, because, either, or, that, though, which, who, etc.

As soon as I perfect my formula, the world is mine!

Never begin a sentence with the words and or but

This is something that will *lose* you *easy marks* in your Exam work — so avoid this mistake.

1) *Never* begin a sentence with *and* or *but* — just don't do it.

This is *easy* if you *think* about it: a conjunction joins two words or clauses, but there's *nothing* to join a word with at the *beginning* of a sentence — so you *can't possibly* use and or but.

2) Sometimes you may read sentences beginning with *because* or *although* with a main clause following them — these sentences are used for *emphasis*, but *don't* do it in *your* written work. You will *lose marks* if you do.

a) Here the order of the *main* clause and the *dependent* clause have been *changed* for emphasis:

Although he is a Martian, he doesn't like space travel.

is an *emphatic* version of 

He doesn't like space travel although he is a Martian.

MAIN CLAUSE — DEPENDENT CLAUSE

Because I am a Martian, I am green.

is an *emphatic* version of 

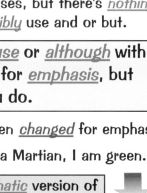

I am green because I am a Martian.

MAIN CLAUSE — DEPENDENT CLAUSE

b) It's called the *dependent* clause because it *depends* on the *main* clause.

RULE 9: never use but, and or because to begin a sentence in written work.

Prepositions — Words that show Relationships

1) Prepositions are words that show the *relation* of a noun or pronoun to another word. This means that they show *where* things are in relation to each other:

   eg *on, at, near, with, onto, to, of.*

Lucy wasn't near anything

2) Be careful. People often put prepositions in the wrong place. Have a good look at the next page and learn how to avoid the most *common mistakes*.

3) *Don't forget* — if a preposition is followed by a *pronoun*, it has to be an *object* pronoun (P.19).

Mistakes with 'of', 'from' and 'to'

Three common little *mistakes* to avoid here — make sure you *learn* how to spot the *traps*.

Two tricky little words — don't confuse of/off

1) *Off* gives the idea of being *away* from something — going away, coming away or being taken away from something, eg a price can have twenty percent *off*.
2) It's also used in some *specific phrases*: eg Come *off* it! The plane took *off*. The milk was *off*.
3) *Of* is a *linking* word in a sentence — a *preposition* — meaning various things, including possession, origin, cause and about:
   eg A friend *of* mine. The works *of* Shakespeare. He died *of* shame. Let's talk *of* other things.

REMEMBER: off is about being away and has two 'ff's — 'of' is a preposition. Think what you are trying to say before you use either one in a sentence.

You must use 'different from' — don't use 'different to'

1) Many people use *'different than'* or *'different to'* in their written work. This is *wrong*. The only correct form is *'different from'*.
2) This makes sense if you learn the rule:

   Different means *'not the same'* — meaning *separate* from the thing described.

   eg Jane is very *different from* Rochester. Holden thinks he is *different from* other teenagers.
3) *'Different to'* is wrong because *'to'* means *'going towards'* — which is the complete opposite of the idea of *'separation from'*. *Think* about it.
4) *'Different than'* is an *American* form, and that means it is *wrong* to use it in your written work.

Two/to/too — they Don't Mean the Same thing

1) These three words are easily *confused* because they all *sound the same* — be very careful.
2) *Two* is a *number* — just think of the word *twice*:
   eg There were *two* ravens.
3) *Too* means *also* — remember to add *'o'* for also:
   eg I ate *too* much.
4) *To* is a *preposition* meaning *towards*, or part of a *verb*:
   eg I went *to* town. You went *to* eat.

These two are getting to me, they're too much

RULE 10: to means to-wards or is part of a verb; too adds an 'o' to mean 'also'; two is a number — so think twice.

'To Try To' — a Phrase to Remember

1) The verb *'to try'* is used with the *infinitive form* of other verbs: eg to do, to eat, to see.
2) Don't ever write *'to try and'*. This is completely *wrong* and will *lose marks*. You must *always* use the form *'to try to'*: eg She decided *to try to* become a star.

A Short Note on Separation

Separation is a word that people often *spell incorrectly* — eg seperation. In fact it's very *easy* to ensure you get it right *every* time, if you learn the rule:

RULE 11: Separation means apart, so spell it with par.

Avoiding Common Spelling Mistakes

You'll really *lose marks* for *bad spelling* in the Exam — so learn these simple rules.

The Top Two Spelling Rules for the letter 'e'

1) Use *'i'* before *'e'* except after *'c'* — but just when it rhymes with *'bee'*.

When you try to spell a word with an *'e'*, say it in your head and think about whether the *'ie'* part sounds like *'bee'*. This is the easy way to make *sure* you *spell* these words *correctly*.

eg

believe ➡	the 'ie' sounds like bee
thief ➡	the 'ie' sounds like bee
achieve ➡	the 'ie' sounds like bee

but:

leisure ➡	'ei' doesn't sound like bee
weight ➡	'ei' doesn't sound like bee
receive ➡	use 'ei' because of the 'c'

There are a few key *exceptions* to this rule:
Weird, *weir* and *seize* sound like bee *but* use 'ei'.
Science has an 'ie' that *does* follow a 'c'.
People's *names don't* follow the rules: eg Keith.

IMPORTANT NOTE: remember to learn the correct spellings for 'neither' and 'either', because they can be pronounced in two different ways (to rhyme with bee or to rhyme with eye).

Another useful rule for the letter 'e' is when it comes at the end of a word:

2) Chop off the 'e' at the end of a word when you add *-ing*, except when there's a double '-e' where you just add -ing.

eg dance ➡ dancing wake ➡ waking *but* flee ➡ fleeing see ➡ seeing

Changing the forms of words ending in '-y'

1) Lots of words end in 'y', whether *nouns* like 'day', *verbs* like 'hurry' or *adjectives* like 'happy'.
2) There are *two rules* for changing the forms of these words:

RULE 12: If the letter before the -y is a vowel — a, e, i, o, u — the -y remains.
eg buy ➡ buyer key ➡ keys day ➡ days obey ➡ obeys

RULE 13: If the letter before the -y is a consonant, the -y is replaced by an -i.
eg hurry ➡ hurries easy ➡ easier daisy ➡ daisies happy ➡ happiest

Don't forget — these examples are all sorts of *different* word forms. The word *'daisy'* is a *noun*; *'happy'* is an *adjective*; *'hurries'* is a *verb*. The *only* thing you need to learn here is the *spelling rule* — when to *change* the -y at the end of a word to an -i, and when to *leave* it alone.

Let's take a break — it's time for a recap

Lots of *rules* to remember here — time to go over a few of the key points. Start by looking at *verb forms*, especially when they involve the *auxiliary verbs* 'to be' and 'to have'. You must always remember to use *'could have'*, never 'could of'.

The tricky part about *nouns* and *pronouns* is knowing the *difference* between *subjects* and *objects*. Look through PP.18-19 again if you're not sure. Think carefully when you're using *adjectives* — don't forget your *comparatives*. *Prepositions* are pretty easy to use, the problems come when you get simple words muddled up.

Phew! I know it looks like a lot, but you'll be fine if you know the *key rules*. Go over the first half of this Section now, and write down all the rules. Then spend some time learning them.

More Spelling Tips

A *varied* vocabulary will definitely improve your Essay-writing, but you need to *spell* words *correctly* if you want to pick up the marks.

Watch out for these Four Silly Spelling Mistakes

1) Words that have a 'y' in the middle, especially 'rhythm' and 'rhyme'.
2) Words with a silent 'h' — you don't say it, but you must write it: eg chemistry.
3) Words written with 'ph' and pronounced with an 'f': eg graph or philosophy.
4) Words that end with '-ly 'or '-ally'. Never end any word with '-ley' except when it is a place name: eg Headingley.

Words that Sound the Same but have Several Spellings

These word often get *muddled up* in written work. Make sure that you use them *correctly*.

1) affect/effect

1) *Affect* is a *verb* meaning to act on or *influence* something
2) *Effect* is a *noun* — it is the *result* of an action
3) *Effect* can also be used as a *verb* meaning to *achieve*

eg Global warming is *affecting* Earth's climate. (= influencing/acting on) The *effect* of global warming is climate change. (= result)

He *effected* his escape through a secret tunnel. (= achieved) His escape didn't *affect* me. (= influence/act on)

2) practise/practice

1) *Practise* is a *verb* meaning to make a *habit* of, to *work* at something or to work in a profession:
   eg He tries to *practise* what he preaches. I *practise* the piano daily. She *practises* medicine.
2) *Practice* is a *noun* meaning the *effort* of improving a skill, the usual *way* something is done or the *business* of a professional:
   eg I enjoy football *practice*. The *practice* of polygamy is rare nowadays.
   Practice makes perfect. Dr Killer only has a small medical *practice* now.

3) where/were/wear

1) *Where* is used to talk about *place* and *position*: eg *Where* is the Frenchman?
2) *Were* is a *past tense* form of the verb *'to be'* (see P.16): eg They *were* hidden behind a statue.
3) *Wear* is a *verb* used with clothes, hair, jewellery etc: eg He *wears* armour of burnished gold.

4) there/their/they're

1) *There* is used for *place* and *position* — remember *where* and *there* go together.
2) *Their* shows *possession* — that something *belongs* to them.
3) *They're* is the short form for *'they are'* — look at the page on *apostrophes* (see P.28).
   eg I went there to meet *their* friends. *They're* very charming people.

5) stationary/stationery

1) *Stationary* with an *'a'* means motionless or *still*. Remember; stationary means cars and vans.
2) *Stationery* with an *'e'* means *office equipment*. Learn this; stationery means pens and pencils.

A Mark-Saving Page

Here are some common words that people often get *mixed up* — so learn the simple rules.

Don't use Them when you mean Those

1) Sometimes people try to use the word *'them'* as an *adjective*: eg Let me see *them* books.
2) This is *wrong*; them is the *object pronoun* from the word *they* (see P.19): eg I met *them*.
3) The word *those* must be used instead: eg Let me see *those* books.

RULE 14: never use them together with a noun — you must always use those.

Who is for People and Which is for Animals and Things

Who and *which* are *pronouns* used to *join* two phrases together — they are very *easy* to use.

RULE 15: who is used to talk about people; which is used for animals or things.

eg King Lear had two daughters *who* lied to him. Androcles met a lion *which* did not kill him.

Remember — the pronoun who changes to *whom* with *prepositions*:

eg He was the man about *whom* she wrote her poems.
To *whom* am I speaking?

As and Like follow a Strict, Simple Rule

RULE 16: like is always followed by a noun or a pronoun on its own; as is followed by a noun with a verb.

eg Othello did *as* Iago told him. He sings *like* an angel. She looks *like* him.

1) *Don't forget* — you *can't* use like in place of as: Othello did *like* Iago told him = *WRONG*.
2) Some people say *'like'* at the *end* of a sentence: eg He seemed a bit confused, like.
3) This sounds odd in *formal* English and you should *never* write it — you'll definitely *lose marks*.

When to use Lend and when to use Borrow

1) These words are easily *confused*, but in fact they are *opposites* in meaning.
2) *Lend* means to *give* something out for a while; *borrow* means to *take* something for a time.
3) Learn the simple *rule*:

RULE 17: you lend something to a person or borrow it from them.

eg John has *lent* me his new Ferrari. She has *borrowed* my shotgun for her wedding.

The difference between Teach and Learn

RULE 18: the verb to teach means giving out knowledge; learning means taking knowledge in. Don't muddle the two.

Between is always followed by 'and'

1) People often try to write 'between him *or* her'. This is *wrong*.
2) Make sure you *always* use *'and'* with between:

   eg She must choose between Leo *and* Matt.

3) *Remember* that *between* always takes *object* pronouns (see P.19 and P.22):

   eg between *you* and *me*, between *you* and *her*.

Punctuation

Punctuation is the collection of *symbols* used to *break up* groups of words. If you don't know how to use them *properly* your writing will be difficult to understand and you'll *lose marks* in the Exam. *Learn it all*.

Ending a Sentence — the Full Stop

1) Full stops mark a definite *pause* at the *end* of a sentence.
2) A *sentence* is a group of words that makes sense on its own — it usually contains a *subject* and a *verb*.
3) A sentence asking a *direct question* is closed with a *question mark*: eg Where are you going?
4) If the sentence tells you *about* a question but *doesn't* ask it, then it is an *indirect question* and has a *full stop*: eg The reader asked the rider where he was going.
5) *Exclamation marks* are used to *emphasise* sentences — to show a strong *reaction* or to give an *order*: eg I don't believe it! Stop!

RULE 19: don't use too many exclamation marks — they are only for special cases of emphasis. Never use more than one at a time.

A Comma separates clauses, and items in a list

1) Commas are used to *separate* words or groups of words so that the *meaning* is made *clear*:
   eg In the valley below, the villages appeared very small.
   Without a comma, the sentence would say, 'the valley below the villages' — a *different* meaning.
2) In very *long* sentences they come *before* the joining word *'and'* or *'but'*.
3) They are also used to *separate* items in a *list* — the *last two* items *don't* have a comma but must be joined by the words *'and'* or *'or'*:
   eg I ordered soup, cheese, chips and fruit.
4) They can be used to separate *additional* phrases or words added to a sentence to give *extra information* or effect, but which aren't *essential*:
   eg I fell in love with Juliet, who is alas a Capulet, at the party last night.
5) Be careful that your sentences don't trail on for *too long*. It's important to know when a clause would look better as a new sentence.
6) A comma *isn't* just where you would stop for breath when reading the sentence *out loud*.

This is gonna be a long sentence.

Colons divide sentences and introduce lists

1) Colons are used to *divide* two clauses in a sentence when *both* clauses would make sense as sentences *on their own*.
   eg 'It took me an hour to drive to work this morning: the road was flooded.'
   but 'I was late, as I said, because of the floods.'
   'The road was flooded' makes sense as a sentence in its own right.
   'As I said' *doesn't* make sense as a sentence on its own.

2) Colons are used to *divide* sentences in two when the second half *explains* the first half:
   eg The ballroom had become very empty: most of the guests had left.
   It allows the writer to *illustrate* or *explain* a point — to say the same thing and make it *clearer*.
3) Colons can also be used to *introduce* a list.

RULE 20: use commas to join two clauses in a sentence. If the two clauses would make sense as separate sentences you must use a colon.

Apostrophes

Apostrophes always seem to cause massive problems — *learn these rules* to stay out of trouble.

Apostrophes can show Possession

1) Apostrophes are used to show *possession* — when a person *owns* something:
   eg The Queen's English is posh. Orwell's vision of the future was wrong about the right things.

RULE 21: an apostrophe for possession must come before or after an 's'.

2) To *use* an apostrophe you must decide what the *basic* word is *without* one. In the examples above, the basic words are the *Queen* and *Orwell*. Then add apostrophe and 's':

   eg The Queen ➡ The Queen's = belonging to the Queen.
   Orwell ➡ Orwell's = belonging to Orwell.

Dudley's dress sense wasn't always perfect

3) *Remember* — you should only use an apostrophe of possession *after* the *owner's* name.
4) If the *basic* word already ends in *'s'*, you should *add* an apostrophe and another *'s'*. Sometimes people only add an apostrophe after the first 's', but this can be *confusing*.
   eg James ➡ James's = St. James's Park.
5) If the *owner* is *plural* and the basic word ends in *'s'*, *only* put an apostrophe after the 's':
   eg He stole the ladies' hearts with his wit and charm. She was brave despite the tigers' roars.
6) If the *owner* is *plural* and the basic word *doesn't* end in *'s'*, add an apostrophe *and* another *'s'*:
   eg Estella ruined men's lives. He lifted the oxen's yoke. (men and oxen are plurals without 's')

IMPORTANT NOTE: there is *no apostrophe* with the possessive pronouns his, hers, ours, yours or its — so *don't* use apostrophes with these words. The words its and it's are *completely different* — see below.

Apostrophes can fill in for Missing Letters

1) This means that the apostrophe goes *in place* of the missing letters to run two words *together* and make a *shorter* form:
   He is a brave man ➡ He's a brave man — the apostrophe *replaces* the letter *'i'*.
   I do not like you ➡ I don't like you — the apostrophe *replaces* the letter *'o'*.
2) Other *common* forms are I've, I'm, you're, they're, who's (who is), I'd (I had), could've.
3) *Unusual* forms include: shall not = shan't, will not = won't, I would = I'd, let us = let's, of the clock = o'clock etc. A *special case* is 'I would have' which *could* be shortened to 'I'd've' — but *don't* try to write it, even in dialogue, because it looks far too *confusing*.

RULE 22: apostrophes can be used to run two words together when letters are missed out — but never do this in essays. Use full forms for formal work.

Don't ever confuse its and it's

1) These are *different* words. Learn the rule:

RULE 23: it's means it is or it has — nothing else. Its is like his, and shows something belongs — it shows possession and doesn't have an apostrophe.

2) *Learn* this practice phrase: I hate the apostrophe; it's had its day.
   = it has ↗ ↖ = possession

RULE 24: never use apostrophes to form ordinary plurals. Some people use apostrophes with plurals of numbers — eg 2's, 3's, 1970's. This is correct but can be confusing. It's safer not to use them for this at all.

Using Quotation Marks

It's *very important* to be able to use quotation marks properly — they are used to show when someone is *actually speaking* in a piece of writing, or to *quote* from a book in essays.

Direct Speech is shown by Double Quotation Marks

1) Double quotation marks are used *before* and *after* someone *speaks* in a piece of writing.
2) When the speech starts, the *first word* inside the quotation mark must have a *capital letter*.
   eg "Don't forget," he said. "it's under the cactus."
   "What cactus?" asked Miguel, confused.
3) If the speech comes at the *end* of a sentence, there must be a *comma* before the *first* quotation mark and a *full stop* before the *final* quotation mark:

   eg He said, "It's under the cactus."
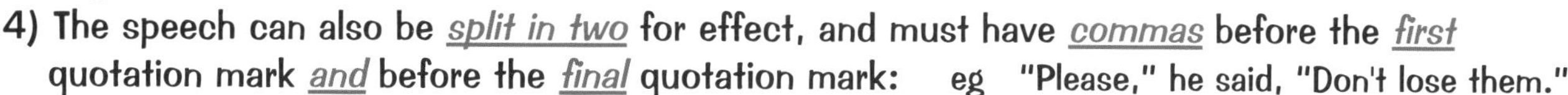
4) The speech can also be *split in two* for effect, and must have *commas* before the *first* quotation mark *and* before the *final* quotation mark: eg "Please," he said, "Don't lose them."
5) If the speech is an *exclamation*, you must use an *exclamation mark* instead of a comma. If it is a *question*, use a *question mark*: eg "No!" screamed Tess. "Why?" asked Hamlet.

Reported Speech Doesn't Use Quotation Marks

1) Reported speech is when you *write* what someone has said in your *own words* — it's also called *indirect speech*, because the original speaker isn't talking to you directly.
2) Reported speech *never* has *quotation marks*; the speech is introduced by the word *that*.
3) If the verb in the *original direct* speech is *present* tense, it must change to a *past* tense in *reported speech*. If it is *future*, *'will'* becomes *'would'*. Look at the *example*, and you'll see.

DIRECT SPEECH	REPORTED SPEECH
Desdemona said, "I like that fellow."	Desdemona said *that* she *liked* that fellow.
= comma before first quotation mark	= that replaces comma; = past not present
"I know I've seen him before," she said.	She said *that* she knew she *had seen* him before.
= comma before last quotation mark	= pluperfect not simple past

Quotation Marks have Three Other Uses

1) You *must* use quotation marks when you want to *quote* exact words from a *book* in an essay.
2) Use quotation marks with *titles* of *songs*, *poems*, *essays* or *articles*, but *not* with the *names* of *books*. Book titles should be *underlined*, and the *key words* should have *capital letters*:
   eg "To be or not to be, that is the question:"
   "The Lady of Shallott" *The Catcher in the Rye*

It's a fair cop, guv!

3) They should be used with *slang* or *technical words*:
   eg The thief knew that the "pigs" had caught him.

IMPORTANT NOTE: single quotation marks *can* be used instead of doubles; but be *consistent* and *careful* — they can easily be *confused* with *apostrophes*. If there are two sets of quotation marks in one sentence, you must use *doubles* for the *outside marks* and *singles* for the *inside marks*.

Brackets, Hyphens and Dashes

Three final punctuation marks to revise here. Be especially careful not to confuse *dashes* and *hyphens* — they have very different jobs.

Brackets are used to Explain and Expand

1) Brackets are used to *include information* which is not directly part of the main sentence.
2) This means that the sentence must *still* make sense *without* the phrase in brackets.

RULE 25: brackets always come in pairs; at the beginning and the end of a phrase which explains or expands on the main sentence.

eg They were determined to find the bag (it was full of money).

3) If the brackets come at the *end* of the main sentence (as above) then there must be a *full stop outside* the end bracket.
4) If there is a *complete* sentence *inside* the brackets and it comes between *two other* sentences, then there should be a *full stop inside* the end bracket:

eg He had spent months looking for the bag. (It had been hidden by the thieves after the raid.) At last his search was over.

Don't confuse Hyphens with Dashes

RULE 26: hyphens are symbols used to join words or parts of words — dashes are used to separate one part of a sentence from another.

Dashes can be used Singly or in Pairs

1) Dashes look like this: — . A dash must always have a *space* before and after it.
2) *Pairs* of dashes are used in the *same* way as *brackets*; they *separate* a phrase which explains what went before, but *only* in the *middle* of a sentence:

eg He was never seen again — he died alone in the desert — and new rumours began to spread.

3) *Never* use pairs of dashes at the *end* of a sentence.
4) A *single* dash can be used instead of a *colon* — this sentence is a good example.
5) It can also *link* two clauses that wouldn't be sentences by themselves, especially in *headings* or *titles:* eg The internet — the future of education.

Hyphens have Three Main Uses

1) Hyphens are used to *join* words that are part of the *same idea* to make them *one word*, and with *numbers*: eg gold-rimmed, up-to-date, free-for-all, duck-billed, eighty-two, twenty-one.
2) These are usually *adjective* phrases, and the separate words form part of *one main idea*: eg 'a free-swimming duck,' means something different from 'a free swimming duck'.
3) Hyphens are also used to join *prefixes* to words. These are fixed to the *beginning* of words to *change* the *meaning:* eg anti- anti-drugs, re- re-record, de- de-icer, co- co-write.
4) Hyphens help to make words *easier to read*, and help avoid *confusing* two possible meanings:

eg sword-dance, de-icer, fifty-odd people, he resigned but later re-signed.

- sword-dance: two 'd's = hard to read
- de-icer: clearer than deicer
- fifty-odd people: fifty odd people means something else
- resigned / re-signed: these are opposites

Negatives

Negatives are simple to form in English, but there are two very *common mistakes* that you must make sure you *avoid:* mistakes with *double negatives* and mistakes with the word *none*.

Don't use Double Negatives

1) A *negative* sentence is where you want to say *'no'* or *'not'* — the opposite of a positive:
   eg I like everyone in this room = *positive*
2) *One way* to make this sentence *negative* is using a negative form of the verb *to do* = *do not*. We also need to change the word *'everyone'* to the word *'anyone'*.
3) Alternatively we could keep the *same verb* and *change* the word *everyone* to *no-one*.
4) The negative sentences are: I do not like anyone in this room *or* I like no-one in this room.
5) Some people try to give more *emphasis* by using *more than one* negative word.
   eg I do not like no-one in this room.
   In this case there are *two* negatives — so they *cancel* each other out: I do not like no-one actually means 'I do not not like anyone', which means 'I like everyone'. *Learn* the rule:

RULE 27: two negative words in the same phrase will make it positive; you should only use one negative at a time.

eg I don't want anything *or* I want nothing (I don't want nothing = *WRONG*)

6) The set phrase 'neither...nor' is *not* a double negative — it is used to talk about more than one object in the sentence.
   eg I haven't seen either Demetrius or Lysander *or* I have seen neither Demetrius nor Lysander.

The Word None

1) None is a *pronoun* used to mean *'not one'* or *'not any':*
   eg — Do you have any in blue?
   — I'm afraid there are *none* left, Madam.
2) None should *not* be used with *other* negative words (see double negative rule):
   eg He has none (He's not got none = *WRONG*). We saw none (We didn't see none = *WRONG*).
   Remember, you say *'hasn't'* or *'haven't'*, but you *don't* use apostrophes in formal *essay* work. You must write *'has not'* or *'have not'*.
3) You can also use none as an adverb, where it means *'not at all'*:
   eg Surprisingly, the fish were *none* the worse for living in a different kettle.

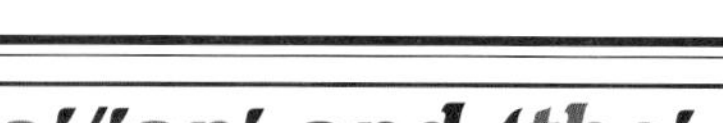

The Key Words we haven't covered — 'a'/'an' and 'the'

1) The words *'a'* and *'the'* are called *articles; 'the'* is the *definite* article, 'a' is the *indefinite*.

RULE 28: the is the definite article, used for something you definitely mean; a is the indefinite article, used when you don't have anything specific in mind.

eg *the* car = specific car, *a* car = any car, not a specific one.

2) The word *'a'* is used with *all* nouns *except* those beginning with *vowel sounds* — a, e, i, o, u. These words take *'an'* instead: eg *an* orange, *an* undertaker, *an* hour.
3) *Don't forget* that words with silent *'h'* take *'an'* — people often get this wrong: eg *an* hour, but *a* hospital. The rule is: if you pronounce the 'h' you can use 'a', but if the 'h' is silent you must use 'an'. Whichever you do, you must be consistent in your writing.

Sentences

A *sentence* is a *group of words* which makes total sense *on its own*. The keys to writing *good* sentences are making sure that *subject*, *verb* and *tense agree*, and using the right *word order*.

The Subject and Verb must agree

1) This is really *very easy*. When the *subject* is *singular*, the *verb* must be *singular*; when the *subject* is *plural*, then so is the *verb*. Follow the rule:

RULE 29: look at what you want to say and ask who or what performed the action. This is the subject, and the verb must agree with it.

eg The sword is poisoned = *singular* subject and verb. These swords are poisoned = *plural*.

2) Things can become *slightly tricky* when the *subject* is a *group* of words: eg a sack of potatoes. Just remember the rule — ask yourself whether the subject is '*sack*' or '*potatoes*', and make the *verb* agree: eg A *sack* of potatoes only *costs* five pounds.

singular subject — singular verb

3) If there is *more* than one *subject*, linked by the word '*and*', then the *verb* is *plural*, even if *both* individual subject nouns are *singular*:
eg Romeo *and* Juliet *are* happy.

4) If there is *more* than one *verb*, then remember the rule and look at the *subject*:
eg This new recipe *looks* delicious but *tastes* like elephant dung. (recipe is a singular subject)

5) If there is a clause separating subject and verb, look back at the subject to see if it is singular or plural. In the example below, ask yourself *who* is meeting us.
eg *Lee* and *Robbie*, who both used to be in the same class as Sam, *are* meeting us at the Sports Centre.

Learn these Special Words with Special Agreement Rules

1) Everyone, someone, anyone, no one, and each = SINGULAR subjects ➡ SINGULAR verbs
eg If someone lends me five pounds, I'll be able to go and see the film that everyone's talking about.
Everyone has to do some housework.

2) Many, both, few and several = PLURAL subjects ➡ PLURAL verbs
eg Both of my brothers play rugby.
Several of the farmers have already sold their sheep and bought llamas instead.

3) Collective nouns, such as team, class, and family = SINGULAR subjects ➡ SINGULAR verbs
eg My class is going on a trip to Whitby to find out more about the British fishing industry.
Steve's team has lost yet another match.
My family is very close.

4) Neither...nor... ➡ If both subjects are SINGULAR, use a SINGULAR verb
➡ If both subjects are PLURAL, use a PLURAL verb
eg Neither Alan nor Jodie knows about the secret plans for Alan's birthday.
Neither the cats nor the hamsters know that we're going on holiday next week.

Sentences and Word Order

It helps if you know some of the *technical names* for bits of a sentence. Remember, *word order* is important if you want to say what you *mean*.

Use Sentences Carefully

1) Sentences can be used to *state facts*, to *ask questions*, to *make exclamations* or to *give commands*. They can contain several *clauses* or just one.
2) Each sentence should contain *one main idea* — no more: eg Let's go racing! Did you like it?
3) All *new* sentences should *begin* with a *capital letter* and *end* with a *full stop*, *exclamation mark* or *question mark*.

Different Kinds of Sentence

1) *Simple* sentences have one subject and one object. You can add adverbs and adjectives to the sentence if you like.
   eg The cat played with the ribbon.
   The *fat, furry, tabby* cat played with the *blue* ribbon *on the carpet at lunchtime*.
2) *Compound* sentences are made from simple sentences joined with a *conjunction* or a *comma*.
   eg Claire likes tea. June prefers coffee. James just drinks water.
   Claire likes tea, June prefers coffee *and* James just drinks water.
3) *Complex* sentences have a *main clause* and one or more *dependent clauses*.
   eg Vivek, who has a sweet tooth, ate three bars of chocolate while walking home from school.

'Vivek ate three bars of chocolate' is the main clause. 'Who has a sweet tooth' and 'while walking home from school' are dependent clauses.

Sentences also depend on Clear Word Order

1) Many sentences will *change in meaning* if you alter the *word order*. You need to be particularly careful with adverbs. Adverbs have to go right next to the word they describe. Look at this example:

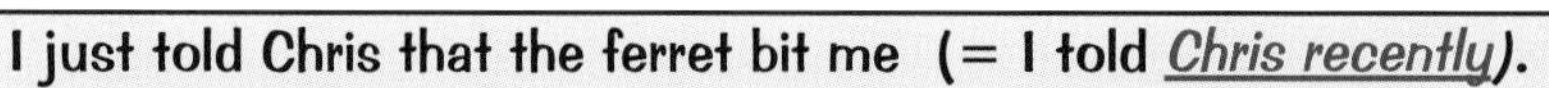

I just told Chris that the ferret bit me (= I told *Chris recently*).
I told just Chris that the ferret bit me (= I told *only Chris*).
I told Chris just that the ferret bit me (= I told Chris *only the fact* that it bit me).
I told Chris that the ferret just bit me (= I told Chris that *it bit me recently*).

2) Think what you *want* to say, and whether you are really saying what you *mean*.

3) Verbs ending in *-ing* or *-ed* must be *close* to the *subject* they relate to:
   eg I saw some snails walking in the park = the snails were walking

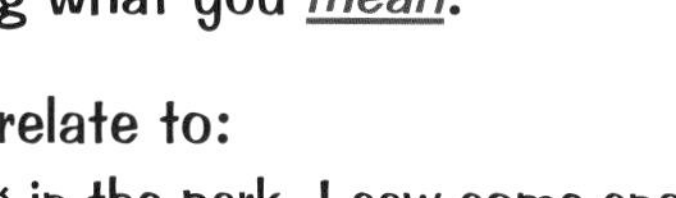

Walking in the park, I saw some snails = I was walking

4) *Avoid* putting subjects a long way from their verbs — the sentence becomes *hard* to follow:
   eg Polonius, hiding behind the arras while Hamlet spoke to the Queen, held his breath.
   = *clumsy* to read, so the *subject* Polonius should go *with* the verb.
   Hiding behind the arras, Polonius held his breath while Hamlet spoke to the Queen.

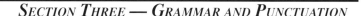

Paragraphs

You've *really got to know* how to put all these words *together*. Using *paragraphs* correctly will get you *more marks*, it's as *simple* as that. If that idea appeals to you, then *learn* this page.

Paragraphs are Groups of Sentences

My paragraph was this big

1) A paragraph is a *group of sentences* about a *related topic*. They are used to break a piece of writing into *sections*, making it *easier to read* (see also P.69 on writing skills).
2) A paragraph is *shown* on the page by setting the *first line* in from the margin — when you write by hand, try to leave the same *gap* as the word '*space*' would take up.
3) Paragraphs can be *any length* — but you should *avoid* very *short* or very *long* paragraphs. *Don't forget* the rule:

RULE 30: if the sentence you want to write is closely related to the last one you wrote, put it in the same paragraph. If you are talking about a different idea or topic, start a new paragraph. Make sure your paragraphs aren't too long.

Example of Paragraphs in an Essay

space | one main idea in the sentence | one main idea leading on from the last sentence

There was a time when I always used to break the rules. It was a challenge; I didn't like doing what I was told. One experience changed all that.

I was twelve when it happened. My parents had gone out and left me playing football with some friends. I was supposed to keep an eye on my little sister, Katy, who was playing on the patio. She was only seven, but already she was adventurous, and almost as good at breaking the rules as I was.

Anyway, the football match was very exciting. We'd been playing for two hours now, and the score was five-all. It was a hot day, so we had decided that the next goal would win. I was ready for anything — until I looked at the patio. Katy was gone.

margin | paragraph not too long

Remember to Watch your Verbs

1) If you *start* a piece of writing in one *tense*, make sure you *stay* in the *same* tense.

eg I *crept* along the corridor. It *was* almost completely dark, and I *was* terrified that I would knock something over and wake the family up. I *didn't* dare switch on the lights.

2) Be careful with *similar-sounding* verb forms. Think what you *want* to say:

I was eating
= I did the eating

I was eaten
= something else ate me

Revision Summary for Section Three

There are plenty of rules for you to learn here — but they are all make a difference to your writing style. If you learn them, you will avoid making the basic mistakes in grammar and punctuation that lose marks in written or oral work. This will automatically improve your chances of doing well.

You need to practise what you've learned. If you can learn all the rules, your writing will definitely be clearer to read and understand. Try to answer these questions without looking back; see how much you have learned. Don't forget; if there is something you're still unsure about, go back through the Section and revise it again.

1) Why is it important to learn grammar?
2) What do verbs do in a sentence?
3) What's the difference between 'I have been eating cheese, chips and fruit' and 'I had been eating cheese, chips and fruit'?
4) What's wrong with saying 'I done all of these questions already'?. What should the sentence say?
5) What's wrong with saying 'They should of called me'? What should the sentence say?
6) When do you use 'would' and when do you use 'should'? Give two examples using each word.
7) What is a noun? What do we call nouns that name people or particular places?
8) What is a pronoun?
9) What's the difference between the subject and the object in a sentence?
10) What's wrong with saying "My Gran gave some money to you and I"?
11) What is an adjective? What is an adverb? Give three sentences using adjectives and adverbs.
12) What's the rule about using 'and' or 'but' at the start of a sentence?
13) What does a preposition do in a sentence?
14) 'Different to', 'different than' or 'different from': which is the form you should use and why?
15) What's the difference between 'to', 'two' and 'too'?
16) Should you 'try and get it right' or 'try to get it right'?
17) Which is correct: 'happyest' or 'happiest'?
18) When should you use 'practise' and when should you use 'practice'?
14) Why shouldn't you ask someone if they will borrow you their book?
15) When do you need to use a pair of commas to separate a clause in a sentence?
16) Should there be a comma between the last two items in a list?
17) Which punctuation mark is used to link two sentences where one explains the other?
18) What's the difference between it's and its? Write three sentences using each word.
19) What's the problem with writing 'Potatoe's 17p per pound'?
20) Re-write these sentences as reported speech:
"We shall never be evicted," said the squatters. "Leave them alone!" yelled Carl's Mum.
23) What is a double negative? Why shouldn't you use them?
24) What must the subject and the verb in a sentence do?
25) Correct these sentences. Each one has more than one mistake:
Dan and Luke's Mum gave them there tea realy early.
If she'd known they was having a party she could of gone.
They kepted on eating until there wasn't none left.
I asked "were are you going" and she said I'm going to the common.
26) Write a mini-essay on "Three Grammar Rules which I find difficult." Explain each of the rules and why you find them hard. Practise writing clear paragraphs and sentences.

Reading for a Reason

Your reading plays a big part in deciding your *final grade* in English. You need to learn *how* to read — *comprehension*. This means looking for clues in a text to help you understand it and to help you answer questions on it. *Remember* — the more you read, the better your *marks* will get.

Three Reasons why Reading is the Key to Good Marks

1) Reading *well* means that you *notice things* when you read — the way a character is described, or a line of poetry that sticks in your mind. This will help you to *write well* about your reading in essay work and in your Exams.
2) Reading *widely* helps you to see *links* between writers and texts and to *compare* them — eg two poems about the same subject.
3) Reading helps you to spot the little *tricks* writers use to create a *reaction* in the reader. This will help you to write about their *use of language*. You can also start *using* these tricks to improve your *own* writing.

Any Kind of Reading will Improve your Marks

1) You'll have to read some *specific* books for your Exams and Coursework — but if you read *other* things too, you can *improve* your ability to read *well*.
2) *Any* piece of writing can be read and studied — eg a *novel*, a *poem* or a *diary*. When you talk about pieces of writing in this way, you should call them *texts*.
3) You can also read *newspaper* or *magazine* articles, *short stories* and even some *graphic novels*. The best way to improve your reading is to read a *variety* of different types of text.
4) Anything that you *enjoy* reading will help you to practise the skills of *comprehension*. Try using the techniques you learn in this section on all the texts you read — you'll be surprised at *how much* you *remember* and *understand*. Think about how that'll help you in the Exam.

REMEMBER: comprehension is about how clearly you understand a piece of text — and also about whether you can read between the lines.

Learn to Read Between the Lines

1) Writers often *don't say* exactly what they *mean* when they write. Reading between the lines means learning to look for *hidden meanings* in a text.
2) Hidden meanings can take many forms. *Characters* may be *lying* to the reader, or *joking*, or even being *deliberately boring*.
3) What characters *do* is as important as what they *say*.
4) Sometimes the *narrator* of a text may *exaggerate* or say something which is *obviously untrue*.

   eg It is a truth universally acknowledged that a single man in possession of a fortune must be in want of a wife.

These hidden meanings are part of the writer's *style* — you need to learn how to spot them.

Marxist books — better red than read...

We're going to focus on *practical criticism* skills in this Section. This means reading *in detail* and *summarising* what you've read so you can *answer questions* or *write essays* about it. These are the basics of *comprehension* — you'll need them for looking at *fiction* and *non-fiction* texts.

Scanning and Close Reading

Comprehension is tested by short *extracts* from texts. That means you have to recognise all the *main details* of the text. The easiest way to do this is to *scan* the passage quickly, and then read it again *closely*.

Scanning means Reading for the Main Idea

1) The *first* thing you should do with a comprehension text is read it through *quickly*. Don't be put off by a long text — skimming through it quickly gives you a fair idea of what's there.
2) Remember — you are *not* trying to understand *every detail;* just the *main idea* in the text.
3) You should note down any *key points*, and *underline* any sentences and ideas you *weren't sure* about. You can look at them again later. Don't spend too long scanning the text; read it as *quickly* as you can.

For example:

If you are reading a passage describing a room, you should scan the text for the basic details. Look for the main features of the room — some kind of general description; perhaps it has bare walls, a little, barred window and straw on the floor.

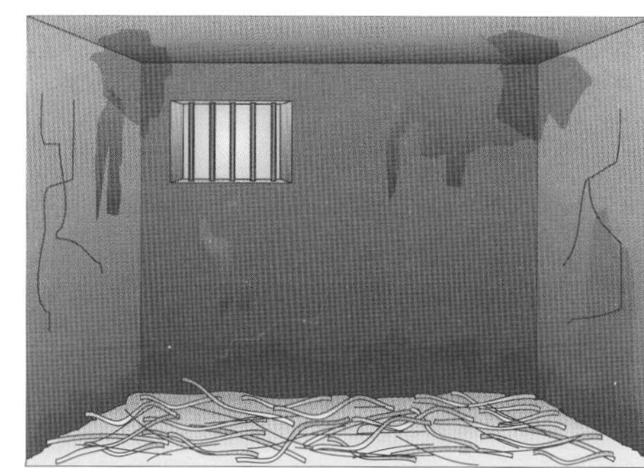

Close Reading Gives You the Details

1) Close-reading means going over the text *in detail* before you start writing about it.
2) You should read each sentence *carefully*, making sure you *understand* it. If you don't, then read the previous sentence *once more*, and then read the problem sentence through *slowly*. Repeat this process until you understand it, and then move on.
3) When you have read the whole thing through, look at the *beginning* and the *end*. If the text is an extract from a book or a longer article, you may not have all of the argument in front of you.
4) Look at any *questions* that are asked about the text; they will help you to see what the *examiners* want you to *notice*. Then go through the text *again*, taking *notes* of the points which will help you to *answer* the questions. Be careful not to miss anything.

Remember — you're *only* being tested on the passage in front of you; that's **ALL** you should write about. Don't add other information *unless* the question asks for it.

For example:

After close reading of the text describing the room, you should be able to give more detailed information about it; there is a skeleton in chains in the corner, a bed on the left and a rat asleep in the straw.

Scanning and re-reading — getting close to a text...

Reading the text through twice might *seem* like twice as much work, but you'll *miss out* a lot of the information if you don't. Scan reading gives you a frame on which to hang the information you get from close reading. If you're asked to *compare* two texts, scan and close read *each* text by *itself* then read them one after the other to look for *similarities* and *differences*. Try a scan read and a close read of *this page* to see how it works — it's the only way to practise.

Making a Summary

One comprehension exercise is writing a *summary* — it may even be part of your *Exam*, so you need plenty of *practice*. Remember — a clear, accurate summary only gives the *vital information*. Any extra, irrelevant details are *left out*; summarizing is about careful reading and understanding.

Firstly, Work Out What is Relevant

1) You *can't summarize* if you *haven't read* the text carefully.
2) Start by *scanning* the text, then reading it *closely*.
3) Once you understand the *whole text*, go through it again *slowly*, working out what is *relevant* for the summary, and which details can be *left out*.
4) Decide what the *main theme* is — look at the *title*, and *where* the text came from to work out the *key details*.

Soccer Star Swede Saves Blaze Baby Faller

City's Swedish goalkeeper Doni Osmundsen was a hero last night after saving a baby from certain death in a terrifying apartment block fire near Surlwick.

The blaze began after a freak kettle accident in long-time resident Maureen Greasby's flat and soon spread out of control, engulfing three floors. The building was quickly evacuated, except for Mrs Greasby and 6 month old son, Wayne, who were trapped on a ledge by the oncoming flames.

"I thought we were done for," said a relieved Maureen later. "Wayne was bawling his eyes out. I really thought it was curtains!"

Then City star Osmundsen, 30, arrived and took control. The soccer star had

seen the thick smoke pouring from the apartment block on his daily jog and sprinted to the scene.

"It was amazing," said an onlooker. "He shouted to the woman on the ledge to throw him her baby!"

"I didn't realise who it was. I hate football," said Maureen.

Osmundsen shouted again: "I am goalkeeper. Throw baby!"

A deadly hot spark hit worried Mum Maureen's hand and she screamed, dropping baby Wayne. Osmundsen dramatically leapt to his right, superbly catching Wayne in mid air. The watching crowd applauded, while two newly arrived policemen prevented the 'keeper from bouncing the baby twice and kicking him over the wall.

Mrs Greasby was later rescued by the traditional fire brigade method.

Police and Fire Chiefs praised Osmundsen's swift action — but modestly the Swede hero was unavailable for comment. His manager Ron Bacardi spoke to the waiting press: "The lad's done well. It means I can finally put him up for a transfer — this is the first thing he's saved all season!"

(by Allan Hack and Selma Reese)

Make Sure Your Summary is the Right Length

1) If the question says *how many words* long the summary must be, you must *never* write *more* than that number. It sounds obvious enough, but people do it every year.
2) Make sure that *all* the *basic information* is there — *don't* include detail when there isn't room.

For example: a 50 word summary of the *article above* will only contain the basic details.

> City Goalkeeper Doni Osmundsen caught a baby thrown from a burning apartment block near Surlwick yesterday. Baby and mother, Wayne and Maureen Greasby, were reunited after firemen rescued Mrs Greasby. The fire spread after a kettle accident, engulfing three floors: no one was hurt. Osmundsen was praised as a hero.

After the spring — it always gets summery...

Remember, writing a summary means keeping the *important* points and *nothing else*. You won't be able to write an accurate summary if you haven't *read* the text through *properly* first.

How To Take Notes

Taking notes when you read is the easiest way to answer questions or write essays about that text — it's a key comprehension skill, so learn to do it well.

Be Clear and Concise — Don't Just Repeat Everything

1) Taking notes is the first step to sorting through a text. You're looking for key information.
2) Notes don't have to be full sentences — just make sure you can understand them.
3) Use underlining and pictures in revision notes to help ideas stick in your mind, like we've done in this book. In an Exam you'll have to make notes quickly.

Pantomimes are Great — Oh no they aren't...

"Christmas wouldn't be Christmas without a panto!" It's what we're told every year, and every year we go along for the same old jokes performed by a different cast of soap-opera stars and local actors — and we love it. So why do the British love a good panto?

Take Notes...

Pantomime originated in Roman times, where it meant an actor who mimed characters and scenes without speaking. In England pantomime began as a stage perfomance without speech but soon developed to include dancing, singing, clowns, topical jokes and certain stock roles — the "principal boy" who is acted by a woman, and the "dame" who is acted by a man. The stories came from fairy-tales.

Modern pantos are very similar — so why do we like them? Perhaps it's because we know what we're going to get. We know the stories and the traditions of a pantomime — like shouting "He's behind you!" The songs chosen are usually popular classics and even the actors are familiar from our television screens. We know that pantos are fun — and they're a great way to show people what the theatre is like, and how enjoyable it can really be.

Concise notes for this piece of writing might go something like this:

Pantomimes — popular; why? Started in Roman times — mime; came to England — mime; then added to — why popular? because we know what to expect — they show what theatre's like.

1) If you're asked about something that doesn't appear in your notes, go back to the text again.
2) You'll find it easier to answer questions quickly if your notes are as accurate as possible.

Draft Your Notes into a Rough Copy

1) Comprehension exercises give questions to answer or an essay to write, based on the text.
2) A rough copy is a rough version of your answer: It doesn't have to be neat or totally accurate.
3) When you have a rough copy, go back over the text and see if you've missed out any information you need, or added anything that the question doesn't ask for.
4) Then check your grammar and your sentences. Make sure your final version is in clear, accurate, neatly-written, standard English.
5) Don't spend too long on notes or rough copies.

Keep your essays cool — with plenty of drafts...

Remember, you write notes to help you understand the text; not instead of the text. If you're in doubt, or you left something out, always go back to the text. Remember to keep notes brief.

Putting Comprehension Skills Together

Time to put the skills in this Section together. Make sure you *learn* how to recognise the *different styles* of questions you may be given, and the kind of answers the Examiners will be looking for.

Start by Scanning the Passage

Pete's method of scanning the text was a little unusual

1) Scan the passage quickly *first*. This should give you the *overall meaning* of the *whole* passage. If something is *confusing*, go *over it* until it becomes clear.
2) REMEMBER — you're only looking for a *rough picture*.

Read the Passage Closely to Understand the Detail

1) Close reading is about *detail* — but only *relevant* detail.
2) *Underline* key words and phrases in pencil, and take *notes* of the *main points* in the text.
3) Go back over the text to check you haven't *missed* anything.
4) Look out for *hidden meanings* — if the writer is saying what they really *mean*.

Answer only the questions you're asked; give the exact answer required for each.

Make Notes to help you Answer the Questions

Sandy knew it was risky. She'd never done anything like this before, but Paul was in trouble. She shut her eyes and jumped.

There was a rush of air and then two hard cracks of pain as her knees hit the ground. She rolled over onto her back and opened her eyes. The barn window seemed a long way up — further than it had looked from above. How had she managed to make herself jump? And was she hurt?

The thought almost made her panic, but she stopped herself by remembering Paul. Carefully she wiggled her left foot. It seemed fine. Then her right foot. Fine again. She moved each of her arms in turn. They were fine too. Relieved, she rolled over onto her front. Time to get help for Paul.

1) PLAIN QUESTIONS — ask you to find out information *plainly written* in the text:

eg *What does Sandy do first after she jumps out of the barn?*

1) *Read* the question carefully to work out *what* you have to do.
2) You need to *look* at the passage to find your answer. Make a *note* of it.
3) Check to see if you've *answered* the question properly — it asks what she does *first*, so if you put "She went for help" you'd get *no marks*.

ANSWER: *After jumping, Sandy checks her legs and arms to see if she's hurt.*

2) OPINION QUESTIONS — ask you to look *closely* at the text to give *opinions*.

eg *What kind of person is Sandy?*

1) You need to *think* about these questions a bit more.
2) You'll have to read the text *closely* and *decide* what Sandy is like from the way she *thinks* and *acts* in this passage.
3) You must explain your answer with *examples* from the passage.

ANSWER: *Sandy is brave — she jumps out of the barn window even though she's never done anything like it before. She is also a good friend, because she is doing everything to help Paul.*

3) PERSONAL QUESTIONS — ask you to write about your *own ideas* or *experiences*:

eg *Write about a time when you did something brave to help a friend.*

Answering the Question

The only way to win *good marks* in comprehension exercises is to *answer the question*. That means looking *carefully* at what it *means* and how many *marks* it is worth.

Answer Only the Questions You Have Been Asked

1) Lots of people don't *read* the questions *properly*. Work out *exactly* what's being asked.
2) Ask yourself what *kind* of question it is.

> eg *How does Lucy feel when Edmund betrays her?*
> = OPINION QUESTION
> *"Sometimes a lie can be a good thing." Do you agree?*
> = PERSONAL QUESTION

3) Don't just retell the events from the text in your answer; you need to show that you've understood *more* than what the story is about.
4) Look at the question and *pick out* the bits of text that are *relevant*. Your *notes* will help you.

Give Enough Detail to Pick Up All the Marks

1) Every question has a *number* beside it showing how many *marks* it's worth. This tells you *how detailed* your answer has to be, and how much *time* to give it in an Exam.
2) If a question is worth *twenty marks*, you'll need to give a *lot* of *detail*, but if a question is worth *five marks*, then don't *waste* time giving *extra* information.

Practise by answering the questions on the following example:

A Little Goes A Long Way in Brazil

by Siobhan Chasey: additional reporting Don Felson and Renee Phelps

Intrepid explorer Sir Simon Little has begun an expedition to chart the course of the unexplored Lower Tiperati river, a tributary of the Amazon in northern Brazil. With a team of local guides, Sir Simon plans to follow the river to its source.

Australian biologist Kate "Mate" Stevens, the famous Bush-Tucker girl, will go with him to collect wildlife specimens. Many of the creatures living in the steamy jungles of north Brazil have not yet been classified.

The team face several challenges, including unfriendly local tribes and the constant threat of attack from drug traffickers, who have many secret plantations in the jungle.

"It'll be tough, but we'll make it," said a determined Little, in an interview last week. "The big problem will be our supplies, especially preserving food in that heat." No doubt this is where Bush-Tucker girl will come in useful.

When we asked Stevens about the food question, she was more relaxed: "Yeah! I'm always able to find something to eat among the plants and bugs. You've just got to know what to look for. Near the Tiperati, they've got some absolutely ripper giant cockroaches. Just right if you're a bit peckish!"

Each to their own. At least Sir Simon won't have a problem carrying food for Stevens: "I suppose you're right. Kate will eat any kind of grub!"

1) What is the purpose of the expedition? (*1 mark*)
2) What kind of character do you think Kate Stevens has? Use the text for examples. (*5 marks*)
3) "Expeditions to unexplored places are a waste of money." What do you think? (*20 marks*)

Looking for answers — searching questions...

Remember — if you read the question *wrongly* you'll be looking for the *wrong* things in the text.

Revision Summary for Section Four

Comprehension is the set of basic skills used for reading any text, whether it is fiction, journalism or poetry. This why we have started our revision of reading skills here. It's all about how you look at a text to find out what it says on the surface, and what may be hidden underneath.

Remember that some comprehension questions in the Exam will be marked for your reading skills, and some will be marked for writing. The questions on the Shakespeare paper are marked for both reading and writing. Writing skills will be tested by personal questions, asking you to write your own ideas in response to the text. Reading questions will ask you to look closely at the text and use only the information you find in it, unless the question itself says otherwise. Only answer the question you are given, not the question you would like to answer.

1) What are the three reasons why reading is the key to good marks?
2) What is meant by 'reading between the lines'
3) What kinds of hidden meaning night you look for?
4) Why do you need to read the text twice?
5) What is scanning?
6) Why is it useful?
7) What four things should you do before you start to answer a Reading question?
8) How long should a summary be?
9) Why do you need to make a set of notes as you read through the text?
10) Do your notes have to be in full sentences?
11) Why is it a good idea to use different colours and underlining?
12) After you've made a rough copy from your notes, what should you do next?
13) What do you need to do if the question asks you about something that isn't in your notes?
14) What are the four points to remember when reading a passage closely for detail?
15) What are the three main sorts of question you could be asked in a comprehension exercise?
16) Do you need to give all the main points of the text in your answer?
17) Why is it important to look at the number of marks a question is worth?

Revision Example for Section Four

My mistress' eyes are nothing like the sun;
Coral is far more red than her lips' red;
If snow be white, why then her breasts are dun;
If hairs be wires, black wires grow on her head.
I have seen roses damask'd, red and white,
But no such roses see I in her cheeks,
And in some perfumes is there more delight
Than in the breath that from my mistress reeks.
I love to hear her speak, yet well I know
That music hath a far more pleasing sound;
I grant I never saw a goddess go,
My mistress when she walks treads on the ground.
And yet, by heaven, I think my love as rare
As any she belied with false compare.

(Sonnet 130; William Shakespeare)

dun = dark greyish-brown
damask'd = mingled red and white
reeks = is breathed out
go = walk
rare = unusual/extraordinary
she = woman
belied = misleadingly portrayed
compare = comparison

Plain Questions on the Extract

1) What does the narrator of the poem say about his mistress' eyes? (1)
2) What does he say about her lips, her hair, her cheeks and her voice? (4)
3) Give a description of the woman from the information in the poem. It may help you to try drawing a picture of her as part of your draft. (8)
4) What does the narrator say about his love at the end of the poem? (2)
5) Give a summary of the main points of the poem. (10)

Opinion Questions on the Extract

1) The poem uses lots of negative images — it says what his mistress is not like, and talks about things which are better then her. Does this mean the poet doesn't love his mistress? (10)
2) "This is a very realistic poem." Explain why. (10)
3) Do you like this poem? Give reasons for or against it. (10)
4) "Poetry is all about false comparisons." Do you agree? Explain your answer using this poem and any others you know. (10)
5) Shakespeare's poems often take an ordinary idea, like a love poem, and then change them into something new. Can you think of other writers or film-makers who do the same thing?(10)

Personal Questions based on the Extract

1) Write a poem about someone you know well, describing them by the things which they are not like. Don't be rude though. (20)
2) Imagine you are a friend of Shakespeare's. Write a letter asking him about this poem — why he wrote it and why he chose this style. Try to bring the letter to life. (20)
3) Write about a time in your life when the right description was very important (clue: think about a time when you were lost, or when you had to meet a stranger). (20)
4) "Shakespeare is boring." Write an essay giving your opinion — and make sure you can back your answer up with good reasons. (20)

Looking at Literature

Literature actually means any *written text*. This section is about *fictional* literary texts — poems, novels and plays — and the *techniques* to use when you *read* them. Your *comprehension* skills (see Section 4) will be useful here; you need to be able to *scan*, *read* closely and take clear and accurate *notes* to pick up good marks.

Four Key Points to Win You High Marks

The following four points are things that you really must do if you want to get high marks for Reading questions in the Exam.

1) You need to be able to discuss the *plot* of a novel or short story. This means *not* just *retelling* the story, but looking at *how* the author *develops* the plot and keeps you interested.
2) You need to discuss *characters* in fiction. There are *clues* in how they're *described*, what they *do*, what they *say* and what *other* characters say about them.
3) You need to be able to talk about the *themes* and *ideas* that come up in a text. For example, two *themes* in *Julius Caesar* are *loyalty* and *betrayal*.
4) The *tone* of a text is very important. You need to be able to discuss how the author's choice of *language* and *language patterns* affects the way you *feel* when you read the text.

Language is a Tool

Ted's tools were giving him problems

1) This Section will help you to discuss writers' use of *language*. Remember: *language* is a *tool*.
2) Authors don't just use it to tell stories, but to make characters *come alive*, to make you feel different *emotions* and to make you *react* in certain ways to characters and events.
3) Your job is to learn to spot *what tricks* the writer is using to create those reactions.
4) Any piece of writing *uses tricks* to make you *react* in a certain way — an advertisement is written to influence you to buy that brand.

Watch out for Language and Spelling in Older texts

1) *Old texts* can cause you problems because the *language* and *spelling* they use is very *different* from modern standard English. Make sure you *know* what words *mean*.
2) Texts written *before* the 19th Century can be *confusing*, because lots of words had a *different meaning* when the text was written. Try reading the text *around* the word to see if it really means what you think it does. Be careful.

Language is a tool — I wonder who the mechanic is...

Literary texts are written to *achieve effects*, and they use many tricks to create them. You need to learn what the tricks are, and how to *spot them*. You can only do that with *practice*.

Looking at Style

Different Styles Can Create Certain Effects

The *style* of a text should tell you what kind of *effect* the author wants. Style is part of any form of text, and it can be broken up into *three features*. Make sure you *learn* what they are.

Written Style has Three Key Features

1) *THE LANGUAGE USED*: the language could be *formal* or *informal*; it may be written like *speech*, or just *descriptive*. The sentences could be *short*, like those of a child, or *long* and rambling like an older person looking back on their life. The text may be in *dialect*, like a poem by Robert Burns. It might contain *dialogue* or none at all. It may use lots of *imagery*.
2) *THE VOCABULARY USED*: the vocabulary could be very *simple*, as though it was spoken by a child or a mentally-handicapped person. It could be *complicated* and full of *technical terms*, such as legal or medical terms. It could *repeat itself* to emphasise points.
3) *THE TONE*: the tone is the way in which the words used *create a feeling* about what is happening; a horror story uses images of darkness, shadows and gloom — nothing is ever clear. *Wuthering Heights* uses the images of the landscape and the weather to represent the emotions of the characters. Tennyson's poems often create a sense of imprisonment and stillness.

Style Affects how we see a Situation or Character

The *style* of a *description* can completely change how we see a situation or a character. Look at these two descriptions of Ms Tique:

Ms Tique was on the phone.
"You're late!" she growled at him. "What time do you call this?"
"I was held up," Dave replied, with a smile.
"What kind of an excuse is that?" Ms Tique looked annoyed.
"The bank I was in...It was held up."

Ms Tique laughed at his joke and winked at him across the table.
"Call me Susanna!" she whispered breathlessly.
Dave swallowed nervously. He had never met anyone as charming.
"Shall we go dancing later?" Susanna raised an eyebrow inquisitively.
She leaned forward and touched his hand.
"Aaarrg!" said Dave. It was all he could think of to say.

Different types of fiction have their own *style*. For example a horror story has a *dark tone* and uses short sharp sentences to build up *tension* and *suspense*. Things happen, but *aren't explained* until later, so that you feel scared for *longer*. A *teenage novel* uses vocabulary that is quite close to the way people *speak*, and often uses quite short sentences.

Reading on situation and character — do it with style...

People often only remember the parts of a text they liked. Surprise, surprise; you'll need to read it *more closely*, so that you can write about it and answer questions on it. That means you need to know *what* to look for. Start by learning the *three key features* of style — and *don't* forget them.

Language and Meaning

Choice of *vocabulary* is a very *important* part of an author's use of language. In the Exam, you have to talk about *how* the author's choice of language has affected the meaning of the text.

The Words used in a Text help Create Meaning

1) Authors try to avoid *repeating* the *same* vocabulary, which would be *boring*.
2) You need to be able to recognise *different* words that mean the *same* thing.
3) The best way to do this is by *learning new words*.
4) Look up new words in a *dictionary* when you're reading — that's a book of word definitions.
5) There is also a special *dictionary of synonyms*, called a *Thesaurus* (*Synonyms* are words that mean the same thing). When you look up a word, all the different synonyms are listed. See if you can find one in your local library. Look at P.4. for how to use a thesaurus.

Effects of Different Vocabulary Choice

Words with *similar*, but slightly *different* meanings can give different *impressions*. For example:

1) She was very tall and blonde, or...
2) She was a tall, straw-topped beanpole of a girl.
3) Her large, vivacious body and mane of tangled locks belonged to a Valkyrie rather than a teacher.
4) She loomed over me, and her pale skin and blonde hair gave her an unreal, ghostly look.

The effects of different vocabulary choices can be seen very clearly in poetry. For example:

In Xanadu did Kubla Khan
A stately pleasure-dome decree:
Where Alph, the sacred river, ran
Through caverns measureless to man
down to a sunless sea.
(*"Kubla Khan," lines 1-5;*
Samuel Taylor Coleridge)

1) The poem's language creates a *mysterious feeling*.
2) The names Xanadu and Kubla Khan sound *exotic* and *foreign*.
3) The words stately and decree suggest that Kubla Khan is very *powerful* and *royal*.
4) A pleasure-dome sounds very *grand*, like the millennium dome perhaps.
5) *None* of these grand things is *explained*.
6) The verb form "did...decree" is *old-fashioned* — it makes the poem sound like an *ancient text*.
7) The river is "sacred," the caverns are "measureless to man" and the river runs to a "sunless sea." These are *strange images* that we're told we *can't understand* — "measureless to man."
8) The *rhyme words* of the poem add to the effect of *mystery* — the rhymes of lines 3 and 4 ("ran","man") *run on* like the river, until they reach "sea" in line 5.

Onomatopoeia is when a word sounds like what it means

1) It *sounds* like a disease, but it's actually a form of *word music* that writers like to use, especially when they describe *noises*: eg words like bang, crash, pop, whisper, and hush.
2) Onomatopoeia is also used to give an idea of *movement*:
eg The vampire *creeps* slowly towards her sleeping victim.
The snake *hissed* and *slithered* away.

Language and Meaning

The Structure of Language in a Text Shapes Meaning

Choice of vocabulary is only one of the ways that a writer can achieve effects in a text.

1) *Sentence structure* and *style* can also be varied to produce various effects, and you need to be able to *recognise* this.
2) Sometimes, the *structure* of one sentence is *repeated* in the text for added *emphasis*. For example: "Mariana" by Alfred, Lord Tennyson. The first sentence is repeated at the end of stanzas 1-6 — at the end of stanza 7 the *same structure* is used but the *words change*.

She only said, "My life is dreary,
He cometh not," she said;
She said, "I am aweary, aweary,
I would that I were dead." (1-6)

Then said she, "I am very dreary,
He will not come," she said;
She wept, "I am aweary, aweary,
Oh God, that I were dead." (7)

Sound Patterns are used to affect Meaning in a Text

Poetic language uses *sound patterns* to create a kind of music that reinforces what the poet wants to say. Sound patterns are also used in narrative texts and in non-fiction texts like newspaper headlines and advertisements to make a *phrase* or *passage* more *memorable*.

Three Main Tricks of Poetic Language

Rhyme

1) Rhyme means that two words sound the *same*. It's what most people recognise in poetry.
2) Rhymes can come at the *end* of two lines, or in the *middle* of a line. Be careful though; many poems *don't* use rhyme, particularly *modern* works.

Out flew the web and floated *wide*;
The mirror crack'd from *side* to *side*;
'The curse is come upon me,' *cried*
The Lady of Shallott.
(*'The Lady of Shallott' Part III; Lord Tennyson*)

Assonance

1) Assonance means two words sound *similar*, because they share a *vowel* sound. Unlike rhyme, the consonant sound *doesn't* have to be the same.
2) The *spelling* of the words doesn't matter: only the *sound* is important: eg *wheat*, *piece* and *sleep*.

Then a mile of warm *sea*-scented *beach*;
Three fields to cross till a farm *appears*;
A *tap at* the pain, the quick *sharp scratch*
And *blue spurt* of a lighted *match*,
(*'Meeting at Night' Robert Browning)*

Alliteration

1) Alliteration means that a *series* of words *repeat* the same consonant. It is very common in poetry and sometimes in prose texts:
2) Nowadays, alliteration is common in *tabloid headlines:* eg Rock Star in Road Rage Rant Shock.

I caught this morning morning's minion,
kingdom of daylight's dauphin, dapple-dawn-drawn Falcon,
(*'The Windhover' Gerard Manley Hopkins)*

WARNING: don't talk about alliteration in a text if there are only two words that share the same letter. Make sure any example of alliteration you give is clear.

Poetic language — rhyme and reasons...

Phew! All these types of *sound pattern* are used to create effects. When you read a text, you need to *look* for these features and say what *effect* they create; if they give a *clearer image*, or a certain *tone*. Remember, the easiest way to find these features is to *read* the text *out loud*.

Imagery

An image creates a picture. Authors *use language* to *create pictures* in a text — if you learn how to spot them, you'll pick up *a lot more marks* for your reading skills.

All Texts Use Imagery to Create Pictures

1) Images are descriptions that create a *picture* of the thing they *describe*. They bring texts to life:

> 'The coast of Patusan (I saw it nearly two years afterwards) is straight and sombre, and faces a misty ocean. Red trails are seen like *cataracts of rust* streaming under the dark-green foliage of bushes and creepers *clothing* the low cliffs.'
> (*Lord Jim*, Chapter XXIV; Joseph Conrad)

a) The red trails through the forest are described as "*cataracts of rust*." Rust is a red colour and cataracts are waterfalls so the image is of red waterfalls amid the green jungle.

b) The bushes and creepers are described as "*clothing*" the cliffs, a visual image of material.

2) An image can be used *once*, or it can be continued through a passage, and *developed*:

In the poem "Lights Out" by Edward Thomas, the narrator creates a *picture* of sleep as a *dark, unknown forest* which he must enter, even though he knows he will lose his way. The image of the forest runs through the *whole poem*. Here are some extracts:

I have come to the borders of sleep,
The unfathomable deep
Forest where all must lose
Their way, however straight... (stanza 1)

Many a road and track
That, since the dawn's first crack,
Up to the forest brink
Deceived the travellers... (stanza 2)

...The tall forest towers;
Its cloudy foliage lowers
Ahead, shelf above shelf... (stanza 5)

REMEMBER: many poems are divided into fixed groups of lines — each group is called a stanza.

Imagery in Romeo and Juliet

Look at this example from *Romeo and Juliet*, Act I, scene v.

This is the *first scene* where Romeo and Juliet *meet* and speak to each other. Both of them are attracted to the other, and the scene shows them *flirting*:

Romeo: If I profane with my unworthiest hand,
This holy shrine, the gentle sin is this,
My lips, two blushing pilgrims, ready stand
To smooth that rough touch with a tender kiss.

Juliet: Good pilgrim, you do wrong your hand too much,
Which mannerly devotion shows in this:
For saints have hands that pilgrims' hands do touch
And palm to palm is holy palmers' kiss.

TALKING ABOUT THE IMAGES

1) The image of Juliet as a "*shrine*" is used throughout this passage.
2) Romeo says his lips are "*pilgrims*" to the shrine — he's offering to kiss her.
3) Juliet says that pilgrims' hands touch saints' hands. She suggests that they go "*palm to palm*" — an image for *holding hands*.
4) The "*palmers*" she mentions are pilgrims who used to carry palm leaves.
5) This passage is an image of the *instant attraction* between Romeo and Juliet. Juliet answers Romeo by repeating the *style of poetry* he speaks, repeating the *same rhymes* of "his" and "kiss" and using the *same images* of pilgrims, shrines and sin.

More Imagery

The Two Key Forms of Image — Similes and Metaphors

1) *Similes* compare two things — they show that they are *similar*.

eg
My love is *like* a red, red rose
That's newly sprung in June:
My love is *like* a melody
That's sweetly played in tune.
("A Red, Red Rose", Robert Burns)

The narrator's love is similar to a newly grown red rose and a sweet, tuneful melody. The poem tries to give pictures of what it is like to be in love, and how joyful a feeling it is.

Similes must *always* use one of the similarity words: *like, as, as if, as though, as...as.*

2) *Metaphors* are images where one thing is actually said *to be* something else. These images *aren't literally true*, but they create an *impression* of what something is like. They are much more *vivid* than similes:

Three years she grew in sun and shower;
Then Nature said, 'A lovelier *flower*
On earth was never sown...'
(*"Lucy," (iv); William Wordsworth*)

In "Lucy," (iv) the narrator imagines Nature calling the girl a *flower* — she is a flower because she's *beautiful* and because she *will not live long*.

REMEMBER: similes are *like* something; metaphors actually *are* that thing.

Exaggeration is used to Emphasise a Point

1) Exaggeration is often used in imagery, to make something seem *especially important*:

eg "Come not between the *dragon* and his wrath;" (*King Lear*, Act I, scene i)

Lear compares himself to a dragon, *exaggerating* the power of his anger against Cordelia.

2) Exaggeration is also used for *comic effect*, to make something seem *ridiculous*.

Jonathan Swift uses *comic exaggeration* in an essay called "A Modest Proposal" (1729), where he suggests that rich people should *eat* the children of the poor in Ireland, since they are treated so badly anyway: he says that this would be "innocent, cheap, easy and effectual." Obviously he *didn't* mean this literally; he is exaggerating to make a point about how the rich treat the poor in Ireland and he uses a *vivid image*.

Personification — describing Things as People

John Keats' poem "To Autumn," describes Autumn *as a human being* with human features, like hair:

Sometimes whoever seeks abroad may find
Thee sitting careless on a granary floor,
Thy hair soft-lifted by the winnowing wind,

1) Making an *idea* or an *object* seem human helps the reader to *identify* with it more closely. This is why sailors call their ships, "she," as though the ship was a woman.

2) It's also why we talk about Father Time and Mother Nature. These names began as *superstitions*.

A poetic adviser — must be an image consultant...

Imagery is all about making a text interesting — *bringing it to life* for the reader. When you read texts, you should be *looking* for all these kinds of image. Make sure you learn *how they work*.

Understanding the Text

The Six Billion Dollar Questions

Exams will ask you all sorts of questions about a text. What they all have in common is: *who*, *what*, *where*, *when*, *how* and *why*. These are the questions *you need to answer* if you want a higher grade on your Reading questions. The first four are quite straightforward, but the *last two* need a lot of *thought*, and it's for the last two that you'll *really earn the marks*. Now you know *why* they're important, it's time to *learn* them.

1) Who Appears in the Text and Who is Speaking?

Stefan liked to be where the action was, which made him unpopular with the other boys

Paddy preferred to comment from a safe distance

1) You have to find out *who* the characters are, and *how* they are described. Remember, you'll have to *take notes* here.
2) In a *play* the *stage directions* tell you who is speaking.
3) For poems, novels and short stories, ask yourself who the *narrator* is. Sometimes the narrator is a *character* in the book, like Pip in *Great Expectations*; sometimes the narrator is someone *looking on* from a distance, like the narrator in *The Mayor of Casterbridge*.
4) Some books have several *different* narrators, like *Wuthering Heights*.
5) Some narrators are *biased*, and give their *opinions* on events.

People often confuse the author with the narrator. The author is the real person who wrote the text, the narrator is a voice created to talk to the reader. Even when the text addresses the reader directly, the voice that is speaking is a narrator.

NEVER CONFUSE THE AUTHOR WITH THE NARRATOR

2) What Happens and What does Each Character Do?

1) You must *make notes* on the main *events* in the text; for example, there may be a murder.
2) Make a *list* of the *characters* and underneath each name *write what they do* in the text. You can even do this for poems.
3) *Make a note* of things that happen by *accident* . Nothing in a literary text is really an accident — there must be a *reason* why the author included it. *Anything* that happens may be *important*; even if it is only the weather outside. Nature and the weather often help to set the tone of a text.
4) It can also be *important* when characters *fail* to do something: for example in Shakespeare's *King Lear*, Edmund fails to send a message in time to save Cordelia's life.

Where, When, How and Why

Here are the other four major reading questions. *Every time* you look at a text, ask yourself these questions and *note down* your answers. Make sure you *learn* the questions...

3) Where does the Action Take Place? — Use the Clues

1) The *setting* of a text is *always important*; sometimes it isn't actually mentioned, but you can usually *guess* it from the text. There are always *clues*.
2) Sometimes texts are deliberately set in *one place*, such as Tennyson's poem "Mariana". Others are set in *several places*: Oscar Wilde's *The Importance of Being Earnest* moves between town and country.

4) When does the Action Happen and When is the Narrator Speaking?

1) You've got to know *when* things *happen* in your text. When you've made notes on '*when*', you can start to see the reasons *why* things happen in a certain order.
2) Remember, texts can cover a period of *many years*, like *Wuthering Heights*. Others cover a *short* period of time; many *poems* try to capture *one moment* in time.

3) Narrators may be immediate eyewitnesses, or they may be looking back on their own past, like Laurie Lee in *Cider with Rosie*.
4) Some texts present *two* views of events, an *eyewitness* version, and a second version, *reflecting* on the *same events* much *later*. In *Great Expectations*, the narrator, Pip, sometimes speaks as a *child*, and sometimes as an *adult*.

5) How does the Action Happen and How is it Described?

1) Close reading (see Section 4) will help you understand the *plot*. You need to make notes on *how* the action happens and how the *events* of the text *fit together*.
2) You should also ask how the action is described; whether the tone is angry or joyful. It's *really important* to make notes of the *tricks* used to create the *tone*, the *characters* and the *descriptions*.

He's back, and this time he's peeved

6) Why do things Turn Out the way they do?

1) You need to keep the *plot*, the *characters*, the *setting* etc in mind.
2) Here you are really asking what the text is trying to say: for example, *All Quiet on the Western Front* is about the mindlessness of war, and the waste of young lives.
3) You need to ask *why* the text has been *written* in the *way* it has: your notes on *who*, *what*, *when*, *where* and *how* will help you.

Understanding texts — a questionable practice...

When you read a text, you've got to *make sure* that you ask yourself the *six major questions* and *make a note* of your answers. Then you'll understand what you've read and you'll be able to answer Exam questions about it. Don't forget to ask the GOLDEN QUESTION: *how* does the text make you *react*, and *what tricks* did the author use to make you react that way?

Extra Exam Hints

These are all hints about how to *read* a text to get the answers you need. For help on how to actually *write* your essays, have a look at Section 7. If you *don't* go about answering the questions the *right way*, the marks will just *slip* through your *fingers*.

Questions that ask How the writer does something

1) For these questions, you need to read the text very *closely* and *carefully*.
2) When you read the text, notice the *tone* of the text, and the reaction it creates in you.
3) You've also got to look at the *style* of the text very carefully, so that you can say *exactly how* the writer has achieved their effects.
4) See whether the *vocabulary* used is simple or complicated — if it gives a lot of detail or just the plain facts.
5) Look at *how* the characters in the text *speak*. The author may be trying to show that they are *foreign*, or *posh*, or *stupid*.
6) Use the six big questions (P.50-51).

I'm the eighth Duke of Windsor don't you know

Questions that ask you to write as a Character

You really need to *understand* the character you're writing about. There will be a lot of *clues* in the text. You need to think about these two things when you read the text:

> 1) The *descriptions* of your character in the book or play.
> 2) The way your character *relates* to the *other characters*.

1) Make sure you've got a *really good grasp* of the *events* in the scene you're asked to write about.
2) Make sure you know *what* happened, *how* it happened, and *why* it happened the way it did.
3) Pick out the *important bits* of the text. Look for the *events* that are most important to your character, and make sure can explain how he or she is *feeling*.
4) Look at the *language* that your character uses, and try to use *similar language* in your answer.

Now is the winter
of our discontent
Made glorious summer
by this son of York...

Questions that ask you to write as a Director

1) For these questions, you have to *understand* the way *language* is used in the play to create *feeling* and *atmosphere*. You need to say what you would do to *suggest* the atmosphere to the *audience*.and where you would get the actors to *stand*, and what they would *do* during each scene
2) You also need to have a good *understanding* of the *characters* so that you can tell the actors how to say their lines.
3) Don't forget to support your answer with *references* to the *text*.

Answering literary questions — going by the book...

If you have a think about how to tackle these questions now, *before* the exam, you'll be *prepared* for them *in* the Exam. Take it step by step and it'll soon seem easy.

Extra Exam Hints

How to write a Subtext to a Scene from Shakespeare

Writing a *subtext* to a playscript is writing down what the characters *really think* or *really feel*.

1) You need to understand the *motivations* of the characters. This means you need to read the scene very *closely* and look for *clues* in the way the characters relate to each other.

Ooh, I know how you feel!

2) Think about what you know about the characters from the *rest* of the play as well.
3) You have to analyse the *language* that the characters use. Obviously, that means that you've got to *understand* it all. You'll get *more marks* if you say in your answer *how* Shakespeare's use of language gives you *clues* about the characters' attitude and motivation.
4) You must look at the *ideas* in the scene. You could say how one character has *power* over another, or how a character has *divided loyalties* and wants to *please two people at once*.
5) *Don't* just translate the text into modern English — that *isn't* what you're being asked to do.

Quote from the Text when you need to

1) Whatever you say about a text, you need to *support* your answer by *referring to the text*. If you *don't* do this, you won't get as many marks for your answer, *even* if it's right.
2) Also, if you *make sure* your answer is *firmly rooted* in the text, you *won't* be tempted to wander and *get off the point*.
3) You've got to remember to *quote* from a text. This shows the person reading your essay *exactly* what bit of the text you're talking about. (See P.73. for how to quote in essays.)
4) *Don't worry* about learning long extracts from the *Shakespeare* plays you've studied, though. In the exam you will be *given* the scenes that you're asked questions on.
5) It's not a good idea to learn great chunks of text for the sake of it.

I've learnt this speech so I'd better put it in

6) First of all, you don't get marks for knowing the text word-perfectly, but for being able to *understand* it and *respond* to it, using *all* the *techniques* you've *learned* in this Section.
7) Secondly, if you answer a question with quotes that just *aren't relevant*, you won't get *any* marks *at all*. That's not what you want.

Giving your Opinion of a Text

1) You can only form an *opinion* of a text by reading it.
2) You must be ready to *quote* from the text. You will need to give *examples* from the text to *back up* your opinion of it. Look at the Section on Writing Skills to help you here.
3) Don't worry if your opinion *isn't the same* as other people's — but only if you can back it up with lots of *examples* from the text.

Opinions are like hats — always on your mind...

There's a lot to remember when you're answering a *reading* question in the Exam. If you *learn* these methods *point by point*, you won't go far wrong. If you know what you've got to *look* for in the text *before* you start to answer a question, it won't seem half as confusing.

Revision Summary for Section Five

Welcome to another extra large Revision Summary. Work your way through the revision questions on this page until you're sure of all the answers. Don't go leaving any out. Once you've got the facts straight, you can give yourself a bit of practice by reading the extract on the opposite page and answering the questions underneath. Fun on a stick...

1) What are the four things that you really need to do if you want high marks for Reading questions in the Exam?
2) What would you look for in a text in order to be able to discuss the characters?
3) Why might spelling be a problem in older texts?
4) What are the three key features of written style?
5) Why do authors vary the language that they use? (Give two reasons)
6) What is the name for words that mean the same thing?
7) Where would you look to find these words?
8) What is the name for a word that sounds like what it means?
9) What else can be altered to shape the meaning of a text?
10) What are the three main tricks of poetic language?
11) What is assonance?
12) What is alliteration?
13) Why is the structure of one sentence sometimes repeated throughout a poem?
14) What is imagery?
15) What is the name for the groups of lines into which a poem is divided?
16) What is a simile?
17) What is a metaphor?
18) What must a simile use?
19) Why is exaggeration sometimes used in imagery?
20) Why do authors sometimes describe things as if they were people?
21) What do we call this?
22) What are the Six Billion Dollar Questions?
23) Which two of them are a bit harder than the other four?
24) What is the difference between the author and the narrator?
25) Is the narrator always involved in the action?
26) Why is it important to know when things happen in a text?
27) Why do you need to note how the action is described?
28) What is the Golden Question?
29) What do you need to take especial care to look at when reading a text if you're asked how a writer has achieved their effects?
30) What two things do you need to look at if you're asked to write as a character?
31) What is a subtext?
32) If you're asked to write a subtext to a scene from a Shakespeare play, why shouldn't you just write down what each line means in modern English?
33) When do you need to quote from the text?
34) Why shouldn't you put quotations in just to show that you've learnt them?

Revision Example for Section Five

Read this extract from *A Midsummer Night's Dream*, and then answer the questions below.

Enter a Fairy *at one door and* Robin Goodfellow [Puck] *at another.*

Puck - How now, spirit, whither wander you?

Fairy - Over hill, over dale,
Thorough bush, thorough brier,
Over park, over pale,
Thorough flood, thorough fire.
I do wander every where,
Swifter than the moon's sphere;
And I serve the Fairy Queen,
To dew her orbs upon the green.
The cow-slips tall her pensioners be,
In their gold coats spots you see:
Those be rubies, fairy favors,
In those freckles live their savors.
I must go seek some dewdrops here,
And hang a pearl in every cowslip's ear.
Farewell, thou lob of spirits, I'll be gone.
Our Queen and all her elves come here anon.

Puck - The King doth keep his revels here to-night;
Take heed the Queen come not within his sight;
For Oberon is passing fell and wrath,
Because that she as her attendant hath
A lovely boy stolen from an Indian king;
She never had so sweet a changeling.
And jealous Oberon would have the child
Knight of his train, to trace the forests wild;
But she perforce, withholds the loved boy,
Crowns him with flowers, and makes him all her joy,
And now they never meet in grove or green,
By fountain clear, or spangled starlight sheen,
But they do square, that all their elves for fear
Creep into acorn-cups, and hide them there.

Fairy - Either I mistake your shape and making quite,
Or else you are that shrewd and knavish sprite
Call'd Robin Goodfellow. Are you not he
That frights the maidens of the villagery,
Skim milk, and sometimes labour in the quern,
And bootless make the breathless housewife churn,
And sometime make the drink to bear no barm,
Mislead night wanderers, laughing at their harm?
Those that Hobgoblin call you, and sweet Puck,
You do their work, and they shall have good luck.
Are you not he?

Puck - Thou speakest aright;
I am that merry wanderer of the night.
I jest to Oberon and make him smile
When I a fat and bean-fed horse beguile,
Neighing in likeness of a filly foal;
And sometimes lurk I in a gossip's bowl,
In very likeness of a roasted crab,
And when she drinks, against her lips I bob,
And on her withered dewlop pour the ale.
The wisest aunt, telling the saddest tale,
Sometime for three-foot stool mistaketh me;
Then slip I from her bum, down topples she,
And "tailor" cries, and falls into a cough;
And then the whole quire hold their hips and loff,
And waxen in their mirth, and neeze, and swear
A merrier hour was never wasted there.
But room, fairy! here comes Oberon.

Fairy - And here my mistress. Would that he were gone!

(A Midsummer Night's Dream, Act II, scene i, lines 1-59; William Shakespeare)

Plain Questions on the Text

1) Why are the King (Oberon) and Queen of the Fairies quarrelling? *(2 marks)*
2) Name four things that the Fairy says that Puck does. *(4 marks)*
3) Name two things that Puck says that he does to amuse Oberon. *(2 marks)*
4) What was the Fairy about to do before he was interrupted by Puck? *(1 mark)*

Responses to the Text

5) Comment on the differences between the two characters. *(10 marks)*
6) What impression do you form of the fairy world from this extract? Comment on some of the features of poetic language that are used and the effects they create. *(20 marks)*

Non-Fiction and Media Texts

For your English course, you'll have to read *non-fiction texts* as well as fiction. *Don't panic* though — the skills you need are exactly the same.

We Look at Non-Fiction Texts All the Time

My hobby is surfing the internet

1) We see non-fiction texts around us all the time. We read *newspapers* and *magazines*. We watch *news* and *documentary* programmes on television. We use the *internet*.
2) These sources of information are called the *media:* they present us with different views of the world, for entertainment or for news.
3) We see *adverts* on television, in magazines and on posters.
4) So we're *already* used to looking at these texts and *understanding* and *responding to them*, even if we don't realise it.

Not that sort of trick, Eric!

What to Look For in Non-Fiction Texts

1) Non fiction texts are always trying to give a certain *picture* of the facts. They use a lot of the same *tricks* that *fiction* writers use (see Section Five).
2) Look at the *style* of the text. You need to look at the *language*, *tone* and *vocabulary* used.
3) Look at the *vocabulary* used. Is it simple and written so that *most people* can *understand* it, or are there a lot of *technical* or *jargon* words?
4) Look at the *sentences* used. Are they *long and descriptive* or are they *short and snappy?* In some newspapers, each paragraph of a story has a *mini headline* which *isn't* a full sentence.
5) Think about the *tone* of the text. An article about a *new computer game* might make you *excited* about going out and buying it (ah, go on, you know it would). A documentary about a deadly *virus* might make you *worried* about diseases taking over the world. A leaflet about *experiments on animals* might make you *angry*.
6) You've got to be able to say *how* the text makes you feel these emotions.
7) When you read the text, ask yourself the *six* major questions (PP.50-51).

They tried teaching me Japanese

The Top Five Tricks used in Non-Fiction Texts

1) *Leaving out information*, especially statistics. They *don't* tell you as much as you'd *think*. Texts *generalise;* they say something is *always true* when really there are *exceptions*.
2) *Emotional vocabulary* — language is used to make you *feel* a certain way: eg some news reports may say "limited air strikes"; others, "illegal military interference."
3) *Exaggerating* information to make it sound more interesting: eg "Music Star Marriage on the Rocks" sounds more exciting than "Married Musicians have a Tiff."
4) *Tone:* whether the presentation is *serious* or *comic:* eg some interviewers describe the bad habits of the person they interview if they want to present a negative opinion.
5) *Opinions* are often presented as though they were *facts*. This is *difficult* to pick up, but it is *important*. News reports speculate about what will happen in the future — this is opinion.

It's all true — honest...

Reading *non-fiction* uses the *same techniques* as reading *fiction*. *Learn* the *top five tricks*.

Looking At Non-Fiction

It's very important to be able to recognise where a text is *biased*. If you can pick out bias in a text, you'll pick up *more marks* in your Exams and classwork.

Everything We Read or Watch is Biased

1) All media are *biased:* they give an opinion of the truth, not the whole truth.
2) Even *news* programmes are *biased:* Local news focuses on different stories from national news. This is because some stories are more important in the local region.
3) You need to look at information *critically*. That means reading it carefully, using your comprehension skills (see Section Four, P.36); and trying to work out what the text is *saying*, and what *opinion* it is putting forward.

BEWARE: many media texts claim to be unbiased and say that they present only the truth. Don't believe them. Make sure you look at them critically.

An Important Question — Why was the text written?

If you know *why* a text was written, you'll find it a lot *easier* to *understand* it and to discuss how it uses *language*.
Texts can be made to:

1) Where the text *came from* gives you a lot of *clues* about its purpose.
2) A *short story* in the back of a women's magazine is written to *entertain* and to appeal to the reader's romantic fantasies.
3) A *booklet* given to *parents of new pupils* at a secondary school is written to *inform* them about the school, and also to *persuade* them that the school has good discipline and exam results.
4) A *shopping list* is just written to *inform* you what groceries you need. There's no point in making it *entertaining* or *persuasive*.
5) An advert is mainly written to *persuade*, but it can also *inform* you about the product and *entertain* you. Some adverts contain more information than others.

My Really Entertaining Shopping List.
chick peas
carrots
onions
chocolate biscuits

Fiction vs Fact

When you look at any text, you'll have to decide whether it's a piece of fiction or not. Unfortunately, it isn't always that easy.

Non-Fiction texts aren't always Factual

The Rubbish Times

Minister's Toe Stuck In Tap Trauma

Mr. Generico-Politico was found by firemen after a five hour ordeal. (FACT) His landlady is reported to claim to have placed superglue in the tap. (OPINION)

1) Learn the *styles* of different kinds of non-fiction text. Then you need to check *bias* in the text, and any confusion between fact and opinion.
2) Many non-fiction texts are deliberately written as a *mixture* of fact and opinion. A good *essay* contains *both* fact and opinion. *Newspaper editorials* do the same.
3) The *argument* of a text will give opinions *based* on the facts, and use facts as *examples* to illustrate points. Sometimes the text will *say clearly* when it's giving an opinion, sometimes it *won't*. You will need to read carefully for opinions and facts.
4) Many texts use *quotations* from other texts. The source of the quotation must be given.
5) Some texts use quotations *as though* they are facts. Be very careful; many quotations just give *someone else's opinion:* eg the opinion of the *Prime Minister's Press Officer* on the *success* of the *government*.
6) News reports today are a mixture of fact and opinion. Reporters tell the *story* of people involved in a news event — we hear *what happened* and their *opinion* of the event. The report has been written to make you respond *emotionally* — it doesn't just contain facts.

Always look out for the relationship between facts and opinions in any non-fiction text you read. It will give you lots to write about in Coursework or Exam essays.

Some Fiction is written in the Style of Non-Fiction

1) Many authors use the *language* and *tone* of non-fiction texts — some novels use *letters* or *diaries* to tell the story: eg *The Secret Diary of Adrian Mole* by Sue Townsend.
2) Sometimes authors include reports from fictional newspapers, or police reports, to make their stories sound *realistic*.
3) *Soap operas* on TV are often written to make the characters and situations *seem real*, even though they aren't. Of course, some soap operas aren't very realistic at all.
4) Adverts use this sort of real-life presentation: If you *believe* in the people in the advert, you will feel that *you* need the *product* as much as *they* do.
5) When you read a text, look for signs that it might be written in a *non-fiction style*, and ask yourself what *effect* the author is trying to create.

You can improve your English grade — that's a fact...

Phew! There's plenty to watch out for when you're looking at *non-fiction texts*, especially media texts. Read closely for *fact* and *opinion* — it'll help you to work out the *bias* of the text.

The Media

The word media is literally "the means" by which something is done. Nowadays it's used to mean the news media — television, radio and newspapers etc.

Newspapers are either tabloids or broadsheets

1) Newspapers are either *tabloids* or *broadsheets*. Tabloids are smaller, easier to read and tend to focus on *sensational stories* with *big, bold headlines*.
2) Tabloids often *mix fact* with *opinion* in the same article.
3) Tabloids use biased and *emotional language* to either make you *feel sorry* for or *dislike* the person they're writing about.
3) Some tabloids cut down the number of *news* stories so that they can include more stories about famous *stars* or *scandals*.
4) Broadsheets are large newspapers that fold in half. They tend to have a *more serious tone*, and are separated into different *sections* which contain different styles of article.
5) In a broadsheet, *opinion* articles are *clearly marked*, so the reader can tell that they're opinion.

Reading Newspapers to find their Style

Here's a sample extract. Read it carefully and learn how to spot the key features of its style.

Pie in the Sky!

Plane Hit by Flying Pie at 40,000 Feet

by Our Special Correspondent

An Air Linton 747 was dramatically hit in mid-air over Essex yesterday by a large unidentified object, which was later discovered to be a cherry pie.

Pilot Jim Mason, 37, grappled bravely with the controls while passengers screamed in fear.

The pie covered the front window

of the plane, making it impossible for air ace Mason to see. Despite this, Mason and co-pilot Steve Hamley remained calm.

While Hamley radioed Heathrow to warn other planes, Mason prepared to land the plane blind, guided only by top air-traffic controller Ravi Singh.

Ice-cool Singh kept Mason calm with a stream of rib-tickling one-liners, and gently talked him through the stages of his emergency landing.

"Steve and I were both in shock," said plucky Mason afterwards. "There was no radar warning — the thing just hit us and we couldn't see. It's only thanks to Ravi we're safe."

Investigators have no idea why the pie was in British airspace.

Key Features

1) The headline has a *pun* (play on words) to draw the reader in — "pie in the sky" is a saying meaning something will never happen, but the story is about a *real* pie in the sky.
2) The tone of the article is very *emotional* — there are lots of words describing feelings; "bravely", "plucky", "ice-cool". Mason and Singh are described only in these *positive* terms.
3) The story is *biased* towards the *pilots* and the *air-traffic controller* — it *focuses* on what happened to them and hardly talks about the passengers. It *doesn't* even say how many passengers were on board, which would be the first piece of information it would give if the plane had crashed.

People are obsessed with News — except historians...

Learn the *differences* between tabloids and broadsheets. Remember the *top five tricks* from p56. If you can say *what* the extract is *trying to do* and *how* it does it, you'll get *a lot more marks*.

Magazines

Features are the most common kind of article you'll come across in Exams or Coursework. Remember, it's all about using those skills from Sections 4 and 5.

The Difference between Magazines and Newspapers

Flaws
Feared
With New
SuperBike

1) Magazines and newspapers are written for *different reasons*.
2) A magazine has *features* and news about a particular *subject* or written for a particular *group of people*: for example, *football* or *music* magazines, *women's fashion* magazines, *motorcycle enthusiasts'* magazines etc.
3) Newspapers are published *every day* or *every week*; magazines are usually *monthly*.
4) Because magazines are written with a *specific audience* in mind, the articles are often written in a particular *style* or *tone* — when you read a magazine extract, think about where it came from. Look at how the *purpose* of the article affects the *style* — look for the top five tricks.

Recognising the Style of a Feature Article

This sample extract shows the style of a feature article.

The Climber on Top of the World

by Valerie Dale in London and Zelba Reivers in Cumbria

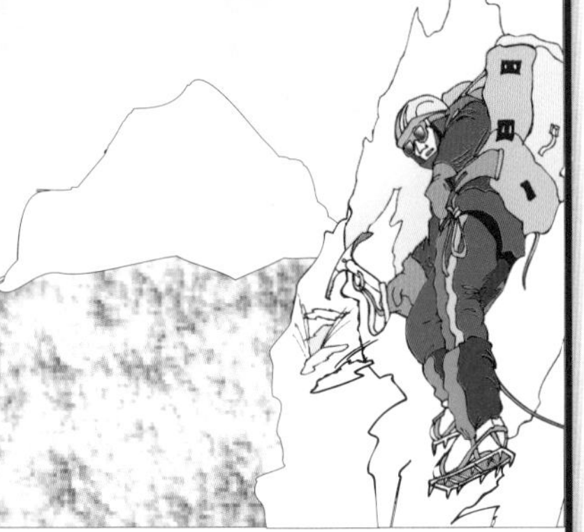

Climbing is a sport dominated by the rich and the young. In recent years, money has come to mean everything; from expensive equipment to huge expeditions with back-up teams, radios and sponsorship deals. Mary Trent is a climber with a difference — she does it all herself.

"I belong to the old school, I'm afraid. None of the great climbers had any of this modern equipment — some of them didn't even wear helmets!" Mary Trent chuckles to herself as she says this.

We are sitting in her Lake District cottage. The walls are covered in photographs of the highest and most treacherous mountains in the world.

I look at all these mountains in amazement. The laughing fifty-year old woman opposite me has climbed them all. I have problems climbing the stairs.

Mary looks at me and taps her nose confidentially: "I'm writing a novel about climbing at the moment. It's about Edmund Mallory. He disappeared climbing Everest in the twenties. A great gentleman amateur, not like today's climbers."

She snorts in derision. "It's all about money now. Real climbers have an obsession. That's why Mallory disappeared. He didn't have the right equipment and the weather was bad, but he kept on anyway — him and one other. The last thing his team saw from the base camp was a solitary figure climbing alone between the clouds. I'd like to think it was Mallory. What a way to go!" cont.

1) The theme is *less obvious* — the headline only makes sense when you start to read the article.
2) The subject of the article, Mary Trent, isn't *introduced* until the *end* of the first paragraph.
3) This is an *interview*, so Mary Trent is allowed to *speak* a lot. The article *describes* her house and the *feelings* of the writer who's meeting Mary — making a *joke* about not being able to climb the stairs.
4) The tone is *slower* than a news report with *more detail*. It's in the *present tense* not the past.

Animal articles — they're creature features...

Feature articles are common in *Reading Exams* — you must learn how to spot the *style* and *tone*. Remember — newspapers and magazines are written in *columns*, so read them that way.

Adverts

You may have to *compare adverts* in a *Reading task*, or write about the effects of advertising. You'll need to know *how* to read adverts critically, so *learn* the points on this page.

Adverts are about Selling Products

1) Sounds simple enough, but some adverts *hide* their product behind a *story* or an *event*. We don't realise they're just selling something.
2) You need to learn to look at them *critically*.
3) Adverts often use the *top five tricks*. Be particularly careful with *statistics* — most are confusing (see below).
4) Adverts appear in many forms: posters, pages in magazines, television adverts etc.
5) The *layout* of an advert is *important* — pictures and text are put together to carry meaning.

Statistics can be Misleading

1) Many adverts use *statistics* to prove a point. They claim that statistics *can't be wrong*.
2) Statistics can be *misleading* though, especially if they aren't very specific.

Example: **"Stoat Toast: Nine out of ten customers prefer it."**

This statistic looks impressive, but you must ask if it's specific enough.

a) It doesn't say *who* the customers are or how many were asked. If we don't know, we *can't tell* if the statistic is impressive or not. The survey might only have asked ten people *altogether*.
b) It doesn't say *what* they prefer Stoat Toast to — there's *no real comparison* between Stoat Toast and their rivals. Perhaps they prefer Stoat Toast to a kick in the teeth, which isn't much of a recommendation.

The advert gives an impressive-sounding statistic which doesn't actually mean much at all. Look out for statistics like this, which give no real evidence.

Some Adverts use Experts to make you believe them

1) Watch out for *so-called experts*. Adverts may use a scientist to recommend a product.
2) It *doesn't matter* that they are experts. They have been *paid* to say how good a product is.
3) Scientific tests may claim to prove a product is better than "our leading competitor" — but won't say *who* the competitor is.

Advertising Slogans Use Sound Patterns

1) Slogans are easy-to-remember phrases which *remind* you of the product in an advert.
2) They often use *sound patterns* (see P.48).
3) They also appeal to our *fantasies* — the kind of lifestyle we want to have — and to our *worries*, such as whether we're overweight or unpopular.

Stoat toast — the anagrammatic snack...

Remember, even though adverts come in *different forms*, they use the same tricks of *tone*, *language* and *style* as other texts to try to *sell* their products. Learn to look at them *critically*.

Posters and Leaflets

You may not think these topics have much to do with English — but you may have to look at a leaflet or a poster when you read an *advertising text*, and that means you need to know about looking at *pictures* and *layout*. Otherwise you *won't* pick up all the *marks*.

Posters and Leaflets are Advertising Texts

The Real Taste Of Fish
ACE FISHY POP
You want fizzy cod!

1) Posters and leaflets use *pictures* and *words* to advertise something. This can be anything from a rock band's tour to a soft drink.
2) A poster is *one sheet* of paper fixed to a wall or a board. It has a *small* amount of *text* and a *big picture* to catch the eye.
3) The language on a poster will be *short and snappy* — it's written to give all the important information as quickly as possible.
4) Sometimes the poster will have a *slogan:* eg "They're here. And they mean business.". These aren't always complete sentences.
5) The *picture* on a poster will be *eyecatching* — a photograph of the band looking cool, or a cartoon-style picture.

Interested in new Turnip Burgers?

6) *Leaflets* explain what they are promoting in more *detail* than a poster. They also need to be eyecatching and clear.
7) *Layout is important*. Look at *where* the information is given — is a free gift offered in *large print* near the *top*? does the price only appear in *small print* at the *bottom*?
8) When a leaflet gives you *information* but *isn't* trying to sell you anything, see if the information is *biased* and look for *opinions* being presented as fact.

Looking at Pictures — Finding a Meaning

1) All pictures try to make you *feel* something. Think about *how* the picture makes you feel — and *why*.
2) You need to know how pictures are used *with text* — in newspapers, posters, leaflets and magazines or on television.
3) Sometimes the *text explains* the *picture*, like a newspaper cartoon.
4) Sometimes the *picture explains* the *text*, like a photo in a news article.
5) Think about *why* the picture has been included — whether it is relevant to the text or not, or whether it creates *bias:* eg An article about lions could show cute cuddly baby lion cubs, or a lioness savagely ripping out the throat of a wildebeest.

Remember — all pictures are biased, even photographs. They create a view of what the world is like using different tricks like lighting and colour.

Layout is Important

But it's right at the bottom, so it can't be that important...
Layout really does make a *big difference* to the way you read a text. Everyone reads the *big bold headlines* first, and then works their way onto the *small print* if they can be bothered.

Old cowboys write adverts — ready with slow guns...

You must learn this page to help you look at *newspaper* or *magazine articles*, and at *advertisements*. Remember that pictures are *biased* — even photos can be *altered* by computer.

Autobiographies, Diaries, Letters

These are often easier to read than fiction, so you can pick up lots of marks here.

Autobiographies give a Personal View of Events

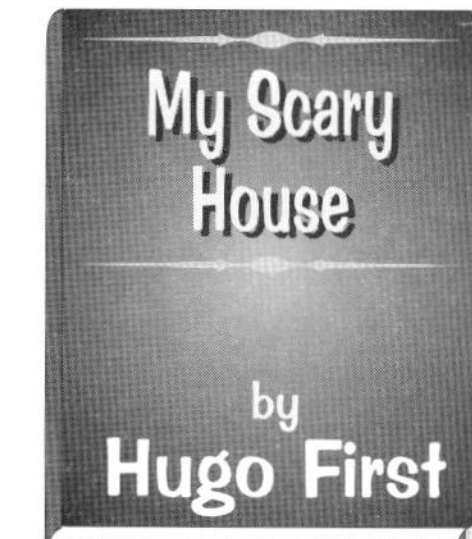

1) Most autobiographies are written by *famous* people.
2) They give a *personal view* of the *events* of their lives, and often include stories about their *careers* and their *private lives*.
3) Most autobiographies are *light-hearted*, but some authors use them to make *serious* points. Recently there have been books about living with cancer, by John Diamond and Ruth Picardie.
4) *Fiction* writers often write in the style of an autobiography. This is called a *first person narrative*, because the story is told using "I" and "me".

REMEMBER: autobiographies are *biased*. Writers *change* the events of their lives to make themselves *look good*, and to *simplify* the past.

Diaries are Personal Daily Records

March 17th I seem to be back on good terms with H. Still not sure what happened at Sally's party though...

1) Don't forget, a diary gives an *opinion*. It's a record of what a person feels.
2) Diaries are *private* books — written for only the author to read. People don't tend to keep secrets from themselves, so they often admit things in diaries that they wouldn't admit in letters or formal writing to other people.
3) Diaries are written in a very *direct style*, as if the author were *talking* to someone — sometimes they address the diary as if it were a real person. *Anne Frank* called her diary "Kitty".
4) Diaries often use *abbreviations* and some use *code* that only the author understands.
5) They are *not* always written in full sentences.
6) The best diaries give a sense of what it *felt like* to be alive at a certain time — *The Diary of Anne Frank* records the life of a young Jewish girl living during the Second World War. She tells us about life hiding from the Nazis. She died in a Concentration Camp.

Looking at Letters

You might be asked to look at a letter and comment on it.

1) Remember to think about *why* the letter was written. Is it trying to *explain*, *inform*, *persuade* or *apologise*? There are always clues in the text.
2) Look at the *tone*. Is it formal or informal?
3) Look at the *vocabulary* used.
4) You should be able to work out *who* the letter might have been written to — a *friend*, a *relative*, a *customer* etc.
5) Look at the section on writing styles for more details about formal and informal letters. See P.91.
6) Often letters written by *famous* people are published after the writer's death — in books of *Collected Letters*: for example, the poet Philip Larkin's letters.

> Dear Ms Hallam,
> I am delighted to inform you that you have won first prize in our Name the Hamster competition.

My aunt delivers post — we always let'er go...

These types of book can win you easy marks — if you read about people who *interest you*. That makes them perfect for *Coursework essays*. Just remember to watch out for *bias* and *evidence*.

Film and TV

Part of your Coursework may include writing a review of a film or TV programme you've watched, or doing a role play in the style of a TV programme. To pick up good marks, you'll need to use your critical skills to interpret them.

Television and Film are Texts Too

1) It might seem *strange* to talk about film and TV as texts, but they are.
2) Even though people seem to be talking naturally in film and TV, they are usually speaking from a *script* — written to make it *sound* like they are making it up as they go along.
3) TV and film include other things apart from language: visual pictures, music, sound effects, sets and lighting. You need to recognise *how* these make you *react* in certain ways.

Film and TV are not the same

1) Films are shown in cinemas and people *pay* to see them.
2) TV is shown on television sets, and shows all kinds of programmes. It's paid for either by *advertising* or by a *licence fee*, like the BBC.
3) Don't forget the *difference* — film makers spend *much more money* making and advertising their product because they need as many people as possible to see it.
4) Most films tell a *complete story*, so that people feel it was worth seeing.
5) Television companies want to have the *biggest share* of viewers, so they try to make a *variety* of programmes that will keep people watching.

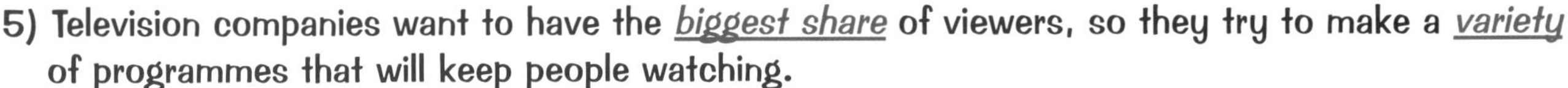

6) Soap operas tell *part* of a story, so you have to watch the *next time* to see what happens.

Films and TV programmes can be *fiction* or *non-fiction* — both use the same techniques to affect you. The *secret* of TV and film is how they make you *feel*.

Watching Television —the Right Way

1) Television programmes come in many *forms* — documentaries, game shows, chat shows etc.
2) Each *form* of programme has its own *style* — chat shows are usually funny and news programmes are almost always serious.
3) Think about how *pictures* and *music* create *tone* — especially in *documentaries*. Remember — documentaries mix *fact* and *opinion*.
4) Listen to the way people on TV talk. On *news* programmes they will sound *serious* and use *formal language*; on *chat shows* people will sound *friendly and jokey*. Listen out for the language and tone.
5) You might be asked to do a *role play* or a *discussion* in the *style* of a TV programme in a Speaking task. You'll get *top marks* if you know the style of that programme, and know *how* you should act and speak.

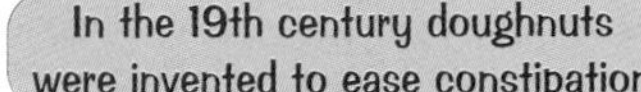

In the 19th century doughnuts
were invented to ease constipation

TV helps you get a better grade — Michael Grade...

Remember — the *words* and *structure* of films or television programmes have been chosen to make you *feel* what the director wants you to feel. To get *top marks* in essays and speaking tasks, you need to show how these *tricks* are being *used*. That means watching carefully.

Texts in the Exam

Here are some hints on how to go about answering questions on non-fiction texts in the Exam.

Unseen Texts are set as Comprehension Exercises

1) Even though you won't see the text until you are in the Exam, *don't panic* — you can do *six things* to improve your chances.
2) You can *practise* the skills you'll need on *any* non-fiction text you've never read before. Practise reading and summarizing newspaper articles. Write a paragraph on the style and the tone.
3) Work out what *kind* of text it is — a magazine, a newspaper or a travel book; a feature article or a critical text.
4) The *key skills* for looking at a text are given in Section Four. Remember to scan the text, read it closely, take note of the important details and be prepared to answer questions.

Six Points to Improve your Marks

1) *Read the questions carefully* to decide what the Examiner is asking you to look for.
2) Check your *notes* and then the *text* to find the answer. If you quote the exact words in the text, make sure you don't forget to use *quotation marks*.
3) Always check to see how many marks are given for each question. Never make your answers longer than they need to be — that's just wasting time.
4) Use *all* the information you're given. If there's a *picture*, make sure you talk about it in any essay question — why it is there, what effect it has.
5) Look for any information in the *introduction* to the question which tells you the *date* and where the piece came from — this will help you look for *bias*.
6) See if the passage is an *extract* from a longer text — this may mean that some parts of the argument are left out. Only write about the text which you've actually been given.

Look out for the top five tricks — especially any confusion between fact and opinion. Always remember to read carefully to see if the text is biased.

Comparing and Contrasting

1) Some unseen tasks will ask you to *compare* and *contrast* two or three texts.
2) The secret is not to panic — scan and read *each text in turn*. Then make a list of what the texts have in *common*, and then what the main *differences* are.
3) The texts will be about the *same subject* from *different* points of view.
4) You need to talk about *why* you think the two texts have different views.
5) The clues are not just in the text, but in the *extra information* you're given about it. For example you might have to compare a newspaper article on a new road being built in a town with a leaflet about the *same road* produced by an *environmental pressure group*.

WARNING: don't *attack* the opinions in an unseen text unless you can give *reasons*. Remember: you *may not* have the *whole argument* in front of you.

I've looked at loads of unseen texts — in the dark...

Talk about details... but they're all important. You need to know *exactly* what you are doing when you get into the *Exam* — that means learning the key skills *now*, so get going.

Revision Summary for Section Six

This is the last Section on Reading skills, so make sure that you've got everything sorted, and you'll be ready to move onto Section Seven on Essay writing skills. You'll find it worthwhile to have a look back over Section 4 on Comprehension skills. They're the key to looking at any text, whether it's fiction or non-fiction. Go through these questions until you can do them all — there's no point in leaving any of them out. If you're stuck, then have a look back through this Section for the answers.

1) Name four places where we see non-fiction texts.
2) What is meant by 'the media'?
3) What are the top five tricks used in non-fiction texts?
4) What four things are texts made in order to do?
5) Is non-fiction necessarily fact?
6) Is the news just fact?
7) Why are adverts often made to look like real life?
8) What are the two types of newspaper?
9) Give three differences between them.
10) How is the pace of a feature article different from a newspaper article?
11) Is it always obvious whether a text is trying to sell you something or not?
12) Give two ways in which statistics can be misleading.
13) What are the differences between leaflets and posters?
14) Why is the layout of a poster important to its meaning?
15) How do pictures help create bias in a text?
16) Give two ways in which autobiographies are biased.
17) What is the style of a diary like?
18) Apart from language, what elements are used to create a reaction in film and television texts?
19) What is the difference between the way films are paid for and the way television is paid for?
20) Why are TV dramas broken up into episodes, while films tell a whole story?
21) Are documentaries fact, opinion or both?
22) What six things can you do to improve your chances when tackling unseen texts in the Exam?
23) Why should you be careful if you say that the opinions in an unseen text are wrong?

Revision Example for Section Six

Looking After the Environment — the Attitude Question

It's very easy to say that we care about the environment. In fact, for a lot of people it has become second nature. They think that by using unleaded petrol and by recycling paper, their lifestyle is "environmentally friendly". But is it really? And if it isn't, what should we be doing?

Looking after the environment means having the right attitude. It's not about a list of things that we all need to start doing, although that helps. It's about learning not to be wasteful — and thinking about how we live.

That means we need to look at what we consume — not just food either. How much electricity we use, how much water? Then we need to ask ourselves the really tough question: do we actually need to use all of that?

Perhaps you don't think this matters. Just think about this, though: every time you leave a light on all day, you waste electricity.

Now most electricity in this country comes from power stations, which are either run on nuclear power or fossil fuels. Both of these types of energy production can cause serious damage to the environment. So every time you leave a light on, you are damaging the environment.

Sounds harsh but it's true. Let's take another example. You often see famous models and film stars campaigning against the fur trade. But how often do you see people campaigning against wearing leather? Leather is made from animal skin too. Maybe the fashion world thinks a leather jacket is too cool to worry about the animals which have died to make it.

Environmental issues aren't something you can pick and choose. They shouldn't be confused with fashion. They're about saving the planet. And that means thinking about every aspect of our lives, not just the ones that the media discusses.

So start by examining your own attitudes, because that's the only way to save the planet.

Questions on the Extract

1) What does the author say is the key to looking after the environment? (1)
2) Is this an opinion or a factual piece? Explain your answer. (3)
3) What does the piece say happens when you leave a light on all day? Why? (3)
4) What reason is given for famous people not campaigning against wearing leather? Do you agree with this reason? Explain your answer. (5)
5) Summarize the argument of the passage. What does it ask us to do? (10)

Writing Tasks based on the Extract

Answer any two of the following questions:

1) "Looking after the environment means changing our attitudes." Do you agree? Give reasons for your answer. (20)
2) Write about your experiences of looking after the environment. (20)
3) Write a formal letter to the Prime Minister expressing your concern about the environment. Think about nuclear power, waste-disposal and road-building. Give a list of practical steps that the government could take to help the situation. (20)
4) Imagine that you could solve three environmental problems in the world. Which ones would you solve and why? (20)

How to Write an Essay

An essay is an attempt to *answer* a *question* — it's a short piece of writing on a particular subject. You'll have to write *essays* for your *Coursework* and in your *Exams*. This Section is about *how* to write a *good* essay, and the common essay *mistakes* to avoid.

Your Essay Work will always begin with a Question

1) Essays are always about *answering questions* — there are *two* main kinds you will come across during your English course.
2) *Literary* essays are essays about specific *texts* that you have read. You'll have to *respond* to the text — you must show you have *read* the text, and *use* it to answer questions and *give opinions* about it.
3) *Personal* essays are essays about a specific *topic* — like *Fox Hunting*, *UFOs* or the *Internet* — where you have to give your *personal opinion* on the topic, giving *reasons* to support what you say.

Essays are about Giving Answers

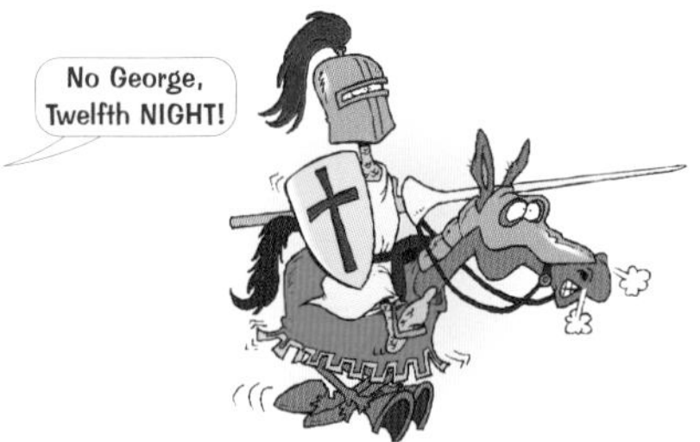

1) The biggest *mistake* that most people make with essays is *not answering* the question. *You mustn't* fall into this trap.
2) Sometimes the question is given to you *clearly:*

> eg What does it mean to be a "gentleman" in *Great Expectations*?
> Does *Twelfth Night* really have a happy ending?

3) *Read* the question *carefully* before you begin your answer. Then give your answer *using* the *words* of the *question*, giving *reasons* and *examples* to support your argument.
4) Sometimes the question will be *unclear* — you'll have to work out *what* it's asking you to do:

> eg "The problem with Romeo and Juliet is that they are too impatient." Discuss.
> Give your opinion on circuses.
> Give reasons for and against road-building.

5) You need to *rephrase* these statements *as questions* — this will tell you *what* you need to think about, and how to start answering them:

> eg Are Romeo and Juliet too impatient? Is this a problem?
> What do you think of circuses?
> What are the reasons for and against road-building?

6) *Be careful* — the first example is actually asking you to think about *two* ideas. Examiners often try to *catch people out* with this kind of question, so keep your *eyes open*.
7) Look at any *extra information* that's given — if there's a *quotation*, see if the *source* is given. If the essay question comes at the *end* of a *comprehension* exercise, then it'll definitely be *based on* the extracts given — read them *closely* and use any *relevant* information in your answer:

> eg The example question about road-building would probably come at the end of an exercise about the Environment. You should read the extracts again to find out what information is given about road-building policy in this country. Then use that information to answer the question, giving your opinion at the same time.

Essays about a blind stag — no eye deer...

This is where you really need to *concentrate* — if your *essay skills* are good, your *marks* will be good too. Remember your *reading skills* from Section Four — if you don't, go over them again.

Essay Style

You must make your essays *interesting* and *clear* to read. If the Examiner can *understand* what you're saying and *follow* your *argument*, you'll pick up more marks.

Write Clear Sentences in Paragraphs

1) *Good* essay style means writing in *proper sentences* — revise PP.32-34.
2) Don't just write *short* sentences or *long* ones, but a *variety* of lengths. The important thing is that they're *clear* to read.
3) Write in *paragraphs*. Every time you introduce a *new point* or a *different idea*, you must start a new *paragraph*. Don't let your paragraphs get *too* long or your essay will start wandering about and will *lose its point*.

Don't Keep Using the Same Vocabulary

1) Try to use plenty of *different* vocabulary in your essays — the Examiner will get very *bored* if you keep using the *same* words over again.
2) Make sure you use words *properly* — if you're not *sure* about a word then think of *another way* to say it. Just be *clear*.
3) *Begin* your sentences in different ways — *don't* just begin every sentence with "The" or "Then" — it's so *boring*.
4) Remember the *two key rules* for using *adjectives* and *adverbs*

> **1) When you use words like *beautiful*, *lovely* and *wonderful*, you must explain *why* you have used them. Without explanation they don't mean *anything*.**

It's not specific enough to say 'This poem is beautiful'. You must *explain why* it is beautiful:

> **2) Avoid *technical-sounding* words like *realistic*, *important*, *poetic* or *stylish*, unless you can explain *why* you're using them. This is a very common mistake.**

People often write things like, '*Wuthering Heights* is a very poetic novel'. This means *nothing* unless you can explain *why* it is poetic:

5) If you use a *technical* word, you should explain what it means in *brackets* (see P.30 on how to use brackets).

You must Use Formal English

The carp were killed in a tragic fatal accident that resulted in loss of life.

1) Your essay has to *prove* to the Examiner that you *know* about the subject and that you can *organise* your *argument*.
2) This means you must use *formal language* — don't be chatty.
3) You need to be *accurate* and *clear* .
4) If your essay seems *confusing* then give a brief *summary* of what you've said so far, and how it *answers* the *question* you were given.
5) *Avoid* using *clichés* (see P.2) and *vague* words, like "nice", "very", "lovely" and "pretty".
6) Watch out for *tautology* — saying the *same* thing *twice* in the same sentence:
   eg The annual boat race is held every year — *annual* and *every year* mean the same thing.

Teachers repeat themselves — that's tautology for you..

Phew! There's a lot to learn on these two pages. If you want to do well in *literary essays*, you must *quote* from the text. Make sure you know how to do it *properly*. Watch the *style* of your essays too — silly mistakes will *cost you marks* even if your argument is clear and well-supported.

Planning and Drafting

I know it's boring, but the *secret* of essay writing really is *good planning*. The stupid thing is that most people *practise* planning, learn how to do it well and then *forget* to do it when they write.

Proper Planning will pick up Better Marks

Edwin's rock cakes weren't going to plan

1) Some people say that planning is a waste of time — it is if you want to *throw marks away*. In fact it can *save* you *time* and *energy*.
2) Planning means *organising* your material to help you *answer* the question.
3) The whole point is to *help* you to work out the *relevant* material for your answer, and the *right order* in which to present it. A good *plan* will help you write a clearer *essay* — and that means *more marks*.
4) A *good* plan will tell you what your *argument* is and which *examples* you need to *support* it — that'll save you *loads* of time when you write.

The Six Steps to Planning a Good Essay

1) Work out *exactly* what the question is asking you to do — *don't panic*. It *doesn't matter* if you have *no idea* what you're going to write. Just *stop* and *think* for a moment about the *exact words* of the question.
2) Scribble a *rough list* of everything you think might be relevant. *Number* each point just so you can *find* it later.
3) Look at the *key* word of the question — *how*, *what*, or *why*. *Choose* the points on your list that *answer* the exact question.
4) If the question says *compare*, divide the list into *two columns* — *similarities* and *differences*.
5) Look at the *whole* question again. Check that you haven't *missed* anything. Then decide what *your opinion* is. You must use your points to *support* your opinion — this is your *argument*.
6) Draw up a *new* plan — write the *question* at the *top*, then your *opinion*. Give your *best* point *first*. Think of *examples* to support your first point, then *link* it to the *next point* you want to make. You'll need at least *five* points.

REMEMBER: if you're not sure what your opinion is, state the arguments for and against. Answer the question by comparing the views on each side.

Drafting means Writing a Rough Version

Tim wasted his time continually redrafting his message

1) This sounds like a real pain — but if you want to do *well* it's *worth doing*. Drafting can *stop* you from writing a *bad essay*.
2) Once you have your *plan*, you should have your *basic argument* and your *key points* and *examples*. Drafting is an *easy way* to see if your plan *works*.
3) Write a *rough version* of your essay. Think what you want to say and *follow* your *plan*. Start by *giving* your *answer* to the question and a short *explanation*, then introduce your *best point*.
4) Give *examples* to support your argument. *Stop* after you've written a *page*. If you think the essay has gone *wrong*, stop *straight away*.
5) Ask yourself if your draft *answers the question*, and if the examples *really* support your points.
6) Think about whether your opinion is *right* and whether your *first* point is really the *best* point. If you're *not* sure then write a *new* plan. It's better to start again *now* than have to do it later.

Be careful of drafts — like planning your chess moves...

Planning and *drafting* saves you time and effort — *thinking* before writing means *fewer mistakes*.

Introducing Your Argument

First you need to know how to *begin* your essay — that means *starting* your argument *right away*.

Essay Structure — getting your point across

1) A good essay has a *beginning*, a *middle* and an *end*, just like a good story.
2) The *hardest* part is *beginning* your essay. The *first sentence* has to start *answering* the question, and tell the Examiner that your essay is going to be good. All that from *one* sentence — so you'd better start *practising*.
3) The middle part of your essay *develops* your *argument*. Follow your plan.
4) The end *sums up* the points you've made and rounds the essay off nicely.

Your Introduction needs to Grab the Attention

1) A good introduction does *two things* — it states clearly *what* the essay is *about* and *how* you are going to *answer* the question.
2) Don't *waste* words — Examiners want you to *get on with it*.
3) That means grabbing their *attention* and showing them that you *know* what you're talking about.

How to write a Good Introduction

1) Answer the *question* in your first sentence, and explain your answer in the rest of the essay, using the points you made in your plan.
2) If you can't answer it *straight away*, then say how you are *going* to answer it in your essay.
3) Then make your *best point* and begin your *argument*.
4) Use the *exact words* of the question. This shows the Examiner that you've *understood* the question fully.

Example of an Essay Introduction

Is Macbeth a wholly evil character? Explain your answer in detail.

Macbeth is not a wholly evil character — he wouldn't be a tragic figure if he were just evil. In fact, Macbeth's character changes during the course of the play; from being a hero and a loyal servant to King Duncan in the opening scenes of Act I, to an unwilling murderer convinced by the prophecies of the witches and the persuasion of his wife. Even at the end of the play, Macbeth is not completely evil. He realises he has lost, and accepts his fate, but he is still prepared to fight and die like a man: "At least we'll die with harness on our back." (Act V, sc. v, line 51). It is because we see him struggling with his ambition and the results of his evil deeds, that Macbeth becomes a sympathetic and tragic hero.

1) The opening sentence gives a *clear answer* to the question. It sounds *sure* of itself. The rest of the opening paragraph *explains* the first point.
2) The introduction links the idea of an *evil character* to the idea of a *tragedy* — if Macbeth is a *tragic figure* then the audience must feel *pity* for him, which means he *can't* be wholly evil.

Essays — more introductions than a Jane Austen book...

Writing *introductions* takes practice — you really must sound *interested*, *organised* and *clear*.

Your Argument

This page is about how to *organise* your writing and *develop* your ideas to get *top marks*. Learn the *Five Points to Avoid*, and make sure you avoid them...

A Good Essay is about being Clear not Right

1) English essays have *no right answers*. It doesn't matter what essay *question* you're given — there's no single *correct* answer.
2) That means you *don't* win marks for being *right* in essays — you win them for making *sense*.
3) This means writing a *good*, *clear* argument and *supporting* it with examples from the text.
4) In *literary* essays the Examiners want you to *show* them that you've *read* the texts, that you've *understood* them and that you can *answer* questions on them, giving *examples*.
5) In *personal* essays you need to *show* that you've *understood* the question, and answer it giving *examples* to support your *own* opinion.

Pete was too clear at times

Your Argument must Make Sense

It was a good night, a bit rubbish really, I really enjoyed it.

1) Don't *contradict* yourself. This means saying one thing and then saying the *opposite* later on in the essay — the Examiner will just think you're *confused*.
2) Keep your argument *logical* — but don't be afraid to *change* your mind. If you realise that your argument is *wrong* halfway through the essay, *don't panic*.
3) Just *add* a sentence saying that your argument up to that point is *one opinion*, but that there's also *another*. Then *explain* what's *wrong* with your first argument, giving *reasons*, and continue the essay with your *new* argument.

Five Stupid Mistakes to Avoid

1) In *literary* essays, don't just tell the *story* in the text — this is a *waste* of time and you'll only get *low marks*. You need to *answer* the question and *argue* in support of your opinion.
2) Don't *wander* — stick to the point and *answer* the question. Don't start talking about *irrelevant* points. Essays are about *answering questions* to get the marks.
3) Don't *change* your argument without explaining *why* to the Examiner. If you *don't* explain what you're doing, it'll look like you don't know what you're talking about.
4) Don't *generalise* — you must give *detailed* examples to back up what you say. Always give *more* than one example. *Never* make sweeping statements about an author or a text.
5) Don't give *irrelevant* or *incorrect* examples — you'll *lose marks*. You must always explain *why* you've included an example and *why* it's relevant to your argument. If it's a *quotation*, check that it *really* means what you think it does.

IMPORTANT: Just retelling the story is a waste of time. Use your comprehension skills (Sections 4, 5 and 6) and talk about the text. ANSWER THE QUESTION.

No correct answers — it just isn't right...

English essays are about *how you argue* — the secret is *learning the skills*, not the answers. Learn the *Five Points to Avoid* — if you don't, you'll just be *throwing marks away*.

Examples and Quotation

To pick up the *marks*, you need to give *examples* to support your *argument* — especially in *literary* essays, where you have to be able to *quote* from the text.

A Quotation is a Phrase taken directly from the Text

1) You must quote *exactly* what the original text says.
2) If you can't remember exactly what the original text said, then put it into your *own words*. Be careful — don't use quotation marks when you do this.
3) Always say where the quotation came from — for *novels* give the *title*, the *chapter* number and the *page* number; for *poems* give the *title* and the *line* number; for *plays* give the *title*, the *Act* and the *scene*. The *first* time you quote from a particular text in an essay, you should also give the *author's name*.

No, Mr Jones,
Juliet did not say,
"Nick Ross by any
other name would
smell as sweet."

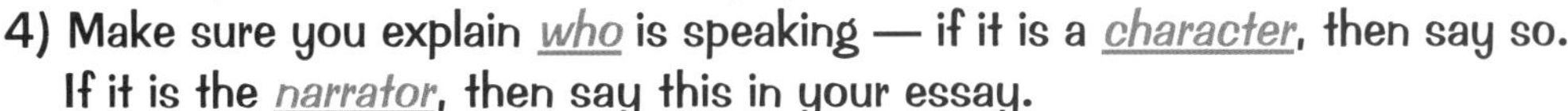

4) Make sure you explain *who* is speaking — if it is a *character*, then say so. If it is the *narrator*, then say this in your essay.

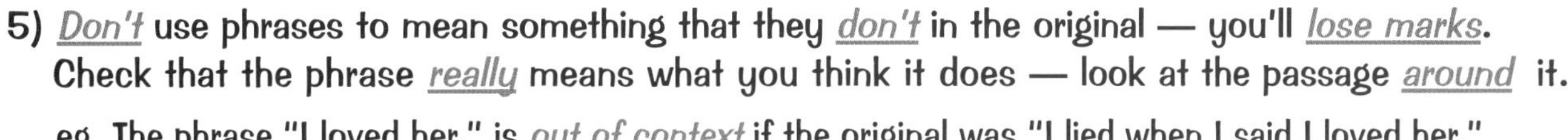

5) *Don't* use phrases to mean something that they *don't* in the original — you'll *lose marks*. Check that the phrase *really* means what you think it does — look at the passage *around* it.

   eg The phrase "I loved her," is *out of context* if the original was "I lied when I said I loved her."

How to Quote from the Text in Essays

1) The *secret* of quoting is choosing *short*, *relevant* phrases that are easy to *remember*.
2) Keep short quotations as *part* of your paragraph, and add *quotation marks* — then give the *reference* in brackets: eg "Sweet sister, let me live." (*Measure for Measure*, Act III, scene i)
3) Leave the *spelling* and *punctuation* exactly the *same* as they are in the original text.
4) Quotations *longer* than a whole *line* should be given as a *separate* paragraph. Leave *space* before and after, and *don't* use quotation marks.

> ...can be seen in the last lines of the poem:
>
> Better by far that you should forget and smile
> Than that you should remember and be sad.
> (*"Remember", lines 13-14; Christina Rossetti*)
>
> The speaker says life should be joyful, even after a loved one dies...

5) When you quote poetry, *don't* just run the lines together like prose. If you quote a sentence where the line *ends* in the *middle*, draw a *slash* / to show where *one line ends* and the next *begins*: "Life's but a walking shadow, a poor player,/That struts and frets his hour upon the stage."

Giving Examples in Personal Essays

1) It's easy to *forget* examples where you're giving your *own opinion* — but unless you include them, your essay *won't* pick up the *marks*.
2) Think about examples from your *own experience* — things that happened to you which are *relevant* to the *question* and relevant to your *argument*.
3) Think about *books*, *films* or *articles* you've read that *support* what you say. If you can, *quote* the *exact* words, otherwise just *explain* what they said in your own words, but give the *source*.

This'll help you — and you can quote me on that...

Your essays need to give *examples* to prove the *points* of your argument. Remember, you get more marks for choosing *relevant* quotations — this shows that you've *read* the text *carefully*. *Never* put a quotation in just because you have learned it — it must be relevant to the essay.

Concluding Your Essay

Once you've made *all* of your points, you need to *close* your essay and *sum up* your answer to the question — you must be *focused*.

Summing Up means bringing together the Key Points

Summing, not
Plumbing!

1) Start a new *paragraph* by looking at the original *question* again.
2) You need to *explain* to the Examiner how you have *answered* the question, restating the *main points* of your argument briefly.
3) Don't go on and on, though. Once you've *summed up*, just write a final *sentence* as your *conclusion*.

Go Over Your Essay When You've Finished

1) *Read through* your essay quickly to check that it *makes sense*, and that it says what you *want* it to say.
2) Check the *grammar*, *spelling* and *punctuation*. If you find a *mistake* then cross it out *neatly* and write the *correction* above. Don't be *messy* — you'll *lose marks*.
3) If a sentence isn't *clear*, then cross it out and put an *asterisk* * beside it. Put another asterisk in the *margin* beside the sentence, and write what you *meant* to say in the margin.
4) If a whole *paragraph* is unclear, write the *page* out again. Rewrite the paragraph so it is *clear*.
5) If there are *lots of mistakes*, then *rewrite* the essay — you won't have time for this in Exams.

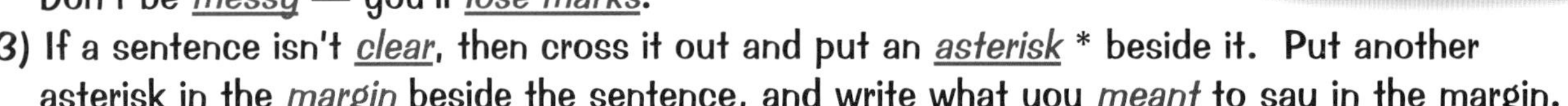

REMEMBER: planning your argument properly means that you won't have to rewrite it at the end. Always plan and draft before you start the actual essay.

Don't Panic if You Realise Your Essay is Wrong

I must
panic less...

1) It's everybody's *nightmare* that they read through an essay and realise that their answer is *completely wrong*.
2) Sometimes it's not until you actually start *writing* that you have your *best* ideas, so your argument should be *flexible*.
3) Don't be afraid to *adapt* your argument as you go along. Every so often, *stop* and *read* what you've written up to that point. If it seems to *answer* the question then keep going.
4) If it *doesn't* answer the question then *stop* writing — work out what the *problems* with the argument are, then *carry on*, saying the *opposite* to what went before.
5) If you realise you've *forgotten* something really *obvious* and *easy*, then write a *note* at the bottom of the *final* page, *explaining* what you've done — you'll pick up some *marks* for *realising* your mistake. If there's time, write an extra *paragraph* at the end of your essay, explaining what your answer to the question *should* have been and *why*.
6) *Never panic* — you'll have *plenty* of chances to write *more* essays. Ask if you can *rewrite* any essays where you made big mistakes — this will help you practise *planning* your argument and *answering* the question. *Learn* from your mistakes.

Always try to answer the question — even if you haven't got much to say. The Examiners will give you marks for keeping to the point. Never make things up.

Fighting about cricket — arguing the toss...

Keep your conclusions *to the point*, and *check* your essay so that you don't make *silly mistakes*.

Writing about Narrative

You'll need to look at *themes*, *style* and *language*. In your SAT Exams, you'll usually be asked questions on specific passages from the texts you've studied.

Looking at Passages in Detail

"Let's get this revolution spic and span," thought Shirley.

1) This means using your *comprehension skills* — look at Section Four again.
2) You need to *read* the text *closely* so that you can *explain* exactly what *effects* it creates and what *language* and *tone* are used.
3) You're giving *examples* to illustrate larger points in the *argument*, but you're also showing the Examiner that you've *read* the text and *understood* it.
4) Remember to ask the *six major questions* (see Section Five, PP.43-44). Work out *who* the *narrator* is, and what the *style* of the passage is — for example, a *descriptive*, *narrative* or *dialogue* passage.
5) Look at *how* the text involves *you* in the action — whether you're told what the characters *think* or you *see* them doing things *without* any explanation.

An Example of Writing about a Specific Passage

...Nothing moved. The fronds of palms stood still against the sky. Not a branch stirred along the shore, and the brown roofs of hidden houses peeped through the green foliage, through the big leaves forged of heavy metal. This was the East of the ancient navigators, so old, so mysterious, resplendent and sombre, living and unchanged, full of danger and promise. And these were the men. I sat up suddenly. A wave of movement passed through the crowd from end to end, passed along the heads, swayed the bodies, ran along the jetty like a ripple on the water, like a breath of wind on a field — and all was still again.

(*'Youth', from the Collected Short Stories of Joseph Conrad*)

This passage creates a *contrast* between *movement* and *stillness*. It opens with *nothing* moving, and describes the stillness of the trees and the foliage which hide the houses. Then it gives an *image* of this stillness — the leaves are said to be "forged of heavy metal." This is a *metaphor* for the still, heavy atmosphere, which the narrator tells us is the *ancient East* — "living and unchanged". These lines make it seem as if *time is standing still*.

Suddenly the narrator *sits up*, and there is an *instant movement*. This movement is described in terms of a *chain reaction* — it is caused by the narrator (an outsider) moving suddenly. When he sits up, he creates a *wave* which passes *through* the crowd before returning to *stillness* ("...and all was still again."). This creates a *picture* in our minds of exactly what happens — the way that the still, unchanging East suddenly *reacts* when confronted by *outsiders* like the narrator.

Writing about the Structure of a Novel

1) Writing about the *structure* of the novel means looking at the *effect* of the *whole* book.
2) See if there is *one* narrator or *more*, and if the narrator is a *character* or a *detached observer*.
3) Write about the main *themes* of the book — the *ideas* that keep coming up in different places.
4) You must make *connections* — you need to be able to *link* different parts of the novel which are about the *same* thing. That means you have to *read* the text *closely* and take *good notes*.

DON'T FORGET: you must give examples to support your arguments about the structure of the novel. Write about specific passages in detail as evidence.

Writing about novels — pure fiction I reckon...

Remember — *don't* just retell the story. You *won't* get *any marks* for doing this.

Writing about Plays

Writing about plays doesn't just mean looking at *what* the *characters say*, but *how* they say it and what else they *do* on stage. Plays were written to be *performed* — never forget this.

Write about How a Play would look On Stage

1) When you read a play, you need to *imagine* how it would look *on stage*.
2) Read it *out loud* or even *act* the scenes out, using the *stage directions*.
3) Stage directions are *information* telling you what the characters are *doing*, where they should *move* and how they *say* their lines.
4) *Remember* — all the information a play gives about the *characters* and *story* must be spoken by the cast *on stage*. The *audience* doesn't get to see the stage directions. *Think* about this when you're *writing* an essay on how you would *direct* a scene.

Julian took acting out too far

Dialogue in a play tells us what the characters _think_ about _themselves_. The way they _speak_ and _behave_ tells us whether they are telling the _truth_ or _lying_.

Plays use Unrealistic Tricks

1) Plays try to create a picture of the *real world*. This can mean lots of *unrealistic* things happen, like people speaking *poetry*, *music* in the background and shifts in *time* and *place*.
2) *Older* plays, such as *Shakespeare's* works, tend to follow the story from *beginning* to *end*. Some modern plays jump around in time between the past and the present.
3) Often characters *alone* on stage speak *directly* to the audience — the *fancy* name for this is a *soliloquy*. In these speeches, characters *explain* what they're *thinking*.
4) *Hamlet* and *Mark Antony* (in *Julius Caesar*) have soliloquies explaining what they're going to do. Talking directly to the audience *involves* us in the *plot* — we *know* things the characters on stage *don't* know.
5) Some plays only have *one* character who tells the *whole* story — these are called *monologues:* for example *Talking Heads*, by *Alan Bennett*.

Five Key Features to Write About in Plays

1) Look at *how* the audience is *involved* in the action — whether *you* know things that the *characters* on stage *don't* know. This can be *comic* or *tragic*.
2) Think about how the play makes you *feel* — whether it makes you *happy*, *sad* or *angry*.
3) Look at the *language* — whether the play is written in *verse*, or the language sounds *normal* and *realistic*, or there's a *mixture* of styles (like in *Shakespeare*). Look at the *imagery* (P.47).
4) Write about *what* the characters *say* and *how* they *sound* to you — telling the *truth* or *lying*.
5) Write about any *performance* of the play you've seen, including *films* and *videos* — how it made you *feel*, and whether you *reacted* differently when you *saw* the play from when you *read* it. *Remember*, any play you see is only *one interpretation* — the *director* has read the play and *told* the actors to perform each scene a certain way (see PP.52 on Direction and 88 on Reviews).

A method-acting doughnut — jammy role-playing...

Plays can be hard texts to write about. You have to look at *more* than just the words on the page, and try to imagine *how* the play would be *performed*. The secret of this is *putting yourself* in the position of the *audience* — think about how the play would *appear* to you and how it *involved* you.

Writing about Poems

Poetry can be *tricky* to write about because a *lot* is said in a *small* amount of *text*. That means you have to read it *carefully* — especially for the *language* and *tone*.

Writing about a Poem — Style, Tone and Meaning

"You can't be too careful when you're reading poetry," said Ken.

1) *Begin* by reading the poem *through*. Ask yourself how it makes you *feel*.
2) Look at what the *question* wants you to *do* and concentrate on that. If it's a *comprehension* exercise then you need to look at *everything*. Make sure you *answer* the question.
3) Read the poem again. Read *each* sentence *carefully* until you've worked out what it *means*. Remember, *even though* a sentence may be on two or more *lines* of a poem, it's still a *whole* sentence that has to *make sense* by itself.
4) *Good* poetry doesn't *waste* any words, so if you don't *understand* any of the words in the poem, look them up in a *dictionary*. In an Exam, try to *work out* the meaning from the *sentence* around it — think about a meaning that would *make sense* in that sentence.
5) Remember to write about the tricks of *poetic language* that are used (See P.47).
6) Look for *hidden meanings* — sometimes the main *theme* of the poem *isn't* mentioned clearly. You need to look at what *happens* and work out what it *means* from the *tone* and the *style*.
7) Every poem has an *argument*, just like an essay. If the argument doesn't seem to make *sense*, there could be a *hidden meaning* in the poem. If the poem *contradicts* itself, then this may be a deliberate *trick* by the poet which you need to spot.

Don't just write about what happens in the poem in your own words. You won't get any marks for that — you have to tell the Examiner what it means.

Older Poems are Easier to Write About

1) You may think that *older* poems are *hard*, but they're actually much *easier* to write about. That means you can win *higher marks*.
2) Older poems often use more *poetic language* and *vivid images* (P.).
3) They generally have strong *rhythms* — so it's much easier to write about the *style* and use of *language*. See how the *rhymes* work.
4) The hard part is understanding the *tone* and some of the *vocabulary*. This comes with *practice*.
5) *Modern* poems are *easier* to understand. This can make it *difficult* to find much to *say* about them — if they're very *clear* then there are no *hidden meanings* to look for. Just remember to look at the *language* and the *images* used.

Writing about word music — going for a song...

Writing about poetry can be tough. Learn the rules on this page, and read the poem through carefully. Take it *step by step*. Remember to write about *tone* — how the poem makes you *feel*. See Section Ten for a *practice example*. You must practise reading *older poetry*.

Writing Exam Essays

Exam essays are *different* — you won't have as much *time* and you'll have to make your *argument* as *clear* as possible. Practise some *timed essays* before sitting any Exam. If you're *well prepared* there's *no reason* to panic.

Always Read the Question Carefully

Pam launched straight in without a clue what she was doing

1) In the Exam you *mustn't panic* — read the *whole* Exam paper through *first*. *Don't* just start writing without *thinking*.
2) Then read it through *again* and *mark* the *questions* you think you can do.
3) Work out *exactly* what the question is asking you to *do*. Then *plan* your essay. *Don't* write without a plan — it should only take a *few minutes* to scribble one, and your essay will be *clearer* for the Examiner to follow.
4) Start with your *best point* and begin your answer *straight away*. Don't *waste* time with a *long* and *irrelevant* introduction.

Poor Presentation will lose you Marks

The Best Essay In The World Ever

My essays are the best in the world ever because (~~I am an absolute genious~~) I practised*.

*the key skills

1) Your essay must look *neat* and *tidy* so the Examiner can read it.
2) Your *handwriting* must be *clear* and *readable*.
3) *Space* your essay out *neatly* — write the *title* at the *top* and *underline* it, then leave one line *blank* underneath it.
4) Remember to write in *paragraphs* — leave a *gap* between the *margin* and the beginning of each paragraph.
5) If you make a *spelling mistake* or write the *wrong word*, put *brackets* around it and *cross it out* neatly with *two lines* through the word. *Don't scribble* all over it or use a *whitener*.
6) If you *re-read* your essay and realise you need to *explain* something, put an *asterisk* * at the end of the *sentence* you need to explain, and write a short explanation in the *margin*. This is the *only* time you should write in the margin.

Never Make Any of these Six Mistakes

As Lord Byron wrote, "You can't beat a pig in a poke with a blind bat."

1) *Never invent* things — *don't* invent *examples* or *quotations*. Even if you don't know any examples, you'll *get marks* for trying to *answer* the question.
2) *Don't* get *sidetracked* — *stick to the point* and *answer* the question.
3) *Don't* write without *thinking* or *planning* — a good Exam answer *isn't* about how *much* you write, it's about whether you *answer* the question *clearly*.
4) *Never* learn an *essay plan* in *advance* — it *won't* answer the Exam question you're given, and you'll *lose marks* for an *irrelevant* argument.
5) *Don't quote out of context* — the Examiner will *mark you down* because it shows that you haven't read the text *properly*.
6) *Never cross out* your *whole essay* if you realise it's *wrong* — this is just a *waste* of time. *Don't panic*, just think about *why* the essay is wrong, and *continue* the essay, *explaining* to the Examiner why it's *wrong*, and if there's time, what the *real answer* is. *Never give up*: even if you only have *five* minutes left, that's *still* time to pick up some *extra marks*.

I hate Exams — they're such a testing time...

This is a really important page to learn. Exams terrify people, and that makes them *careless*. The first things they forget are the *basic skills* — reading the *whole paper* through, reading the *question* carefully, *planning* their essay and *timing* it. Just keep *calm* and *answer the question*.

Revision Summary for Section Seven

Another big Section to revise — but don't panic, these questions are here to help. Essay writing is one of the basic skills of English — without it, you'll be lost. Spend some time going over the Section, then look at these questions for some practice. Don't look back for the answers — see how much you can remember without looking first.

1) What are essays for?
2) What's the biggest mistake that people make in their essays?
3) What should you do when a question doesn't look obvious?
4) What's the most important thing to look at when you read the question?
5) What should you vary in your essays to keep them interesting?
6) What should the tone of an essay be like?
7) What are the two key rules for using adjectives and adverbs?
8) What are the six steps to writing a good essay?
9) What is drafting? Why bother writing a rough draft?
10) What does your introduction need to do?
11) What are the four steps to writing a good introduction?
12) What is meant by the argument of an essay?
13) Why must you take care not to contradict yourself in your argument?
14) What are the five big mistakes to avoid?
15) Are there right answers to English essays?
16) Are there wrong answers to English essays?
17) Do you need to give examples in personal Essays as well as literary essays?
18) Why do you need to quote from the text?
19) How should you write a quotation that's longer than a whole line?
20) How should you write lines of poetry when you quote them in an essay?
21) How would you finish your essay?
22) What do you do if you find your essay is completely wrong?
23) What three things do you have to look at when writing about narrative?
24) How would you go about writing about the structure of a novel?
25) What are the five key features to write about in plays?
26) What is a soliloquy?
27) Why are older poems easier to write about?
28) How should you prepare for an Exam essay?
29) What should you do if you make a spelling mistake?
30) When are you allowed to write in the margin?
31) If you need more than two asterisks on a page, what's gone wrong, and what should you do about it?
32) What are the six big mistakes to avoid in Exam essays?
33) Write an essay on the advantages and disadvantages of living at home with your parents. Remember to plan your essay and give examples to support your points.

Personal Writing

Personal writing means any written work about *yourself* and your *opinion*. It includes *fictional stories* you write, or *real-life experiences* you write about, as well as your opinions. This section tells you how to *improve* your *style* to get a *better grade*. Read on...

Personal Writing Must Always be Clear

1) When you give your own opinions, you still have to be *clear*. That means your *punctuation*, *spelling* and *grammar* must be *correct*. Go over those in Section Three.
2) The *secret* of good writing is knowing your *audience*. This section is about audience and using the right *style* for different writing tasks.

You Have to Write in the Right Style

Dear Hamlet, that Claudius is bang out of order

1) You need to choose the *appropriate style* to use for every piece you write — that means *looking carefully* at what the *question* asks you.
2) If you're asked to write about an *experience* you have had, then you should use a fairly *formal* style, but you should also write about your *feelings* — what it was *like* to be in that situation.
3) If you're asked to write a *letter*, decide whether it should be *formal* or *informal* — for example, if you're writing a letter to a *character* in a *play* as a *friend*, you should write an *informal* letter; if you're writing to the *editor* of a *newspaper* you should write *formally*.
4) Some personal writing questions ask you to *imagine* you're in *contact* with a *character* from a *book* or a *play*, or to imagine yourself in the same *situation*. You need to think about *how* the characters *talk*, and try to write in a *similar style*.

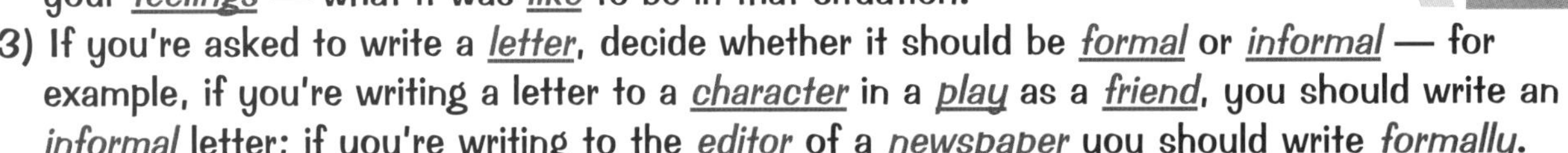

Choosing the right style means knowing your audience — using the right vocabulary, explaining difficult ideas clearly and keeping people's attention.

Five Elements of Style to Watch Out For

1) **LANGUAGE**: make sure your readers *understand* what you're writing about — especially if you're describing something *technical*, like *sport* or a *hobby*. Vary your sentence structure to keep your writing interesting.
2) **VOCABULARY**: use a *variety* of words and don't *repeat* yourself if you can avoid it — make sure you use new vocabulary *correctly*.
3) **TONE**: keep the reader *interested* by varying the *tone* of your writing — try using some *fiction* and *non-fiction* techniques (see next page).
4) **HUMOUR**: be careful with *jokes* — they're a *good* way to keep people reading, but think about whether they'll *offend* anyone. If they're *not* funny to the Examiner, you could *lose* marks — so *think* before you make a joke.
5) **OPINION**: if you give an *opinion* you should try to *support* it, even in a *descriptive* essay. The Examiner doesn't just want to know *how* you *felt*, but *why* you felt that way too. Try to *explain* it clearly.

I love writing — personally speaking...

Personal writing sounds easy — it's only writing about yourself. Unfortunately, that's why most people do it *badly* and throw away lots of *easy marks*. You have to write your *personal pieces* just as carefully as *your essays*. Learn the *five elements of style* off by heart.

Persuasive Language

This is the way you use words to *argue* a case, especially *exaggerated* language. It's a key skill in *personal writing* and in *public speaking* (see PP.9-10) — in the Exam, you might be asked to write as if you were giving a talk to a *school assembly*.

You Can Persuade People With Over-the-Top Language

Everything about the British way of life depends upon chickens...

1) Persuasive language is one of the main *tricks* used in *fiction* and *non-fiction* texts to cause a *reaction* (top five tricks on P.56).
2) You can use it in your writing to *argue a point*, or to make the reader react in a certain way.
3) You can also use it in *public speaking* — in *debates* or *speeches*. *Politicians* try to make their points *sound* more *important* than they really are.
4) People exaggerate *feelings* when they describe them: for example, *journalists* will say things like "This result is the *final nail in the coffin* of English football." They don't *mean* it literally — they're using *over-the-top* language to make the reader *react*.
5) Journalists and politicians use *questions* without giving the *answers*. The reader will often just *accept* what they say and *agree*.
6) You can also *repeat* words and phrases to *emphasise* them for the reader.
7) You can also *attack* the *opposite* view to your own, by making *jokes* about how *wrong* they are, or by finding an *extreme example* of that view in order to *outrage* your audience.
8) You can use a *slogan* — or *soundbite* — which is easy to *remember*.
9) One of the *cleverest* tricks is to *identify* yourself with your audience — when you write about *your* feelings use "*we*" and "*us*". This encourages the *audience* to *agree* with *your* view.

Two Examples of Writing Using Persuasive Language

Look *closely* at these texts — see *how many* of these *tricks* you can spot in them.

It's time to look to the future. Let's face facts; unless we join a United Europe, this country is going to find itself isolated, with high unemployment and no trade prospects. Over the last few years we've sold off our national industries to private companies. There are very few British companies left. The only way to compete is by working with the rest of Europe. If we don't, we'll end up as part of the United States of America!

Those people who support a United Europe tell us about the benefits it will bring. But what about the cost? I don't see many pro-Europeans in our town centres on a Saturday night, explaining to people why their tax bills will double under a United Europe. You may think that's an exaggeration, but being part of Europe means subsidising smaller countries, paying more taxes and having to follow rules made in Brussels by people who don't understand that life in Britain and life in France is different. You can't just make one set of rules to cover all of Europe.

Europe — more united than Manchester...

This is a really useful trick to practise for your personal writing. Remember — it's about *persuading* the Examiner to *agree* with you — and to give you *high marks* for your writing.

Writing about Experiences

Writing about *experiences* means trying to put down on paper a particular *moment* in your life when you felt a certain *feeling*, or something specific *happened* to you.

Answer the Question You're Given

1) *Experience* pieces come with some sort of *guideline question:* for example, *Write about a time when you got lost somewhere.*
2) These questions could come up after you've been reading a *text* in class, or as part of a *comprehension exercise* in your *Exam*.
3) Start by *looking* at any *texts* you were given — look for the *feelings* you need to *capture* in your writing.
4) Think about *your* experiences and try to come up with one where the *same* thing *happened* to you.

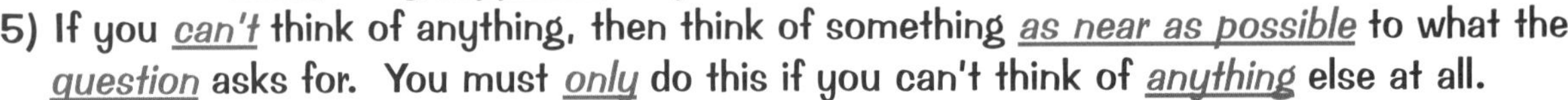

5) If you *can't* think of anything, then think of something *as near as possible* to what the *question* asks for. You must *only* do this if you can't think of *anything* else at all.
6) *Start* your piece by explaining *why* your experience is *relevant* to the *question:* for example, "I remember when I got lost in the supermarket when I was five."
7) If your experience isn't *exactly* the same then *say* so *immediately*, but *explain* why your experience is *similar* and *relevant:* for example, "Although I have never actually got lost, I used to worry that my sister and I would go too far from home when we were playing outside and not be able to find our way back, which was similar in some ways."

Galahad realised he'd found the wrong round table

REMEMBER: you must make your experience relevant to the question — and interesting for the Examiner to read. Think about the tone and the style.

Good Style and Tone will Win You High Marks

The air rushed past as I soared through the sky. "I can see all the way to Wigan," I thought.

1) Even though this is a *personal* piece, the *style* of your writing is a *major factor* in how good a *mark* you get.
2) You need to make the experience *come alive* for the Examiner — that means describing it *accurately* and *interestingly*.
3) It also means *varying* the *style* — the *length* of *sentences* you use, putting in *dialogue* as well as *description* and using lots of *different vocabulary*.
4) You'll need to *vary* the *tone* — use the text to make the Examiner *feel* the way you *felt*, make it *funny*, *sad* or *frightening*.

Start off by Grabbing the Examiner's Attention

1) You need to make an *immediate impression* on the Examiner — showing that you're writing a *relevant answer* to the question, and making your piece sound *interesting* so the Examiner keeps reading.
2) *Don't* tell the Examiner *everything* about the experience *right away* — just give a *hint* to show that it's *relevant* to the question and to make the Examiner *want* to read on: for example, "My experience of getting lost involved two policemen and left me with a fear of eggs."
3) You need to make the Examiner ask the question *"why?"* If they're *curious*, they'll *want* to read on to see *what happens* in the piece.

Bev's pets always made an impression

Personal writing in the Exam — a fun experience...

If you *learn* the main points on these pages, you can really *improve* your *personal writing marks*.

Descriptive Writing

After *grabbing* the Examiner's *attention*, you need to *keep* it — this means *varying* your *style* and *tone*, especially in your *descriptive* writing.

Descriptive Writing means Saying What's Going On

1) *Good* descriptive writing makes a scene *come to life* — it *doesn't* mean you have to describe *everything* you can think of.
2) You need to give the Examiner *enough* information to *explain* what is *happening* and who is *involved*, but keep your story *moving* too.
3) You should also try to *set the scene* — talk about the *place* where your writing is set. You could describe the *weather* .
4) You must try to describe your *feelings* — this is what the piece is *about*. It's not just *what* happened, but how it made you *feel*. The piece *isn't* just a *report* of the facts — it's also about your *opinion* of them.

It was fairly hot and quite sunny

You Can Give Two Sorts of Opinion

1) You can describe your *opinion* at the time — what it was *like* to be there, how you *felt*, whether you were *afraid* or *excited*. Try to *imagine* yourself *back* in the same situation:

I saw a group of five or six children, all quite a bit younger than me, gathered round an old woman. They were shouting at her and calling her a witch. She looked frightened and upset. She caught my eye and her look seemed to plead with me. I didn't need any pleading.

I could feel the hairs on the back of my neck stand up, and my heart was already pounding. My whole body felt like it was buzzing with rage. I marched over to the crowd and started yelling.

"Who do you think you are? What gives you the right to talk to people like that?" As the words came out of my mouth I realised that I had no idea what I was going to say next. I suddenly felt very afraid that the children would turn on me now.

2) You can describe your opinion *now*, looking *back* at the experience — whether you're *embarrassed* at what you did or *glad* that you did it, and what you *learned* from it:

Looking back, I'm really glad that I told those kids what I thought of them. I wish I'd been able to think of something better to say, something that really made them stop and think, but at least I tried. I think that I'd be sorry now if I'd let them get away with it.

Practise Descriptions Using Your Senses

1) The *key* to description is using your *senses*. Think about the *sounds* you hear, the things you *see*, what things are like to *touch* and *taste*, and how they *smell*.
2) Use these *senses* to write a *paragraph* describing the *room* you're in *right now*. Try to describe as *many* things as you can. *Don't* repeat yourself.
3) You should also try to use *comparisons* — look at P.48 on *imagery*. Try to think of your *own* images instead of ones you've *read* in books. *Never* use clichés (P.2).
4) Remember your *adjectives* and *adverbs* — use them to *express* how things made you *feel*.
5) *Don't* overuse words like "beautiful" or "interesting" in your writing — you must explain *why* the things you're describing were beautiful or interesting. *Never* use the word "nice" — it doesn't *mean* anything. You need to give a *clear picture* of what you're describing.

I can't describe how this page makes me feel...

You'll definitely *pick up marks* for writing about your experiences if you can *describe* them clearly. Don't forget your *adjectives* and *comparisons*, and practise descriptions using the *five senses*.

More on Descriptive Writing

Descriptive writing is also about how you use *language* to create *mood* and *tone* — making the *atmosphere* of your experience *come to life*.

Adjectives and Images Can Affect the Mood

1) If you want to write about a *happy* experience then you should choose the right kind of *language*. Try to make the reader think of happy things. Use images of *colours* and *brightness*, or *spring* and *summer*.
2) If you're writing about a *depressing* experience, then use images of *cold* and *darkness*. Any images of *loneliness* will also help to create the right *tone*.

Three Ways of Describing People

1) Describe what they *look like* — the *shape* of their *head* and their *nose;* the *colour* of their *skin;* their *shape* and *size;* whether they are *good-looking* or *ugly;* even their *clothes*.
2) Describe the way they *act* — how they *walk* and *talk;* whether they seem *confident* and *friendly* or *cold* and *cruel;* whether they have any *annoying habits* like running a hand through their hair or picking their nose.
3) Think of something that they *remind* you of: a *quiet, skinny* man could be like a *lizard;* a *fat* man *exercising* could be bouncing like a giant *beach ball*.

For the last time, I am strawberry-blonde!

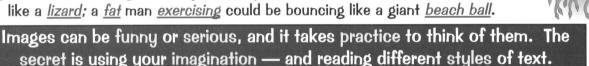

Images can be funny or serious, and it takes practice to think of them. The secret is using your imagination — and reading different styles of text.

Use Sentence Structure to Create Tone

1) If you want to create a tone of *suspense*, use *short*, *sharp* sentences which just explain *one fact* at a time — *delay* the full explanation for as *long* as possible (like ***The X Files***). *Don't* give too much information away. The Examiner will *keep reading* to see what happens:

> *Night fell. Somewhere an animal whined. Lizzie sat very still as the darkness grew around her. The fire crackled in front of her, but behind her back she could hear rustling noises. She moved closer to the fire. Matthew had been gone a long time.*
>
> *There was a loud sharp crack from nearby. Something had stepped on a twig. Lizzie strained her eyes but could see nothing. Then she shivered.*
>
> *From among the trees there suddenly appeared hundreds of tiny points of light, as hundreds of tiny pairs of eyes fixed themselves on her. Lizzie gasped in fear. She turned quickly and ran to the other side of the fire. The points of light followed her. Something stepped out of the darkness towards her. She screamed.*
>
> *"Lizzie! It's me!" said Matthew, surprised. "I've invited the Weasels over for tea."*

2) The passage sounds very *mysterious*. Lizzie hears noises but *can't* see anything; the scene takes place at *night* and she is *on her own*. This means we *sympathise* with her.
3) There are lots of *short sentences*, but they *don't* always give much information — they say there is a noise, but *don't* tell you what *made* the noise, they say there are hundreds of pairs of eyes, but *don't* say *whose* eyes. The passage *seems scary* — until the end.
4) Only *at the end* do we find out that it's alright. The ending comes as a *relief* to the suspense.

Keep the Examiners reading — without paying them...

More for you to *learn* — but you need to *practise* these skills. Try writing *descriptions* of two people you know — make one description *funny* and the other one *serious*.

Writing Dialogue

Dialogue is any part of the text which is actually *spoken* by one of the *characters* in it. You can use it as a *change* from *descriptive* writing — letting the characters *speak* for themselves.

Dialogue Must Be Presented Clearly

1) Every time a *new character* speaks you should start a *new line*.
2) You must use *double quotation marks* to show where the speech *begins* and *ends*. Remember the *rules* for quotation marks (see P.29).
3) Make dialogue interesting by *varying* sentence structure— you can *split* a sentence in two in order to *delay* saying what's happening:

> "The pie thief," said Kieran, "was you...Matt!" *is more dramatic than*
> "The pie thief was you, Matt!" said Kieran.

DON'T **use the word "said" all the time — think of other words like "answered", "replied", "asked", "wondered", "complained", "shouted", "moaned" etc.**

Dialogue Should be Realistic and Create Character

These figures are tip-top-tastic
They're mega-top-a-roony
They're mega-roony-tastic

1) Dialogue has to *sound* like *real speech*.
2) When you're writing about a *person*, think about the *way* they speak — if there are certain *phrases* they use all the time.
3) Try to *use* these *features* when you write dialogue for that person — this will *bring them to life* and can sometimes be very *funny:* "you won't know it's twue till you've twied it"
4) In dialogue you can use *clichés* and *jargon* to show the Examiner the way that a character speaks — but *don't* use them in your *descriptive* writing *at all*.
5) When you *read* texts, *look* at the way that the *characters* speak — if their speech is written in an *interesting* or *clever* way, try using it for the dialogue of one of *your* characters.

Writing a Playscript

> Almost The Greatest Play
> In The World Ever
> Act One
>
> Scene One
>
> (Burnley, 1987, a carpet superstore, there are some rolls of carpet. The lights come on as Jeanie the saleswoman enters wearing a bright yellow boiler suit.)
>
> Jeanie: (To herself.) Oo, look at the pile on that.

Drama is about writing *good dialogue* so that when it's *spoken onstage*, the *audience* will *believe* in the characters and the scene.

1) Start with the *Title* and the *Act* and *scene* number.
2) Then write the *stage directions* — *where* the action happens and *when*, *who* is onstage at the *start* and any *props* which need to be there (like a table or a bed).
3) Imagine that you're writing for the scene to be *performed* — give a direction for when the *theatre lights* should come on.
5) Then write the *name* of the first character to *speak*, and then the first piece of *dialogue*. Each time a *new* character speaks, start a *new line*, and write their name.
6) When a character *does* something, put in a *stage direction*. Write it in the *middle* of the dialogue in brackets, so that the *actor* will do it at the right *time*.

Dialogue — a word in your ear perhaps...

Any dialogue you write must sound *realistic* and give some idea of what the *speaker* is like. Think about *how old* they are and *what kind* of *words* they would use — they should say what they *feel*.

Writing Stories

Some people find this incredibly *hard* — they can never think of anything *interesting* to write about. *Don't panic* though — this page gives you plenty of tips. Writing stories means using the *same skills* you use for writing about your *experiences*.

Stories Use Descriptive Writing and Dialogue too

His toupee slipped, then without warning began to attack his face.

1) *Brilliant news* — this Section has *already* covered *most* of the *key techniques* you need for writing *stories*.
2) There's one *big difference*, though — in a story you *don't* have to write about something that *really happened*.
3) This means you can use your *imagination* — which can be *great*, but it can also be *difficult* if you can't think of anything.
4) The *secret* to story writing is finding a *good plot*.

Finding a Plot and Using it to Write

Sauvignon or Shiraz, squire?

Planet of the Grapes

1) Plots are the *basic outlines* of what *happens* in a story.
2) You'll need to decide on a *plot* and the *characters* — this will help you decide how *long* the story is going to be before you start.
3) *Lots* of people write *bad* stories because they choose a *plot* which takes *too long* to write, so they get *bored* and *end* the story *quickly*. You'll *lose marks* if you do this.
4) You *don't* have to be *original*. There's no such thing as an *original* story. *Every* story you know in *books* or *films* is based on something else — often a *mixture* of different stories.
5) Look at some stories you *like* — think about the *main events* that happen. Then think about the *characters* and the details and try to *change* them. You could write a story like a James Bond *adventure* with a girl as the main character, for example.
6) *Don't just copy* though — you'll lose *lots of marks* if the Examiner can see that you've *copied* the story of a film without *changing* it in any way. You need to take the *outline* of the plot and then write your *own story*, in your *own style* to win yourself high marks.

Writing the Story

This town is somewhat too small to accomodate us both, sir

1) When *choosing* a plot, think about how *long* your piece needs to be, and how much *time* you've got to write it. Don't try to write an *entire novel*.
2) Think about the *style* of the piece,and use the right kind of *language* for the *style* you choose. If it's a *news report* then it should *sound* like one.
3) Make sure you keep to the *same style* — *don't change* style unless you make it *clear* to the Examiner.
4) Think about the *atmosphere* you want to create — how you want the Examiner to *feel* reading the story. Use *descriptive language* and *dialogue* to create the *tone* of the story and to bring the *characters* to life (revise the last four pages if you're unsure).
5) Use you *own experiences* if you can't think of anything else — you can *change* the *names* and the *details*. This can help you to write about the characters' *feelings*.

Guy Fawkes liked stories — he loved a good plot...

Stories need a good plot. Remember, you *can borrow*, but you *can't copy*. You'll need to use your *descriptive* and *dialogue* writing skills here, so look back over the last two pages and *revise*.

More on Story Writing

Here are several more important points to consider when you write stories. Remember — writing good stories takes just as much effort and practice as writing good essays.

Choose a Voice for Your Narrator

As he crosses the line to win the Marathon, the look on his face tells the whole story

1) Your story has to have a narrator — someone to tell the tale.
2) If the narrator is a character in the story then write as if you are that person, using "I" and "we" — a first person narrative.
3) A first person narrative is like a personal experience piece. You'll need to talk about how you felt at the time, and give your opinion on what happens. Look over the last four pages to remind yourself of the skills you'll need to use.
4) Alternatively, you can use a third person narrative. This means describing the characters as "he" and "they". You'll need to write about what they think and feel, not just what happens.
5) Remember — once you've chosen a narrator, you must stay in the same voice. Don't change the style of writing or the Examiner will think you've forgotten who the narrator is.

Start in the Middle and then Set the Scene

It was a dark, dark night. As Katie came nearer, she was gripped by terror as the thing inside the shed started to move.

1) The best stories start right in the middle of the action — they make you want to read on.
2) You need to be direct — you can use dialogue to do this: *"Don't jump!" shouted the soldier.*
3) Don't start off the same way all the time — try to use different tricks in different stories.
4) Your first sentence is important— you need to let the Examiner know that the story is going to be interesting and you're deliberately writing in a certain style to create a particular tone.

What to Put In and What to Leave Out

1) You can't describe absolutely everything that happens — you don't have the time. Don't get sidetracked, and don't describe things that don't matter to the story.
2) Think about the plot of your story — and focus on what's going to happen next.
3) Ask yourself what the Examiner needs to know to understand the story.
4) Think about the style of your piece. If it's in the style of a travel piece, then you can add lots of description and detail. If it's a detective story then don't give too much description — you don't want to give away any clues as to who the murderer really is.

End Your Story Properly — Before You Run Out of Ideas

1) Plan the end of your story before you start writing — this outline will help you decide which information is relevant or irrelevant for your descriptions and dialogue.
2) Don't get sidetracked and forget your plot — you'll lose marks if the Examiner can't follow the story because you're busy describing things. You'll lose marks if you don't describe anything.
3) You must tie up the whole plot at the end — don't leave anything hanging. Never end a story by saying, "Then I woke up — it had all been a dream." Examiners hate that ending.

The neverending story — happened to me once...

Beginning and ending properly will win you marks. Don't just make your story up as you go along.

Writing Responses to Texts

These *writing exercises* are very *popular* with Examiners. You have to *read* a text and then *write* about it as if you *were* one of the *characters*, or as if you were giving them *advice*. Look at Section Five, P.44 for how to *read* the text to help you with these questions.

Writing as a Character from a Text

June's new house helped her to get into character

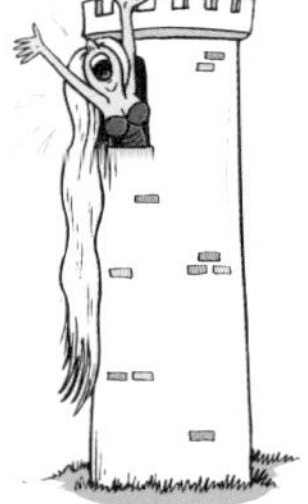

1) The *secret* of this exercise is *imagining* what it's *like* to be the character.
2) You need to think about what the *character* is like — how they *speak*, how they *act*, whether they're *comic* or *scary*.
3) The *only* way to find these things out is to *read* the text *carefully* (see Section Five).
4) These features will help you decide what the character's *point of view* is.
5) When you've *decided* this, you must *answer* any question in the way that you think the *character* would. You should also try to use the same *style* of *language*.

Writing to a Character — Choosing the Right Style

Mary, 34, of Swansea, breathed a sigh of relief at the end of the 10 hour struggle to save the child's life

1) You need to choose the *right style* for your answer — *read* the question *carefully*.
2) It will *tell* you *who* you're supposed to be and what *style* you have to write in.
3) Who you are tells you what *relationship* you have to the character — whether you're a *friend* or a *relative* and can write *informally*; or whether you're a *journalist* and have to be *formal*.
4) You could be asked to write *different styles* of answer — *letters*, *diary entries*, *news reports* etc. *Write* in the *style* you're given in the question, and *stick to it*.
5) Think about the *language* you use . If you're writing a *newspaper report*, think about how *journalists* write (see P.59). If you use the *right style* then you'll pick up plenty of *marks*.
6) Remember to *answer* the question — *only* give advice about the things you're *asked* to.

Use your imagination — talk about the characters as though they're real people. The more imaginative you are at bringing texts to life, the more marks you'll win.

Writing a Diary Entry for a Character in a Play

1) Remember, diaries are written in an *informal style*.
2) Look at how your character *speaks* in the play, and use the same kind of language.
3) Diaries are very *personal*, so your character will write down what they're *really feeling*.

Writing as a Play Director

1) A popular *Exam question* is to ask you how *you* would *direct* a scene from a play. This means you need to explain *where* you would have the actors *standing*, *how* they would *behave*, and what kind of *emotion* they would use when they said their *lines*. You'll need to *practise* this.
2) Try and imagine how a director would talk to actors, and write in that style.

Be like a clear radio — respond well...

Writing in response to texts means writing in the right style. Read the question and write in the style you're asked to. Look through this Section for how to write in different styles. Remember, *careful reading* first, and using your *imagination* in your answer.

Writing Reviews

A *review* is a *short essay* which tells you what a *book*, *film*, *TV programme* or *theatre performance* was like. If you go to see a production of the Shakespeare play you've been studying, you'll probably have to write a review of it in class.

Start a Review with a Brief Description

1) The *first step* in a review is to explain *what* you're *reviewing*.
2) You need to *tell* your reader what the *title* is and what *kind* of *book*, *film* or *play* it is.
3) *Don't* explain the *entire story* — just give an *outline*.
4) Think about your readers — they need you to *explain* to them what the play is like.

Last Thursday night, Little Giggleswick saw the world première of Andrew Freud Weber's new musical, "Catflap." This exciting new work tells the story of Miffy, an orphaned cat who teams up with Dick, a young boy travelling to seek his fortune in London. It is a modern-day version of the Dick Whittington story, set in the thrilling world of Circus performance, where Miffy learns to fly...

A Theatre Review Tells You About the Performance

1) Writing a *theatre* review means talking about the *performance* you saw.
2) Start by making *general comments* about how the *director* has chosen to *present* the play — Old plays by *Jonson* or *Shakespeare* are sometimes performed in *modern costumes*.
3) Write about the *set* — some plays have a *large* set with lots of *scene changes*, other plays have *no set* and the actors *mime* all the props.
4) Look at *costumes*, *music* and *lighting*. These things can *change* the way you *feel* about a *character* or a *scene*.
5) Write about the *acting* — whether it was *good* or *bad* — particularly if there was a *very good* performance by *one* actor. *Remember* to explain *why* you thought it was good.
6) Give *opinions* on how the *performance* went — whether it was *exciting* or too *slow*, whether you could *hear* the actors properly. *Always* give *reasons* for your opinions.
7) Finish with a *final opinion* on whether you would *recommend* the production to other people. Ask yourself whether you *believed* in the *characters* and the *story* — if you *didn't*, then explain *why not*.

Book and Film Reviews Explain What the Work is Like

1) *Book* reviews should look at the *style* of the book and whether it's a *good story*. You should also write about whether it's *easy to read* or *dull*, and whether or not you *enjoyed* it. You must give *reasons* for your opinions, like a short *essay*.
2) *Film* reviews look at the *style* and *story*, but they also look at the *acting*, the *music* and the *images* of the film.
3) *TV* reviews are *similar* to film reviews. They talk about the *style* of the programme and whether it was *enjoyable* to watch. Don't forget to explain *why*.

Book, Film and Theatre reviews — what're they like...

Remember — *reviews* are just like short essays. You need to talk about *style*, *tone* and *language* — and then give your *opinion* on whether you liked it or not. Don't forget to give *reasons* for your opinions, though. Think about *your* audience and what they need to know.

Writing Reports

A report is an *account* of a particular subject — a *description* of the *facts*. You may be asked to write reports about *events* you've been to for your *Coursework*.

A Report Concentrates on the Facts

1) The *difference* between a *report* and a *review* is that a review is about giving an *opinion*, a report is about giving the *facts* of an event or a situation. Always keep this in mind.
2) *Reports* are also about *description* — you need to *describe* what the event or the situation is *like:* for example, a *business* report about a proposed new type of *breakfast cereal* needs to describe *what* the cereal would be *like*, and look at the *advantages* and *disadvantages*.

Why You Need to Practise Writing Reports

Nearly True Gazette

Cumbria Erupts In Fire And Brimstone

Kendal residents were amazed yesterday when a portal to the third circle of the underworld opened beside the local launderette.

1) You may have to write a report about an *event* at *school*, or about a *sports match* that you went to.
2) You may also have to write reports in the *style* of a *newspaper* as an exercise in writing *responses* to texts (see P.88).

How to Write a Good Report

My article gives a true impression of just how brilliant I am

1) *Describe* the facts *carefully*. Try not to be *biased* but explain *exactly* what happened, and if you can, *why*.
2) Describe the *scene* — think about the *six major questions* from Section Five (PP.50-51): *what* happened, *where* and *when* it took place, *who* was involved, *how* it happened and *why*.
3) If you can *answer* all these questions you'll write a *clear* report — make sure it's as *accurate* as possible by *checking* it through.

Example of a Sports Report

Wrestling Legend Pants to Victory

by Our Cumberland Wrestling Correspondent Malcolm Grundy

Cumberland Wrestling legend Chris "Beast" Dennett picked up another title yesterday in the final of the Bowness Wrestling Championships. Dennett came back from a poor run in the tournament to sweep to a deserved victory in the Men's Singles Final, against Polish Champion and favourite Lech Sobieski.

The fight had begun uneasily, with both men warned for using illegal holds. Referee Jeff Turner had been instructed to clamp down on this sort of behaviour, which has spoiled so many big finals in the last few years.

Towards the end of the second minute, however, Dennett was to produce a moment of "Beast" magic. Feinting to his left, he managed to draw Sobieski into dropping his hold. This forced error allowed Dennett to shift his weight and shunt the Pole out of the tournament. This was a magnificent move, the like of which has not been seen since the days of the equally legendary Mickey Rinton.

Yesterday Dennett could do no wrong though: also picking up the prize for best Grapple Pants for a fine pair knitted by girlfriend Jennie Gardner.

Writing Letters

Letter writing is a *skill* you'll need to *practise* for *everyday life* as well as for your *Coursework*. There are *two* main kinds of letter — *formal* and *informal* — and *formal* letters have *strict rules* of presentation.

Learn these Seven Rules for Formal Letters

1) Write your *name* and *address* in the *right-hand corner* of the page, then *leave* a line and put the *full date* underneath — *day*, *month*, *year*.
2) Then write the *name* and *address* of the person you're *writing to* on the *left-hand side* and leave a line.
3) Underneath this write, "Dear Sir or Madam," if you *don't* know the person to whom you're writing, or, "Dear Mr..." or "Dear Ms..." with the person's *name* — eg Dear Ms Jones. Dear Mr Peters, etc.
4) Then write a sentence explaining *why* you're writing the letter:
   eg *Re: Application for a Bank Loan*
5) Start the letter using *formal language* — explain *clearly* and in *detail* your *reasons* for writing.
6) Leave a *line* of space between each *paragraph*, and *don't* let the paragraphs become too *long*.
7) *Close* the letter properly — if you *know* the person's name write "Yours sincerely"; if you *began* with "Sir"/"Madam" you must use "Yours faithfully". Print *your name* then *sign* above it.

grrrr

An Example of a Formal Letter

writer's name and address →

Saskia Tuesday
Tuesday Publishing
Uverdale Road
London
SW10

recipient's name and address

William Shakespeare
Anne Hathaway's Cottage
Stratford-upon-Avon

date → Wednesday 15th March 2004

Dear Mr Shakespeare, ← dear + name

Re: Plays ← subject of letter

introductory paragraph

Thankyou very much for the playscripts of *A Midsummer Night's Dream*, *Romeo and Juliet* and *Julius Caesar* that you sent to us on the 12th February. My colleagues and I very much enjoyed reading them. Unfortunately, we have decided not to publish your plays. Our opinion is that the market for plays set in foreign countries has had its day. We appreciate that your Romeo and Juliet is a beautiful story with a truly tragic ending, but we do not feel that a modern audience will be able to identify with the heroine.

We wish you the best of luck in your career and hope that you find another publisher.

Yours sincerely, ← correct ending

Saskia Tuesday ← print name then signature above it

Saskia Tuesday
Commissioning Editor

Informal Letters Don't Have Strict Rules

Informal letters are letters to *friends* and *family*. You *don't* have to give a *full* address, just the *date*. Call the person by their *first name* and use *informal endings*, like "love" or "best wishes".

Look for a letter-writing job — good post to have...

Writing *formal letters* is easy if you learn the *seven rules*. You may have to write letters in your *Exam*, giving advice to *characters* from literary texts. Practise writing *formal* and *informal* letters.

Presenting Your Work

Presentation is a major factor in picking up *good marks* — whether in *essay* work or *personal writing* pieces. Examiners will give *higher marks* to *neat* work which is *easy* to read.

How to Structure Your Page

Viv was always neat

1) *Structuring* your page means using a *clear layout* so that the Examiner can *read* your piece *clearly* and in the *right order*.
2) Start by writing out the *number* of the *question* in the *margin*. Then write out the question *in full*, or give the *title* of the essay or piece.
3) Leave a *blank line* and begin to *write* the piece. *Only* begin writing *after* you have *planned* what your *answer* is first. Most *messy* pieces of writing are *badly planned*.
4) If you're *not sure* about your plan then write a *draft version* of the piece. Then you can *check* it for *mistakes* before you write the *final* version.
5) Try to write as *clearly* as you can, *without* rushing. If you *rush*, you're *more* likely to make *mistakes* and then you'll have to *cross things out*. You could also *smudge* the ink by rushing.

REMEMBER: **write out neat versions of all the pieces in your final Coursework folder *before* the deadline. Then you *won't lose* any marks for presentation.**

Avoid Any Grammar, Spelling or Punctuation Errors

1) *Any* mistakes in these areas will automatically *lose you marks*, no matter how good the content of your written work is.
2) These *errors* can be *avoided* if you're *careful*, and if you make sure you know the *rules* in Section Three. *Learn* the list of words on P.108.
3) *Practise* any areas where you *know* you're *weak* — the *mistakes* you make *regularly*. If you *don't* learn to *avoid* them, then they could seriously affect your *marks* — so spend some time *working* on them *right now*.

Cross Out Mistakes Neatly

1) This is one of the *worst mistakes* you can make in *presentation*.
2) *Never* scribble all over a mistake or spend ages crossing it out — because it'll make the page look *messy* straight away. In fact, the Examiner's attention will be *drawn* to the *mistake*.
3) When you *cross out* a mistake, you want the examiner to *ignore it* and carry on reading what you've written instead.
4) Put *brackets* around the mistake and draw *two horizontal lines* through the word or phrase. This will make it *clear* that you want the Examiner to *ignore* it. *Don't* draw *crosses* over everything.

52nd Brigade kept vigilant watch for grammatical errors

Read the Instructions for Presentation Tips

1) This is a *stupid* thing to *lose marks* for, but people do it every year.
2) *Before* you begin an Exam, *read the instructions* carefully to see if they mention *presentation*.
3) Sometimes the *instructions* will say that you should only write on *one side* of the paper — if you *don't* you will *lose marks*. Reading the *instructions* is part of your Exam too.
4) If *nothing* is mentioned then you can write on *both* sides — but make sure you *check*.

Examiners are shallow — they like good-looking work...

Bad presentation can cost you *lots of marks* — so *structure* your work and *read the instructions*.

Revision Summary for Section Eight

There's plenty for you to learn in this Section. Personal writing sounds easier than essay work, but in fact it's just as difficult. Make sure you know the skills you need, particularly for descriptive writing and writing about your experiences. Remember — you're trying to bring the experience to life for the Examiner. Never forget to read the instructions you're given, though — that could cost you lots of expensive marks. This set of questions will help you revise the key information from the Section — as long as you read them through carefully before you answer them and follow the instructions exactly.

1) What are the five elements of style you need to use in your personal writing?
2) What is personal writing about?
3) Explain briefly what rhetoric is, and how you can use it: a) in personal writing b) in essays.
4) List four rhetorical tricks and explain how they work, giving an example of each from the two texts on P.81.
5) Why should you vary the style and tone when you write about your experiences?
6) Why do you need to grab the Examiner's attention immediately? How do you do that?
7) What two kinds of opinion can you give in your experience writing?
8) What does descriptive writing do? Give two tricks you can use in descriptions.
9) What are the three ways of describing people? Write three short descriptions of someone you know using each of the three ways in turn.
10) Write a short passage about a dungeon. Try to describe it clearly, giving a sense of what it's like to be there.
11) Write a short passage about a big party, describing it in detail.
12) Write the opening paragraphs of a novel. Try to grab the reader's attention immediately and introduce the story, using description and dialogue. Only give the key information.
13) How do you decide on the plot and style of a story?
14) Write the outline for a plot about a masked bandit helping the poor. Don't just copy a famous story — think of your own version.
15) Write a short first person narrative about a race.
16) Write a short third person narrative about a fight.
17) How should you lay out a drama script? Give a brief example of the opening of a scene.
18) Write a review for the last film you saw.
19) Write a review for the last book you read.
20) Imagine that you live in Verona. You have just found out that your friend Romeo Montague has fallen in love with Juliet Capulet. Write a letter to him giving him advice on what he should do. Try to think of ways to avoid the same tragic outcome as the play. Try to make the letter believable — you're playing a role.
21) Write a report for a sports match you saw recently.
22) Write a report on a big news story. Remember to give the facts as clearly as you can.
23) Write a formal letter to a famous living writer, asking them for any tips they have for writing. Remember to follow the rules for formal letter writing.
24) Write an informal letter to a friend telling them about a typical day at school, and what your ideal day would be if you could do anything you wanted.
25) Give five key features of good presentation.
26) Only answer the questions with odd numbers in this revision summary. If you've done all of them then you obviously didn't read all the questions through before starting. Don't make the same mistake again.

Talking About Culture

Many of the texts you will read for your English course come from *different cultures* around the world. The *ideas*, *themes* and *images* of the texts come from their *own cultures*.

Every Text is Grounded in a Culture

...So I said to Brigadier Cholmondely-Smythe, you'll never get that filly into the jolly gate, what?

1) It *doesn't matter* where in the world you are, a text is always *affected* by the *culture* in which it *was written*.
2) The *ideas* and *themes* important to people in *England* have always been the source of literature *in England*. The same goes for *Wales*, *Ireland* and *Scotland*. Even though these countries share the *same* language, their literature can often be very *different*.
3) The same thing is true of *any* literature written in English; whether it comes from *India*, from *Africa*, from *Australia* or the *USA*.
4) People in *Britain*, *Australia*, *New Zealand*, the *USA* and *Canada* all speak English but they come from a variety of *different cultures* from all over the world. This is reflected in the literature from these countries.

English is Spoken all over the World

1) *Many* countries around the world have English as a *native language* or as one of the *official languages* of that country. This *doesn't* mean their *culture* is English.
2) These countries are mostly *former colonies* of the British Empire, now *independent*.
3) This is one of the reasons why English has become the *unofficial language of the world*.
4) The other main reason is the *power*, *wealth* and *influence* of the *USA*, particularly in the *media*.

Be Aware of Other Cultures When You Read Texts

1) Many of the *expectations* of our culture are *irrelevant* to texts from *elsewhere*.
2) Don't *judge* before you *read* — try to *understand* what it's like to *live* in another culture.
3) You will have to look for clues about the *characters* and *situations* in the way they are described. Use the *reading skills* you developed in sections 4 and 5.
4) Don't assume that just because someone is the same *age* and *gender* as you that they have a similar kind of *lifestyle*.
5) Look for clues about the sort of *jobs* people have and the *everyday tasks* they have to do.
6) Look for clues in the *food* that people eat. People in different countries often have *different diets* — they may eat lots of rice and hardly ever eat potatoes.
7) *Don't forget* — the *themes* of literature are *similar* all over the world, in *any* language. People will always fall in *love*, make *friends*, *betray* each other, *fight enemies* and try to live their lives in *freedom*.

Bob and Barney couldn't have been more different

8) When you read texts from *other* cultures, you must try to *identify* with the *characters*, just as you would with any other text.

Cultures — even you have one...

One last topic to go. You'll *definitely* have to look at texts from other cultures during your course — so make sure you learn the *key skills*. Remember — *don't judge* a text before you read it.

Cultural Context

The central skill in this Section is *empathising*. It means reading *without prejudice*, and trying to *identify* with characters from *cultures* and *situations* in which you've never been.

Cultural factors create Identity

Long time no see,
me old china

1) **LANGUAGE** — Every culture identifies itself by the it uses. This is why many different cultural *groups* in Britain today still *keep up* their *own* languages alongside English: for example, *Urdu*, *Hindi*, *Arabic*, *Hebrew*, *Welsh* and *Gaelic*. It's also why different *areas* of Britain maintain their *dialects:* for example, *Yorkshire*, *Geordie*, *Cockney*, *Scots* etc. This is very important for literature: the poets *Benjamin Zephaniah* and *Derek Walcott* use *Jamaican* dialect for much of their writing.

I worship flowers

2) **RELIGION** — When you read texts from other cultures you should always look for *clues* to the *religion* of that culture. Many religions have sets of *rules* and *customs* that people living in that culture have to *obey:* for example, women *dress* differently in *Islamic* cultures, and many religions *forbid* the eating of *pork*.

DON'T FORGET: Many famous texts have been influenced by religious culture and imagery — including Irish texts like the novel *Portrait of the Artist as a Young Man*, by James Joyce, and the poetry of the Welshman Dylan Thomas.

3) **WEATHER** — This may sound strange but the *weather* of a country does *affect* its culture. Texts set in *Africa* or *India* may be concerned with the problems of *heat* and *droughts*, or *heavy rains* during a monsoon season. In the same way, texts set in *Britain* are often concerned with *rain*...

VOTE

4) **POLITICS** — Read *carefully* for any information about *politics*. Many books discuss the *inequalities* that people face in other countries. *Maya Angelou* and *Toni Morrison* write about the political situation faced by *black people*, and particularly by *black women* in the *USA*.

5) **GENDER** — This is partly a *political* issue, but it's also *general reflection* of different societies, where *women* are often expected to conform to *traditional ideas* of *marriage* and *motherhood*. When you read a text from another culture, look at the way men and women *relate* to each other. Ask yourself if the women and the men are *treated differently*.

I treat everyone the same

6) **LIFESTYLE** — Different cultures have different *expectations*. In some cultures, everybody must *work*, and education comes second to *survival*. Some cultures in the past were built on *slavery*, and the lives of slaves was *harsh* and *cruel*. Even though the *main events* of people's lives are often the same — *birth*, *marriage*, *family*, *death* — the *culture* they live will affect what kind of opportunities they have during their lives.

Cultural texts — books about opera and ballet...

It looks pretty daunting, I know, but cultural context is really very easy to spot when you're reading a text. Just look out for these *six factors*, and see if they're *different* from your culture.

Multicultural Societies

Any text you read has its own *cultural context* — it doesn't matter who wrote it.

Writing about Different Cultures

1) British authors often write about the *clash* between *different* cultures in *Britain* where people come from all sorts of *ethnic* and *cultural* backgrounds as well as being British.
2) An example is *Farrukh Dhondy's* collection of short stories, *Come to Mecca*, about the relationship between the traditional *white* community and the *Bengali* community in London.
3) Some authors try to bring their two cultures *together*: *Salman Rushdie* writes about India *and* Britain.
4) Even in the past, Scots authors like *Walter Scott* and *Robert Burns* wrote in Standard English *as well as* Scots, so as to appeal to *larger audiences*.

Sir Walter Scott

Remember the Two Rules of Cultural Context

When you look at texts from other cultures, there are *two rules* you should always keep in mind:

RULE 1: Think about your own context, and how it affects your understanding of the world, especially your understanding of what is right and wrong.

RULE 2: Look at the context of the text you're reading. Be sure you understand the view of the world presented, and how it's different from your own view.

Look out for Vocabulary

1) *Don't forget* to check that you have understood any *new vocabulary*, especially *dialect* forms.
2) *Always remember* that English written in other cultures *may not* follow the same *grammar rules* as you need for your *Exams* — read it carefully, but *don't copy it* when you write.

I knew a stick once — he wanted to dialogue...

Texts from other cultures are specifically mentioned in *all syllabuses*, so you'll certainly have to study them. I know it sounds hard work to find out all about cultural context, but you can pick up a lot of *easy marks* here if you do your *research* thoroughly. *Coursework essays* on texts from other cultures are always *popular* with Examiners.

Revision Summary for Section Nine

Texts from other cultures form an important part of your Syllabus, which is why we've looked at them briefly in this Section. In fact, the skills you need for looking at the texts are exactly the same as for any other. The only difference is the context they were written in, and the context in which you read them.

Make sure you understand the idea of cultural context, and how it affects the way people write. Don't forget that a lot of literature written in English doesn't come from England, and doesn't follow the same rules of grammar and spelling. Just remember that your answers to Exam and Coursework questions must be written in standard English. Try reading some books from other cultures — you could also read translations of books from other languages. All your reading will help your critical skills and improve your writing — which means better marks.

Look over these summary questions quickly, to ensure that you've understood everything in this Section. If you're not clear about something, then go back and look at the relevant page again.

1) Is all literature in English part of the same culture? Explain why not?
2) How does cultural background affect a text?
3) What is your own culture? Think about where you live and what your daily life, your family and your friends are like.
4) Give the two reasons why English has become the unofficial language of the world?
5) What shouldn't you do when reading texts from other cultures?
6) Why is it important to look for the similarities between you and the characters in the text, as well as the differences?
7) What are the six factors that create cultural identity?
8) What does the weather have to do with culture and texts?
9) What should you think about when you look at gender issues in a text?
10) Why do different groups of people have different dialects?
11) Why is cultural conflict a common theme in literature today?
12) How do authors sometimes try to bring two cultures together?
13) What are the two rules for looking at cultural context?
14) Why is it important to think about your own context when you read a text?
15) Do texts from other cultures always follow the rules of standard English?
16) What should you do if you come across unfamiliar vocabulary in a text?
17) What should you avoid doing in your own work?
18) Write a comparison of your own culture with a different culture. Try to find five similarities and five differences between the two. What effect do these differences have on life in these cultures?

Looking at a Novel Extract

Let's go through some *examples* of how to look at texts. Think about reading the text carefully and answering the *exact questions* which are asked.

Looking at an Extract from a Novel

Mr Sherlock Holmes, who was usually very late in the mornings, save upon those not infrequent occasions when he stayed up all night, was seated at the breakfast table. I stood upon the hearthrug and picked up the stick which our visitor had left behind him the night before. It was a fine, thick piece of wood, bulbous-headed, of the sort which is known as a 'Penang lawyer'. Just under the head was a broad silver band, nearly an inch across. 'To James Mortimer, MRCS, from his friends of the CCH', was engraved upon it, with the date '1884'. It was just such a stick as the old-fashioned family practitioner used to carry — dignified, solid, and reassuring.

"Well, Watson, what do you make of it?"

Holmes was sitting with his back to me, and I had given him no sign of my occupation.

"How did you know what I was doing? I believe you have eyes in the back of your head."

"I have, at least, a well-polished, silver-plated coffee-pot in front of me," said he. "But tell me, Watson, what do you make of our visitor's stick? Since we have been so unfortunate as to miss him and have no notion of his errand, this accidental souvenir becomes of importance. Let me hear you reconstruct the man by an examination of it."

"I think," said I, following so far as I could the methods of my companion, "that Dr Mortimer is a successful elderly medical man, well-esteemed, since those who know him give him this mark of their appreciation."

"Good!" said Holmes. "Excellent!"

"I think also that the probability is in favour of his being a country practitioner who does a great deal of his visiting on foot."

"Why so?"

"Because this stick, though originally a very handsome one, has been so knocked about that I can hardly imagine a town practitioner carrying it. The thick iron ferrule is worn down, so it is evident that he has done a great amount of walking with it."

"Perfectly sound!" said Holmes.

"And then again, there is the 'friends of the CCH'. I should guess that to be the Something Hunt, the local hunt to whose members he has possibly given some surgical assistance, and which has made him a small presentation in return."

"Really, Watson, you excel yourself," said Holmes...

(from The Hound of the Baskervilles, Chapter One; Sir Arthur Conan Doyle)

What the Difficult Words Mean

Bulbous = with a bulging or rounded shape like a bulb. (*adjective*)
Dignified = commanding honour and respect. (*adjective*)
Ferrule = a ring or cap fitted on the tip of something like a walking stick. (*noun*)
Notion = idea or opinion. (*noun*)
Occupation = activity/what someone is doing. (*noun*)
Practitioner = someone who practises a profession, eg medical practitioner. (*noun*)

Questions on the Novel Extract

Time for you to show *how well* you've read the passage, and to *practise* those *reading* and *comprehension* skills from Sections Four and Five. Answer the questions carefully.

Answering Plain Questions on the Extract

These first questions are pretty *easy* as long as you have *read* the extract carefully. Remember to look at *how many marks* each question is worth *before* you start answering them.

1) Who is the narrator of the passage? *(1 mark)*
2) Who are the two characters who appear in the scene? *(2 marks)*
3) How does the narrator describe the stick which has been left behind? *(4 marks)*
4) What reasons does Watson give for saying that the owner of the stick is a successful country doctor? *(5 marks)*
5) Why does he guess that the local hunt gave the stick to the doctor? *(3 marks)*

Opinion Questions based on the Extract

Here you have to give *your opinions* based on your *close-reading* of the extract — but don't forget that your opinions should *only* come from the *extract*, unless the question *says different*.

1) Describe what impression this extract gives of Sherlock Holmes' character.
2) How does Watson come to his conclusions about the owner of the stick?
3) Watson says he is using the "methods of my companion." Explain what you think Sherlock Holmes' methods are. Use this extract and any other evidence you know to help you.
4) When Watson suggests that the stick was presented to its owner by a local Hunt, what evidence does he give? Are these reasons convincing?
5) At the beginning of his final point, Watson says he is guessing. Do you think that this is part of Sherlock Holmes' methods? Explain your answer. *(10 marks for each question)*

Personal Questions related to the Extract

Now you have to answer questions on your *personal opinions* about subjects which are *related* to the extract. Answer any *two* of the following questions:

1) What are the characteristics of a good detective? Discuss, giving reasons for your answers.
2) "Let me hear you reconstruct the man by an examination of it." Describe an object that one of your friends or relatives owns — for example: a pen, a car or a hat. What does the condition and appearance of this object tell you about its owner?
3) Compare the methods of Sherlock Holmes with the methods of any other fictional detective.
4) 'Every good detective needs a less intelligent assistant.' Do you think this is true? Give examples to prove your point.
5) Write a short detective story where Dr Watson has to solve the case on his own.

(20 marks for each question)

A Big Hint about the Extract

The key point about this extract is that Watson starts off his examination of the stick very well, but by the end he is *not backing up* his arguments properly. He gives *no reason* why the owner of the stick should be elderly, and when he looks at the engraving Watson tells us he is *guessing* what the inscription means. Holmes praises Watson for his deductions, but *never* tells him that he is right. When Watson talks about the stick being worn away, Holmes says that his reasons are *sound* — this *doesn't mean* they're right, it means they've been worked out logically from the evidence. Remember — Watson is *narrating* the story.

Looking at a Drama Extract

When you look at *drama extracts*, read the *old language* carefully, especially in Shakespeare.

Read the Extract Carefully

Duke Senior - True is it that we have seen better days,
And have with holy bell been knoll'd to church,
And sat at good men's feasts, and wip'd our eyes
Of drops that sacred pity hath engend'red;
And therefore sit you down in gentleness,
And take upon command what help we have
That to your wanting may be minist'red.

Orlando - Then but forbear your food a little while,
Whiles, like a doe, I go to find my fawn,
And give it food. There is an old poor man,
Who after me hath many a weary step
Limp'd in pure love; till he be first suffic'd,
Oppressed with two weak evils, age and hunger,
I will not touch a bit.

Duke S - Go find him out,
And we will nothing waste till you return.

Orlando - I thank ye, and be blest for your good comfort! [*Exit*]

Duke S - Thou sees't we are not all alone unhappy:
This wide and universal theatre
Presents more woeful pageants than the scene
Wherein we play in.

Jacques - All the world's a stage,
And all the men and women merely players;
They have their exits and their entrances,
And one man in his time plays many parts,
His acts being seven ages. At first the infant,
Mewling and puking in the nurse's arms.
Then the whining schoolboy, with his satchel
And shining morning face, creeping like a snail
Unwillingly to school. And then the lover,
Sighing like furnace, with a woeful ballad
Made to his mistress' eyebrow. Then a soldier,
Full of strange oaths, and bearded like the pard,
Jealous in honor, sudden, and quick in quarrel,
Seeking the bubble reputation
Even in the cannon's mouth. And then the justice,
In fair round belly with good capon lin'd,
With eyes severe and beard of formal cut,
Full of wise saws and modern instances;
And so he plays his part. The sixt age shifts
Into the lean and slipper'd pantaloon,
With spectacles on nose, and pouch on side,
His youthful hose, well-sav'd, a world too wide

knoll'd = rung (*ringing the bells told people to go to church*)
engend'red = caused
ministr'ed = administered/given
forbear = avoid/keep away from
suffic'd = satisfied/given enough
pageant = a spectacular show illustrating historical events
players = actors
mewling = crying like a cat
ballad = love song/poem
pard = leopard (Mid. English) *The image means that the soldier has whiskers like those of a leopard*
capon = a castrated cockerel fattened and eaten like chicken
saws = proverbs/sayings (*from* Old English)
pantaloon = foolish old man (*character in Italian comedies*)
hose = stockings worn by men

Questions on the Drama Extract

For his shrunk shank, and his big manly voice, — *shank* = lower part of leg
Turning again toward childish treble, pipes
And whistles in his sound. Last scene of all,
That ends this strange eventful history,
Is second childishness, and mere oblivion,
Sans teeth, sans eyes, sans taste, sans every thing. — *sans* = without (French)
[*Enter* **Orlando** *with* **Adam**.]
Duke S - Welcome. Set down your venerable burden, — *venerable* = respected because of old age
And let him feed.
Orlando - I thank you most for him.
Adam - So had you need,
I scarce can speak to thank you for myself.
Duke S - Welcome, fall to. I will not trouble you — *fall to* = fall to eating
As yet to question you about your fortunes...

(*As You Like It, Act II, scene vii, lines 120-172;*
by William Shakespeare)

This scene takes place in the Forest of Arden, but the language is very *formal*. It is all in poetry so the *word order* isn't always the same as modern English. *Read it through* carefully first.

Plain Questions

1) What does the Duke say about his former life? *(3)*
2) Why does Orlando ask the Duke and his men not to eat for a while? *(2)*
3) What is the Duke's response to Orlando's story? *(2)*
4) What are the seven stages of man that Jacques lists? *(7)*
5) What happens at the end of Jacques' long speech? *(2)*

Opinion Questions

1) What impression do you get of Orlando's character from the extract — particularly from the way he treats Adam?
2) Jacques' speech lists the seven stages of man. Do you agree with all of them? Why?
3) What kind of person do you think Jacques is? Give reasons for your answer.
4) Jacques finishes his speech saying that old age is like "second childishness". When he finishes speaking, Orlando comes onstage carrying Adam. Do you think Orlando and the duke agree with Jacques' ideas about old age? Explain your answer based on the extract.
5) This scene is written in verse (poetry). Comment on some of the features of poetic language used and the effects they create. Why do you think the scene is in verse?

Personal Questions

Answer any *two* of the following questions:

1) Write your own modern version of the seven ages of man or woman.
2) Write an account of a time when you were desperately in need of help.
3) Imagine that you are Orlando. Write a diary entry describing the events of this extract and your impressions of Duke Senior and his men.
4) Imagine you are a theatre director. Write an account of how you would direct this scene.
5) Write a story about what you think it is like to be old.

Looking at a Non-Fiction Extract

Now it's time to look at a *non-fiction text* — a descriptive piece. Read it carefully.

The Thames river is the most famous in England, running from its source at Thameshead all the way to the great city of London. On its path, it passes through the long, low valley of Southern England, and one of the country's most famous cities: Oxford.

Oxford is celebrated for its University, but its name comes from a less intellectual source. The area where the city now stands was one of the few places where the Thames was shallow enough to cross. As late as the Seventeenth Century, writers refer to the city as "Oxen-ford" — a place where oxen could ford the river. The root of the name can be seen on the crest of the city; a shield marked with a red ox crossing a blue stream.

Dominated by the famous University, Oxford has historically been a centre for power and learning. Founded in the 1200s, it is the oldest University in England, and many of its ancient traditions are still in place today. Some, however, are not. The tradition of gentlemen at the University being exempt from classes has long since been abandoned, much to their regret.

The prestige of the University has often led to conflict between students and the townspeople, who resent the invasion of scholars. During the Middle Ages, this once erupted into open battles on the street, something not seen again until Oxford United briefly became a successful football club in the mid-nineteen eighties.

Oxford is more than its University, as the inhabitants are always keen to tell you. In the 1250s it was a key site in the civil war between King Stephen and his rival for the throne, Matilda. Besieged in the old walled city, Matilda escaped at night, wearing a white cloak to camouflage her against the snow.

During the English Civil War, Charles I made Oxford his capital city, after fleeing from riots in London. Oxford fell after a long siege, and after the defeat at Naseby in 1645, Charles fled to Scotland, before being sold back to Parliament by the Scots and later executed. It is said that he saw his wife for the last time in Abingdon, seven miles to the south of Oxford.

Apart from this bloody past, Oxford has been the home of many great writers, from Lewis Carroll, who wrote *Alice in Wonderland*, to J.R.R. Tolkien, who wrote *The Lord of the Rings*, to A.A. Milne, creator of Winnie the Pooh.

The city was also the site of William Morris' car factory, and even today, the Rover company still builds cars at the Cowley works to the east of the city. Recently, the short distance between Oxford and London has meant that many businesses have moved out of the capital and into the science parks around the city. The University is also a major research centre.

For all that, Oxford is still a small town, curled around the banks of the Thames and its tributary, the Cherwell. In fact, if you ever visit, the best time to see Oxford is first thing in the morning, from the hills outside the city. Looking down into the valley, you can see the white mist clinging to the fields, and the ancient, limestone spires of the college towers peeping through towards the morning sun. Seeing that view, you might almost believe you were still in the Middle Ages — if you weren't thinking in the back of your mind that you've seen it all before on *Inspector Morse*.

List of Difficult Words

abandoned = given up
exempt = free from
prestige = reputation/fame
resent = show anger at
erupted = broke out
besieged = surrounded/under siege
camouflage = disguise to blend in with surroundings

Questions on the Non-Fiction Extract

Question time again, I'm afraid. I know it seems boring but this is the *only way* to practise your reading and comprehension skills. If you can sort them out now, then you *won't* drop any silly marks when you're doing the *real thing* — so keep practising.

Plain Questions on the Extract

Don't forget to *read* the questions through first — and check *how many marks* you can win for each one:

1) According to the extract, where is Oxford? *(2)*
2) Where does the name "Oxford" come from? *(2)*
3) What is the design on the crest of the city? *(2)*
4) Which tradition of the University is no longer in place? *(2)*
5) How has Oxford been involved in two civil wars? *(8)*
6) Name two famous authors who lived in Oxford and a book that each one wrote. *(4)*
7) What two reasons are given for the increase in businesses moving to Oxford? *(2)*

Opinion Questions on the Extract

Remember to *back up* your answers using the text — and *plan* them carefully *before* you start writing:

1) How does the extract describe the best time to see Oxford?
2) The extract compares the battles between students and townspeople in Oxford to the behaviour of football fans. Is this a good comparison? What are the similarities between the two groups?
3) Write a short summary of the main points of the extract.
4) The extract gives information about several historical events. What else does it do?
5) What impression of Oxford do you get from the extract?
6) Does the extract make you want to visit Oxford? Explain your answer, giving reasons.

(10 marks for each question)

Personal Questions based on the Extract

Answer *any two* of the following questions:

1) Write a description of a town or city that you have visited, giving as much detail about the history, the main features, the buildings and the people as you can.
2) Imagine you could change five things about the place where you live. What would you change and why?
3) Write about a tradition — in your town, your school or your family. Explain what the tradition is and why it began.
4) "History and tradition are a waste of time." Give arguments for and against this statement.
5) Write a story about a lucky escape from a tricky situation, like Matilda's escape from Oxford.
6) The extract talks about the relationship between the people of Oxford and the students. This is still an issue today. Do you think this is because the townspeople resent the students coming to the town when they don't belong there? Or is it because the students treat the people of the town badly? How would you try to solve the problems between the students and the people of the town?

(20 marks for each question)

Worked Example of a Poem

Time to look at a poem — but *before* you answer the questions, we'll *work through* the poem, looking at the key features of *style* and *content*.

Read the Poem through Carefully

Thou shalt have one God only; who
Would be at the expense of two?
No graven images may be
Worshipped, except the currency:
Swear not at all; in, for thy curse
Thine enemy is none the worse:
At church on Sunday to attend
Will serve to keep the world thy friend:
Honour thy parent; that is, all
From whom advancement may befall:
Thou shalt not kill; but need'st not strive
Officiously to keep alive:
Do not adultery commit;
Advantage rarely comes of it:
Thou shalt not steal; an empty feat,
When it's so lucrative to cheat:
Bear not false witness; let the lie
Have time on its own wings to fly:
Thou shalt not covet; but tradition
Approves all forms of competition.

The sum of all is, thou shalt love,
If anybody, God above:
At any rate shall never labour
More than thyself to love thy neighbour.

("*The Latest Decalogue,*" *Arthur Hugh Clough*)

1) *Decalogue* means the *Ten Commandments*, like those given to Moses in the Bible — so this poem is about writing a *modern ten commandments*.
2) The language is deliberately *old-fashioned*, with lots of "thou" and "thy" — this is to make it *sound more like* the language of the Bible.
3) Every few lines gives a *different rule* to follow — and then gives a *reason*.
4) Each reason is a *joke* — when a rule is given, the reason for following it is a *selfish one*: eg "Thou shalt not steal," *only* because you can make more money by cheating.
5) If the reason *isn't* selfish, then it usually *reverses* the rule: eg "Thou shalt not kill; but need'st not strive/Officiously to keep alive:" (which means don't kill people, but don't work too hard to keep them alive!)
6) All of the rules given are from the *original Ten Commandments* — the difference here is that they are made *meaningless* by the reasoning that goes with them.
7) Instead of being rules to *improve* people's behaviour, these rules do exactly the *opposite* — they *justify* people behaving in a *cruel*, *selfish* and *unfriendly* way.
8) This creation of the opposite view is *ironic* (be careful when you use this word). The poem gives a very *negative* view of human nature.

Questions on the Poem

Answer any *three* of the following questions:

1) What does the poem say is the most important rule for life? Do you agree?
2) This poem is about saying the same thing in different ways so as to support your behaviour. In modern society this can happen a lot: the allied forces talked about "collateral damage" during the Gulf War when they meant civilian casualties around a military target. How does the kind of language we use change the meaning of an idea? Think of some other examples.
3) Give a list of ten rules that you think everybody should have to follow. Make sure you give reasons explaining why you think each of these rules should be followed.
4) Write about a time when you were supposed to follow a rule, but didn't.
5) Write a story about someone who makes a list of fair rules for daily life and tries to get everyone else to follow them.

Index

A

A Midsummer Night's Dream 55
a waste of time 72
'a'/'an' and 'the' 30
abbreviations 3, 63
accents 2, 5
accident 50
acting 12, 52, 76, 85, 88
acting out 76
AD 3
adapt as you go along 74
adjectives 20, 30, 69, 85
adverbs 20, 33, 69
adverts 61, 62
affect/effect 25
agreement 33, 81
alliteration 47
although 22
am 3
and 22, 27
answering questions 40, 68, 71, 72, 74, 78
antonyms 4
any 31
anyone 32
apologise 63
apostrophes 28
appropriate style 80
argument 70, 71, 72, 73, 75, 77, 78
argument of a poem 77
arrogant 7
articles 31
as and like 26
as soon as 22
asking permission 17
asking questions without giving answers 81
assonance 47
asterisk * 74, 78
at 22
atmosphere 86
attitude 53
audience 10, 76
autobiographies 63
auxiliary verbs 15, 16, 17

B

bad/worse/worst 21
BC 3
be 15, 16, 20, 25
beautiful 68
because 22
been and being 14
beginning a sentence 22, 33, 69
beginning an essay 71
being able to 17
being clear 72
being deliberately boring 36
better/best 21
between 26
bias 57, 58, 62
big, big mistake 68
biggest bird in the World 21
body language 7, 12
book reviews 89
books 1, 89
books — titles 29
books you like 1
borrow and lend 26
both 32
brackets 30, 31, 78
British Empire 94
broadsheets 59
but 22, 27

C

can 17
cannot 17
capital letter 18, 29, 33
chairperson 9
changing your argument 72
characters 44, 52, 53, 85
chat shows 64
checking the grammar, spelling and punctuation 74
cheese, chips and fruit 1
choice of vocabulary 46
cinemas 64
clauses 33
clear not right 72
clichés 2, 6, 69, 85
close reading 36, 40
clues 51, 52, 57
code 63
collective nouns 32
colloquial 4
colons 27
comic effect 49
comma 27, 29, 33
common spelling mistakes 24, 25
comparatives 21
compare 21, 65, 70
compare and contrast 65
completely wrong answer in an essay 74
complex sentences 22, 33
compound sentences 33
comprehension 36, 68, 75, 77
comprehension skills 36-41, 75
concentrate 7
concluding an essay 74
conclusion 74
conjunctions 22, 30, 33
connecting words 22, 30, 33
constructive questions 11
context 73, 78
contradiction 72, 77
conversations 7
corrections 74, 78
costumes 89
could 17
could have/could've 16
could of 16
creating an impression 49
criticise 7
cross reference 4
cultural context 96
culture 94

D

dashes and hyphens 30
debate 9, 12
definite article 31
dependent clauses 22, 33
describing with images 48
descriptions of characters 52
descriptive writing 48, 52, 83
detail 41
developing an image 48
dialect 2, 5
dialogue 85
diary 63
dictionary 4
did and done 16
different from 23
directing a scene from a play 88
direct questions 27
direct speech 28
director 52, 76, 89
discussion 8, 9
divided loyalties 53
do, do not 31
done and did 16
don't just copy 86
don't panic 10, 65, 74, 78
double negatives 31
double quotation marks 29
doughnuts 64
drafting 39, 70

E

each 32
easy marks 14
eaten/eating 34
eating dog food 15
effect/affect 25
eg and ie 0
ei 25
either 22
emotional language 56, 59, 81
empathising 95
emphasis 23, 27, 31, 47
end your story properly 87
ending a sentence 26, 33
entertain 57
enthusiastic 10
episodes 64
er and est 20
essays 1, 29, 68-73, 78
essay plan 70, 78
essay structure 71
essay style 69
essay writing skills 68
essays — titles 29
etc 3
everyone 32
exaggerating 36, 49, 56
exam essays 78
examiners hate that ending 87
example of an essay introduction 71
example of an extract from a longer text 65
example of a feature article 60
example of a formal letter 90
example of paragraphs 35
example of a sports report 91
example of writing about a specific passage 75
examples 41, 68, 70, 72, 73, 75, 78
exclamation mark 27, 29, 33
explaining 3, 57, 63, 75
explaining technical words 3
explaining your mistakes 74
expressions 12
extra exam hints 52
extra information 65
extra marks 78
extract from a longer text 65
eye contact 10
eyecatching 62

F

f and ph 24
fact and opinion 58
feature article 60
feelings 83
few 32
fewer/less/least 21
fictional stories 80
film reviews 89
first person narrative 63, 87
five key features to write about in plays 76
five major mistakes to avoid 72
fixed groups of lines 48
flexible argument 74
floor debate 9
food 94
formal 6, 69, 80, 88
formal English 60
formal situations 6
formal style 80
four things to do for high marks for reading 44
from 23
full stop 27, 29, 30, 33
funny 85
future 14

G

gaps 34
gender 95
generalising 7, 56, 72
giving a clear answer to the question 71
giving a reference for a quotation 73
giving a talk 10
giving advice to a character from a text 88
giving answers 68, 71
golden question 51
good/better/best 21
grabbing their attention 71
grammar 1, 14-35, 39, 74

Index

groups of sentences 35

H

h 24, 31
had 16
handwriting 78
have 16
he 18, 19
headline 56, 59
headword 4
helps you answer the question 70
her 19
hey nonino 18
hidden meanings 36, 77
him 18, 19
holding hands 48
how a debate works 9
how characters speak 52
how many marks it's worth 41
how something is done 20
how actors say their lines 52
how characters really feel 53
how to ask a good question 11
how to avoid arguments 7
how to lead a discussion 8
how to use a dictionary 4
how to use a thesaurus 4
how, what or why 70
humour 80
hyphens and dashes 30

I

I 19
i and y 24
I and you 19
i before e 24
ideas 94
ideas in a scene from a play 53
identifying with your audience 81
identity 95
ie 3, 24
ie and eg 3
if you find English boring 1
if you want to throw marks away 70
imagery 48, 77, 83, 85, 88
imagination 88
improvising 12
indefinite article 31
index 4
indirect free kick 3
indirect question 27
indirect speech 29
inform 57, 63
informal 88
informal letters 91
ing 24, 33
innit 6
instead 39
interesting essays 69
internet 56
interrupt 7
introducing your argument 71
introducing your key point 70
introductions 70, 71
it 18
items in a list 26
its and it's 28

J

jargon 3, 29, 56, 68, 85
joining words 22, 30, 33
jokes 36, 80
Juan 18
just plain rude 7

K

Katy on the loose 35
keep it relevant 38
keep talking 10
keep to the point 8
key points 75
key skills for speaking tasks 5
key skills of studying English 1
key to grammar 14
kinds of sentence 33
Kubla Khan 46

L

language 77, 80
layout 61, 62
leaflets 62
learn from your mistakes 74
learning the rules 1
lend and borrow 26
less/least 21
letter writing 91
letters 63
letting the audience have their say 9
lifestyle 94
lighting 89
like and as 26
linking words 22
list 70
listening 5, 11
lists 27
literal questions 40
literary essays 68, 72
local words 5
looking at passages 75
looking on from a distance 50
lovely 68
ly 25

M

magazines 56, 60, 61
main clause 22
make the Examiner want to read on 82
make your writing come to life 83
making grammar easy 14
making people believe you 12
making sense 72
making things up 78
many 32
margin 35
mark-saving page 26
marriage 95
martian 22
may 17
me and you 18
meaning 46, 77
media 56, 59
metaphors 49
might 17
Miss Stoat Toast 1999 61
missing letters 29
mistakes 74, 78
modern costumes 89
modern poems 77
monologues 76
mood 84
more than 21
most 21
Mother Nature 49
motion 9
motivation 53
music 89

N

naming 18
narrative 75
narrator 50, 75, 87
NB 3
near 22
neat and tidy essays 78
neatly-written 39
negatives 31
neither...nor 31, 32
never give up 78
never panic 75
new plan 70
news 56-58
newspaper editorials 58
newspapers 56, 58
nice 69, 83
no, not 31
no one 31, 32
no right answer 72
no time to lose 1
non-fiction 56
none 31
not at all 31
not funny 80
notes 39, 75
nouns 20
nouns and pronouns 18
novel 75
numbers 30

O

object 18, 19
object pronouns 19, 22, 26
obvious 7
of 22, 23
of/off 22
OK 6
old texts 44
older poems 77
on 22
on stage 76
onto 22
opinion 53, 57, 58, 70, 73, 80, 83
opinion questions 43
opinions 43, 56
or 22

P

paragraphs 34, 69, 78
passages 75
past tense 14, 16, 17, 25
performance 76
permission 17
personal essays 68, 72, 73, 80
personal questions 40, 43
personal view 63
personification 49
persuade 57, 63
ph 25
physical ability 17
pick up good marks 1
pictures 48, 62
pies 59, 84
plain questions 43, 55
planning 10, 70, 75, 78
planning a talk 10
plays 76
plot 44, 86
plural and singular 32
poems 77
poems — titles 29
poetic language 47
poetry 73, 77
polite questions 11, 16
politics 95
positive 31
possession 16, 23, 25, 28, 29
possibility 17
posters 61, 62
practice/practise 25, 65
prefixes 30
preparation 10
prepositions 19, 23, 26
present 14
presentation 78
preventing bad essays 70
probability 17
pronouns 18, 19, 22, 26
pronouns and nouns 18
pronunciation 2, 4
proposer 9
PS 3
pun 59
punctuation 1, 27, 73, 74

Q

questions 11, 29, 68, 70, 77
question mark 27, 29, 33
quotation 4, 58, 68, 72, 73, 78
quotation marks 28, 29, 73, 85
quote from the text 53

Index

R

Rambo Moose 51
reacting to the text 51
read between the lines 36
read carefully 37
read the question 41, 68, 78
reading 36, 44
reading for detail 37
realising an essay is wrong 74, 78
realistic 68
really think 53
recap 24
relationship words 22
relevant experience 82
relevant quotations 73
religion 94
repeating sentence structure 47
repeating the same consonant 47
repetition 18, 47
replaced letters 29
reported speech 28
responding to media texts 56
responses to the text 55, 56
revision notes 39
rhyme 47, 77
rhythm 77
role play 13, 64
Romeo and Juliet 48
rough copy 39
rough list 70
rough version 39, 70

S

s 28
said 85
saying the same thing twice 69
scanning 36
script 64
secret of essay writing 70
secret of quoting 73
sentence structure 1, 27, 32, 33, 47, 84
sentences 32, 33, 39, 56, 68
separation 23, 26, 30
serious tone 59
set 89
set the scene 83
setting 51
seven rules for formal letters 90
several 32
shall/will 17
sharing a vowel sound 47
she 19
shopping list 57
short and snappy 62
short forms of words 3
short, sharp sentences 84
shortcuts 1
shortened words 29
should 16, 17
should/would 17
sidetrack 8
silent h 24, 31
similarity words 49
similes 49
simple sentences 33
simple way to say things 3
single quotation marks 29
singular and plural 32
six major questions 50-51, 75
six mistakes to avoid 78
six points to improve your marks 65
six steps to planning a good essay 70
skimming 37
slang 2, 6, 29
slogan 62
soap operas 58
soliloquy 76
someone 32
songs — titles 29
sound patterns 47, 61
source of a quotation 58, 68
speaking 5, 64, 76
speaking directly to the audience 76
speaking task 64
special words 33
speech 29
spelling 1, 25, 24, 73, 74, 78
spelling tips 25
spoken English 4
spot the tricks writers use 36
stage directions 50, 76, 85
standard English 2, 6
stanza 47, 48
starting in the middle 87
stating your answer first 70
stationary/stationery 24
statistics 10, 56, 61
stick to the point 53, 72
Stoat Toast 61
structure 75
structure of a novel 75
style 44, 59, 60, 63, 65, 69, 77, 80, 82, 86, 88, 89
stylish 69
subject 18, 19, 32, 33
subject pronouns 18-19
subtext 53
suggest an interesting topic 8
summarize 38
summing up 75
superlatives 21
superstitions 49
support your answer with examples 53, 73
suspense 84
symbols 27
sympathetic 7
synonyms 46

T

table of comparatives and superlatives 21
tabloids 47, 59
taking notes 11, 39
tautology 69
teach and learn 26
technical words 3, 29, 56, 68
tense 14, 29, 32, 34
terrible mistake 14
that 22
the 30
theatre lights 85
their/there/they're 25
them 19, 26
them and those 26
themes 44, 51, 75, 77, 94
there/their/they're 25
thesaurus 4, 46
they 19, 25
they're/there/their 25
think before writing 70, 78
those and them 26
though 22
three key features of style 45
three rules for abbreviations 3
three things that affect the way we speak 6
three ways of describing people 85
timed essays 78
timeline of tenses 14
tired old phrases 2
titles 29, 30
to 22, 23
to ask permission 17
to be 15, 16, 20, 25
to have 16, 17
to try to 23
to/too/two 23
tone 44, 51, 56, 77, 80, 82, 84
top five tricks 56, 61
top two spelling rules 24
tricks 76, 77
try to 23
TV and film 64
two/to/too 22

U

UFOs 68
unclear questions 68
underlining 39
unrealistic tricks 76
unseen tasks 65
us 19
use of language 36, 53
use the words of the question 68, 71
use your own images 83

V

vague 7, 69
vague words in essays 69
varied vocabulary 25, 69
variety 25, 68, 69
verbs 14, 20, 32, 34
vertical slash / 73
vocabulary 1, 25, 46, 52, 56, 63, 69, 77, 80
vocabulary choice 46
voice 12

W

was and were 15
we 19
wear/were/where 25
weather 50, 94
were and was 14
were and we're 14
what to put in and what to leave out 86
when things go wrong 72, 75, 78
where/were/wear 24
which 22, 26
which and who 26
who 22
who and which 22, 26
whom 26
why 69
why was the text written? 56
will 17
with 22
wonderful 68
word music 47
word order 33
words ending in '-y' 24
worse/worst 21
would 16, 17
writing as a character 52
writing as a director 52, 89
writing a rough version 70
writing a summary 38
writing about a novel's structure 75
writing about experiences 82
writing about narrative 75
writing about novels 75
writing about older poems 77
writing about plays 76
writing about poems 77
writing about structure 75
writing an essay 68
writing exam essays 78
writing letters 91
writing reports 90
writing reviews 89
writing stories 86

X

Xanadu 46

Y

y 24
y and i 24
yes or no questions 8
you 19
you and I/me 19
your own experience 73
yours faithfully 91
yours sincerely 91

Commonly Misspelled Words

Here is a list of the most common words that people spell wrongly. Learn them now — if you don't you'll just be throwing marks away.

absence
accelerate
accommodate
accurate
achieve
acquire
across
address
aerial
aeroplane
agreeable
amount
anxious
appalling
appoint
argue
assistant
association
athlete
autumn
awkward
beautiful
beige
belief
benefit
benefited
bicycle
biscuit
build
business
cease
ceiling
chaos
cheque
chief
chimney
choose
chose
college
colourful
column
commit
conceit
condemn
conscience
conscious
criticism
deceive
decision
definitely
desperate
develop
disappear
disappoint
disciple
double
eccentric
eerie
efficient
embarrass
exaggerate
exceed
except
excitement
exercise
extremely
fascinate
February
financial
foreign
forty
fulfil
fulfilled
gauge
gorgeous
government
grammar
grief
handkerchief
height
holiday
humorous
humour
illegible
imaginary
immediately
incidentally
independent
innocence
insistent
install
interruption
irrelevant
its
jewellery
judge
knock
knowledge
laughter
leisure
library
likeable
loveable
manoeuvre
maintain
marriage
mischievous
necessary
neighbour
niece
ninety
occasionally
occur
occurred
panic
panicked
parallel
permissible
personal
personnel
philosophy
possess
prejudice
prescribe
privilege
proceed
profession
psychiatrist
quay
questionnaire
queue
realm
receive
receipt
recommend
resource
restaurant
rhyme
rhythm
ridiculous
secretary
scene
scenery
schedule
seize
separate
skilful
solemn
soliloquy
sophisticated
souvenir
stationary
stationery
style
succeed
successful
temporary
theatre
thieves
thorough
tongue
transfer
tyre
umbrella
unnecessary
unnoticed
until
vicious
view
Wednesday
weight
weird
which
whole
wilful
woollen
wreath
wreck
yacht
yield

Commonly Confused Words

accept and except
affect and effect
buy, by and bye
decent and descent
here and hear
illegible and eligible
practice and practise
of, off and 've
past and passed
stationary and stationery
their, they're and there
to, two and too
where and wear

R. Crumb's

AMERICA

Robert Crumb

KNOCKABOUT
A CRACK EDITION

R. Crumb's America

Published by Knockabout Comics, 10 Acklam Road, London W10 5QZ
The moral right of the author has been asserted

A CIP catalogue record for this book is available from the British Library.
Layout and Design Rian Hughes
ISBN 086166 1141
Printed in Denmark by Norhaven A/S

THIS IS NOT A HAPPY COMIC STRIP.
LET'S TALK SENSE ABOUT THIS HERE
MODERN AMERICA
"And I saw three unclean spirits like frogs come out of the mouth of the dragon, and out of the mouth of the beast, and out of the mouth of the false prophet. For they are the spirits of devils, working miracles, which go forth unto the kings of the Earth to gather them to the battle of that great day of God Almighty... And he gathered them together into a place called in the Hebrew tongue ARMAGEDDON.
—Revelations 16:13-16
LOVE ME OR LEAVE ME!
IT GIVES ME A HEAD-ACHE!
by THAT CRANKY OLD FUDDY-DUDDY, R. CRUMB
-© 1975-
YOW
EEEEK!
SCARY!
HELP! IT'S GONNA GET ME!!
AMERICA THE CRUEL BULLY
U.S. ARMY
ONE SIDE, GOOK!
NO KILL PLEASE!
AMERICA THE GLUTTON
ERP
AMERICA THE GREEDY
COMING SOON
MOUNTAIN VIEW ESTATES
500 CONDOMINIUMS IN BEAUTIFUL RECREATION AREA!
A BOISE-CASCADE DEVELOPMENT
AMERICA THE UGLY!
SAVE MORE
VALUE GIANT
ZIP GAS
JACK IN THE BOX BURGERS
DISCOUNT APPLIANCE CENTER
CLAXTONOLA
PEE CHEE INC.
EXPRESS

LET'S LOOK IN ON JOHN Q. PUBLIC, THE LITTLE GUY, MR. TAXPAYER, AND ASK HIM WHAT HE THINKS!
GRRRR TH' STUPID ASS-HOLES!
IN THE MIDDLE EAST TODAY, SECRETARY OF STATE HENRY KISSINGER BLAH BLAH
I'LL TELL YA WHAT I THINK! I USE TA THINK THIS COUNTRY WAS THE GREATEST... WE COULD DO NO WRONG! BUT NOT ANYMORE! ALL THIS CORRUPTION IN TH' GOVERNMENT AND BIG BIZNIZ HAS OPENED MY EYES!
?
SHAG
NOW I CAN SEE THAT ALL THOSE CRANKS WHO ALWAYS SAID THE COUNTRY'S GOING TO THE DOGS WERE RIGHT!!
IT'S NO WONDER I CAN'T PULL MYSELF TOGETHER!
MISTER BOJANGLES
WHY SHOULD I BUST MY ASS TRING T'DO WHAT'S RIGHT WHEN A BUNCHA FAT CATS ARE RIPPIN' OFF EVERYTHING THEY CAN GET THEIR HANDS ON!!!
FUCK IT!
PEOPLE PEOPLE WHO NEED PEOPLE
THREE HUNDRED YEARS AGO THIS WAS A VIRGIN LAND.... IT DIDN'T TAKE 'EM LONG TO MESS IT UP... ALL TH' GODDAMN PIMPS, PANDERERS, PICK-POCKETS AND PLUTOCRATS!!
ARE THE LUCKIEST PEOPLE IN THE WORLD
WHY SHOULDNT I GRAB SOME KICKS WHILE I CAN?! EVERY BODY ELSE IS...
WHERE ARE YOU GOING, HONEY?
DONT BUG ME, BITCH! GETCHERSELF LIBERATED, WHY DONTCHA!
BRUMMM
NUDES at NOON
GEORGE'S TOPLESS
AMATUER NITE EVERY TUESDAY
NO COVER NO MINIMUM
THIS'S THE PLACE!
YEAH...
I'M ENTITLED
...AND HOW ABOUT THESE KIDS TODAY
THE LATEST POSTURES
LIVE FOR THE MOMENT, MAN!
WISH I HAD SOME COKE.*
FUCK YOU..
* NOT COCA-COLA AS IN MY GENERATION, BUT COCAINE!
OBNOXIOUS, CONTRIVED MUSIC FOR THE SPOILED BRATS OF MODERN AMERICA
OYE' COMO VA!
MOTORCYCLES SO THEY CAN GO OUT AND HAVE FUN AND MAKE LOTS OF NOISE!
GWAUGHNGG
JERKS
I HATE ALL MODERN POPULAR MUSIC AND I HATE MOTORCYCLES... THAT'S RIGHT KIDS, I'M JUST A CRABBY OLD KILL-JOY!

CRUMB RAVES ON...

FAT CAPITALISTS & ALL BIG BUSINESS, NATURALLY!
"BENEVOLENCE IS A SUBJECT WHICH LIES OUTSIDE THE SPHERE OF ECONOMIC PHILOSOPHY..."
THERE HE IS!

IT'S ALL HIS FAULT

SLOGAN-CHANTING RADICALS ALMOST AS MUCH...

ONLY THE CULTURAL WORKERS' COALITION FRONT HAS THE CORRECT IDEOLOGICAL LINE ON THESE FASCIST OPPRESSORS AND THEIR RUNNING DOG LACKEYS!
CHE LIVES
SIDDOWN YA BIG MACHO PIG!

GLAD-HANDERS OF ANY KIND!
HEY YOU'RE BEAUTIFUL! THAT'S WHY I KNOW THAT YOU CAN SEE I'M GREAT!
KNIFE READY FOR YOUR BACK

THE "YOUTH CULTURE" AND ALMOST ALL TEEN-AGERS
THEY'RE LAUGHING AT ME AGAIN...GOD-DAMN LITTLE HERD FOLLOWERS!!

"FASHIONABLE" WOMEN, ALSO "FAG-HAGS" & FAGS...
PATHETIC DUPE
I HOPE I'M UP TO THE MINUTE!
ALL THOSE "BEAUTIFUL" PEOPLE.. I HATE 'EM

PLASTIC SIGNS
Y-NOT CLUB
CLUB INTIMO

CLUB INTIMO
FIRE LITE ROOM
IT'S TOO PLASTIC MAN!

SHOW BIZ PERSONALITIES & MASS MEDIA IN GENERAL

URBAN SOPHISTICATES
SO THEN I TOLD HIM "THAT WAS OBVIOUSLY A META-PHYSICAL INNUENDO"!
AH! HA HA HA HOW GAUCHE!

JET PLANES & OTHER FLYING CONTRAPTIONS

FREEWAYS, TURNPIKES, THRUWAYS, SKYWAYS, ETC.

MODERN ARCHITECTURE & REAL ESTATE DEVELOPMENT

COWBOYS, RednecKS AND OTHER WHITE TRASH, THEIR WIVES & KIDS...

NIGGERS AND MOST BLACK-TYPE COONS...
WUTDISHIT, BITCH!
SHEEMUV FUH!
PUSHY JEWS...
LEMME HANDLE THIS, BUBBIE!
ARROGANT ITALIANS
SNOTTY WASPS, DUM POLACKS AND ALL OTHER ETHNIC GROUPS

I COULD GO ON AND ON, BUT WHY BOTHER? WHAT DO I LIKE ABOUT MODERN AMERICA, YOU MAY ASK? WELL, THE ANSWER IS:
NOT MUCH!
OLD MEANY!
HISSS
DROP DEAD, CREEP!
BOO!
GO LIVE IN RUSSIA!

AND WHAT WOULD I DO TO MAKE AMERICA A BETTER PLACE, YOU MIGHT ASK? WELL, FIRST I'D BRING BACK STREETCARS
DING DING
CAR STOP

DISMANTLE ALL ATOMIC POWER PLANTS AND IMMEDIATELY STOP PRODUCTION OF PLUTONIUM!

MAN WAS NEVER MEANT TO FOOL AROUND WITH SUCH DANGEROUS AND DEADLY ELEMENTS!

SOME THINGS I'D MAKE JUST LIKE RED CHINA... I'D TAKE ALL THE JET-SETTERS, STOCK BROKERS, FASHION DESIGNERS, INTERIOR DECORATORS, FASHION MODELS, PUBLIC RELATIONS EXECUTIVES, BOARD CHAIRMEN, AND THEIR WIVES, ALL OF THESE HIGH-SOCIETY PEOPLE... I'D TAKE 'EM OUT AND MAKE 'EM WORK IN THE FIELDS HOEING BETWEEN THE ROWS FOR A FEW SUMMERS... THEN THEY'D KNOW WHAT LIFE IS REALLY ABOUT!
OH GOD I FEEL SO HUMILIATED! I DONT THINK THIS IS ONE BIT FUNNY!!
TSK! I JUST HATE THIS ENSEMBLE I HAVE TO WEAR FOR THIS WORK!
IS IT ALMOST BREAKTIME YET? I'M UTTERLY EXHAUSTED ALREADY!!
NO ITS NOT EVEN NINE O'CLOCK YET!
I'VE HEARD OF "BACK TO THE ROOTS" BUT THIS IS JUST RIDICULOUS!
WHINE SNIVEL
'COURSE, I'VE NEVER DONE IT MYSELF, BUT THEN, I'M A HARD-WORKING ARTISTE!
I'D BRING BACK CRAFTSMANSHIP SO PEOPLE COULD GET A FEELING OF PRIDE FROM THEIR WORK! NO MORE ASSEMBLY LINES! BETTER QUALITY GOODS, AND LESS QUANTITY! THINGS WOULD LAST LONGER!
THE SUPERIOR MOTORCAR
I'D HAVE ALL THE GIANT CORPORATIONS AND CARTELS BROKEN UP... I'D PUT A STOP TO THE DEFENSE INDUSTRY AND I'D NATIONALIZE OIL, AND... HMM... I WONDER IF THE AMERICAN PEOPLE ARE READY FOR SOCIALISM?!?
HOW ABOUT THE AGED? WHAT COULD I DO FOR THEM? AND THE MEDICAL PROFESSION NEEDS DRASTIC REFORM... HOW 'BOUT TAX CUTS FOR THE SMALL BUSINESSMAN.... ?... HMM.. THIS IS GETTING COMPLICATED...
LEMME THINK
WHAT AM I GETTIN' MYSELF INTO HERE? TRYIN' TO SOLVE THE PROBLEMS OF MODERN AMERICA!!
I'M OVER MY HEAD... IT'S TOO DEEP FOR ME... WHAT THE HELL DO I KNOW!? I'M AS CONFUSED AS THE NEXT GUY...
KNOW NOTHINGS
NEW AMERICAN MOVEMENT
BLACK REVOLUTION BRIGADE
WOMEN'S LIBERATION ARMY
PROGRESSIVE SOCIALIST PARTY
WORKERS LABOR FRONT
BAN THE BOMB
JOHN GALT SOCIETY
AFL CIO
AMERICANS FOR AMERICA
UNITED CARTOON WORKERS
LIBERAL REPUBLICANS
NATIONAL WHITE PEOPLE'S DEFENSE ORGANIZATION
ECOLOGY ACTION GROUP
POLISH ANTI-DEFAMATION LEAGUE
UNITED ANARCHISTS & DADAISTS LEAGUE
GOD'S DUPES
CONSERVATIVE DEMOCRATS
NATIONAL CONSUMERS ASSOCIATION
WELFARE RIGHTS PROTECTION ASSOCIATION
TECHNOCRACY
WEIGHT WATCHERS
ALF LANDON
BOOSTERS CLUB
UNITED POTATO DIGGERS
CHILE PICKERS UNION
THIRD EYE MISSION
MOOSE LODGE
CONCERNED MOTHERS OF AMERICA
MARCH AGAINST RACISM COMMITTEE
HIPPIES FOR PEACE PARTY
LEGION OF DECENCY
STUDENTS FOR CHRIST ALLIANCE
PSYCHO-CYBERNETICS
JEWS FOR JESUS
APATHY & INDIFFERENCE SET IN...
WHO CARES??
WHAT'S ON TV? TONIGHT?
TV GUIDE
MERV
AMERICA'S TOP SELLING 'ZINE
WHAT'S THERE TO EAT AROUND THIS JOINT?
I DONT KNOW.. LET'S GO OUT TO A CHINESE RESTAURANT!
I FEEL MORE LIKE MEXICAN FOOD TONITE...
HMMM... WELL...
OH GOD...
DECISIONS DECISIONS
DOES AMERICA YEARN FOR STRICT DISCIPLINE? ARE THE PEOPLE TIRED OF HEDONISM? WILL A NEW GREAT "LEADER" EMERGE TO TELL US WHAT TO DO?
WE CALL FOR A RETURN TO THE VALUES THAT MADE THIS COUNTRY GREAT! AND WE MEAN BUSINESS!!
NEW AMERICAN MOVEMENT

WHAT DOES THE FUTURE HOLD FOR AMERICA?
I CAN'T LOOK!
THE SCARIEST THING GOING ON RIGHT NOW OF ALL THE SCARY THINGS I'VE HEARD OF IS...
RIP
TEAR
AEROSOL CANS!
LOOK AT JOHN Q. PUBLIC! THE POOR JERK'S GOING BERSERK!
YES, ALL LIFE ON EARTH IS NOW THREATENED WITH EXTINCTION BY UNDERARM DEODORANTS, HAIRSPRAYS, AIR FRESHENERS, SPRAYPAINT AND OTHER COMPLETELY NEEDLESS PRODUCTS IN AEROSOL CANS!
HM!
A BUNCH OF SCIENTISTS HAVE STATED THAT IF THEY DON'T STOP PRODUCING "FREON" IN SPRAY CANS, IT'S ALL OVER BY THE YEAR 2000!!
HA HA HA HA HA HA HA
PSSHHT
FREON DESTROYS OZONE, A THICK LAYER OF WHICH PROTECTS THE EARTH FROM THE ULTRA-VIOLET RAYS OF THE SUN. TESTS HAVE BEEN MADE. EXPERTS IN ATMOSPHERIC RESEARCH HAVE STUDIED THE PROBLEM.. THEY SAY THAT FREON IS DRIFTING INTO THE UPPER ATMOSPHERE... ONE ATOM OF THE STUFF DESTROYS 10,000 MOLECULES OF OZONE! SCIENTISTS SAY THAT FROM THE AMOUNT OF FREON ALREADY IN THE AIR 150,000, OR MORE, PEOPLE WILL GET— SKIN CANCER!
DUPONT CHEMICAL COMPANY MAKES HALF OF ALL THE FREON USED IN AMERICA... A BIG DUPONT EXECUTIVE WAS ASKED RECENTLY WHAT HE THOUGHT ABOUT THE THREAT TO THE OZONE:
"I HAVE FAITH IN THE BIOSPHERE ACTING TO PRESERVE LIFE."
HE HAS FAITH IN THE... BIOSPHERE .... ACTING... TO... PRE.... SERVE.... ......
OH MY GOD!
NOTHING IS BEING DONE... FREON IS BEING MANUFACTURED IN GREATER QUANTITIES THAN EVER BEFORE... THE AEROSOL CAN MARCHES ON!!
MY BABIES!
IT'S MONEY, MY FRIENDS... MONEY MONEY MONEY MONEY MONEY!
NO, THERE'S MORE TO IT THAN THAT... ITS... IT'S...
THE DEEP THINKER
IT'S... IT'S..... WHAT IS IT EXACTLY?
HE'S LOST
M-MAYBE IT WONT HAPPEN! MAYBE THEY'LL FIND OUT THAT THEY WERE ALL WRONG! MAYBE THEY'RE PUSHING THE PANIC BUTTON TOO SOON!
MAYBE... YOU CAN ALWAYS HOPE FOR THE BEST!
EVENTUALLY THEY'LL STOP MAKING THE STUFF IF IT REALLY IS BAD, WONT THEY?...
BEFORE IT'S TOO LATE??
OH EVENTUALLY, MOST CERTAINLY! WE CAN ONLY HOPE THEY'LL STOP BEFORE THE OZONE LAYER IS SO FAR GONE THAT ALL ORGANIC LIFE GETS TOTALLY SCREWED UP!
WELL, MR. CRUMB, IS THERE ANY GOOD NEWS??
SURE THERE IS, LI'L BUDDY! TOMORROW IS GONNA BE A BEAUTIFUL, SUNNY DAY, ONLY, I'D FORGET ABOUT TRYING TO GET A TAN... IT AINT HEALTHY!
WAP
YAK YAK!
...AND THAT'S LIFE IN MODERN AMERICA!
AINT IT A GAS!
BEEP!
SPLAT
THE END
EEK!

Underground Cartoonist & Folk Hero R. Crumb :
FOLKS, I'M GOING TO SPEAK PLAIN; THE FACT OF THE MATTER IS, I KNOW THEY'RE TRYING TO GET ME BECAUSE I BRING YOU THE TRUTH!

... AND THE TRUTH IS THE ONE THING THESE BASTARDS CAN'T TOLERATE!! I ONLY HOPE TO GOD I AM ABLE TO COMPLETE MY MISSION ON THIS PLANET BEFORE THEY SUCCEED IN EXTERMINATING ME!!!

WHY, THIS VERY EVENING, AS I SET ABOUT TO DRAW A CARTOON, I DETECTED A STRANGE ACRID SMELL IN THE AIR
SNIFF SNIFF... NOW WHERE COULD THAT BE COMING FROM...
TRUCKIN

A LITTLE INVESTIGATING ON MY PART AND I REALIZED THE PUNGEANT ODOR WAS COMING FROM MY INK BOTTLE!!
GOOD LORD!
FLO-EZE INK

I GRABBED THE INK BOTTLE AND FLUNG IT FROM THE DOOR OF MY STUDIO!!
THAT WAS POISON GAS!!
NO PEDDLERS
AWARD

AFTERWARD, I TRIED TO THINK BACK... WHO HAD BEEN IN MY STUDIO THIS MORNING? AND THEN, IN A FLASH, I KNEW WHO IT WAS THAT WAS TRYING TO KILL ME!!!
OF COURSE!! I SHOULD HAVE KNOWN ALL ALONG! HE'S A GOVERNMENT AGENT!! IT'S SO OBVIOUS TO ME NOW... I'VE GOT TO BE MORE CAUTIOUS IN THE FUTURE...

I WON'T NAME NAMES HERE, FOR THAT WOULD ONLY GET ME IN DEEPER TROUBLE WITH THEM, BUT LET ME JUST SAY THIS TO THOSE ROTTEN MOTHERFUCKERS!!
IT DOESN'T MATTER WHAT YOU DO TO ME, YOU SWINE! YOU'VE ALREADY SEALED YOUR OWN DOOM!! FREEDOM LIVES ON!!

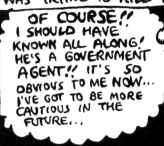

TRASH
what do we throw away?
by R. Crumb ©'82
WE THROW AWAY EVERYTHING! WE'RE THE THROWIN'-AWAYEST PEOPLE ON EARTH! AND WE HAVE SO MUCH TO THROW AWAY! HERE'S A YEAR'S WORTH OF GARBAGE FOR ONE UNITED STATESIAN!
WAIT! HERE'S ONE MORE!
URP
GRRUNCH
DEPT. OF SANITATION

JUST THINK, IF ALL TRASH COLLECTION SUDDENLY STOPPED... PEOPLE WOULD JUST SIT IN THEIR STINK!
PEW
IT STINKS IN HERE...
BUT WHY PICK ON ME!? IT'S NOT MY FAULT THAT ALL THIS CRAP IS MADE TO THROW AWAY! IT'S THESE BIG SHOTS THAT ARE RESPONSIBLE...
HEY, A GUY'S GOTTA EAT 'N' HAVE HIS BEER 'N' WHATNOT!
I GOT NOOZ F'YA, THAT POOR SLOB IS RIGHT! OUR GLUT OF GARBAGE IS THE DIRECT RESULT OF A CONSPIRACY, DON'T KID Y'SELF!!!
WHAT WE COULD USE RIGHT NOW IS A REALLY BIG WAR... THERE'S TOO MANY OF "THEM" ANYWAY!
NAH... OLD HAT... LET'S GET OFF THAT TRACK, J.B... WE NEED FRESH IDEAS.
A.J. IS RIGHT.. BUT OUR MARKETS HAVE "PLATEAUD OUT".. WHERE DO WE GO FROM HERE?
WE HAVE TO GET COZY WITH THE RUSSIANS.. THEN WE CAN OPEN THEM UP TO OUR PRODUCTS... THIS'LL ENTAIL A MORE LIBERAL ADMINISTRATION IN WASHINGTON..
NO PROBLEM THERE, J.S..
NON-SPECIFIC MULTI-NATIONAL CONGLOMERATE
CONTAINER INDUSTRY
PETRO-CHEMICALS
PAPER COMPANIES
BANK BOARD CHAIRMAN
BIG PLANS
I JUST LOVE TO DRAW THESE HEINOUS BUSINESS MEN! —R. CRUMB
BASICALLY MORE TRASH MEANS MORE PROFITS!
TRASH LEFT-OVER AFTER FAST-FOOD MEAL
AND BELIEVE IT OR NOT, THERE ARE STILL A FEW PLACES LEFT IN THE WORLD WHERE THERE'S NO SUCH THING AS "WASTE"!
LOOK, MY GOOD FRIEND, I'LL GIVE YOU THIS SHINY NEW PLASTIC CUP FOR THAT SHABBY OLD HAND-CARVED DOLL!
O.K.! YOU GOOD TO ME MR. BOSSMAN!

IT'S NO WONDER THAT WHEN THIRD-WORLDERS MOVE TO THE "LAND OF PLENTY" THEY MUST LITTER!!
I DO NOT NEED THESE THING!
WHY ARE THOSE PEOPLE SUCH FILTHY BARBARIANS!?
BEFOULING OUR LOVELY TOWN!
GOOD CITIZENS BRAINWASHED BY "LITTER-BUG" PROPAGANDA
THEN ON THE OTHER HAND THERE ARE PEOPLE WHO SAVE EVERYTHING...
DON'T THROW AWAY THAT COTTAGE CHEESE CONTAINER! THOSE THINGS ARE GOOD FOR KEEPING LEFT-OVERS IN THE FRIDGE...
BUT... THE CUPBOARD'S FULL OF THESE DAMN THINGS ALREADY!
ONE WAY OR ANOTHER, THE INUNDATION OF TRASH HAS TO BE DEALT WITH... THE AMOUNT OF PAPER ALONE IS STAGGERING...
GOTTA GET RID OF ALL THESE @**!!! PAPERS!
ONE WEEK'S WORTH
NEATLY FOLDED PAPER BAGS
OLD MAGAZINES
WESTERN GIZMO SALE
"WASTE NOT, WANT NOT."...
WE'LL NEVER USE HALF OF THESE JARS AND BOTTLES BUT I HATE TO JUST THROW 'EM AWAY...
I DUNNO I DUNNO
RECYCLING CENTERS ARE BASICALLY A FORM OF THERAPY FOR PEOPLE OBSESSED BY GUILT ABOUT THROWING ALL THIS JUNK AWAY!
MUSIC TO MY EARS!
RECYCLING CENTER
SMASH
SHATTER
TINKLE
NOW THEY CAN ORGANIZE THE DELUGE OF GARBAGE INTO A SYSTEM THAT SEEMS RATIONAL. EVEN THOUGH IT'S VERY TIME-CONSUMING, AT LEAST THEY'RE IN CONTROL!
SUPPORT YOUR LOCAL CO-OP
SAVE THE
ALUMINUM CANS
TIN CANS
PLASTIC
CLEAR GLASS
BROWN GLASS
GREEN GLASS
WHAT THEY'RE REALLY DOING IS SUBSIDIZING A BUNCH OF LOUSY FOOD-PROCESSING, BEVERAGE AND CONTAINER CORPORATIONS!!

NOT ONLY HAS THERE BEEN A VAST INCREASE IN THE QUANTITY OF TRASH, BUT ALSO A DECLINE IN THE QUALITY... WHEN I WAS A KID IN THE 'FIFTIES WE USED TO FIND WONDERFUL THINGS IN TRASH-CANS AND DUMPS!
WOW! HEY, LOOK WHAT I FOUND!
WHAT!? WHAT!?
BOING
GLOM
BREYER'S ICE CREAM
IN FACT, IT WAS BY PICKING IN BACK-ALLEY TRASH AFTER SCHOOL THAT WE GOT OUR REAL EDUCATION!
HUH! LOOKIT THIS OL' MAGAZINE!
PRETTY NEAT COVER!
GUY! THAT LOOKS REALLY OLD!
THERE'S A WHOLE STACK OF 'EM HERE!
65
LOOKING BACK, IT SEEMS WE SHOULDN'T HAVE THROWN SOME THINGS AWAY, BUT THEN WE COULDN'T SAVE EVERYTHING! WE HAD TO KEEP THE WHEELS OF OUR MASS-PRODUCTION ECONOMY TURNING AT A FEVER PITCH!
SO WHAT IF A CULTURAL HERITAGE WAS LOST IN THE PROCESS... SO WHAT IF RESOURCES WERE MINDLESSLY SQUANDERED... SO WHAT IF MOM NATURE HAD TO BEAR THE BRUNT!
OUF
HURRY UP!
I'M NEXT!
UNH! UNH!
FUTURE GENERATIONS
DRINK UP MY PET.. HEH HEH HEH
GORP SLURP
SHE'LL HAVE THE LAST LAFF ON US!
NUKEY WASTE
END

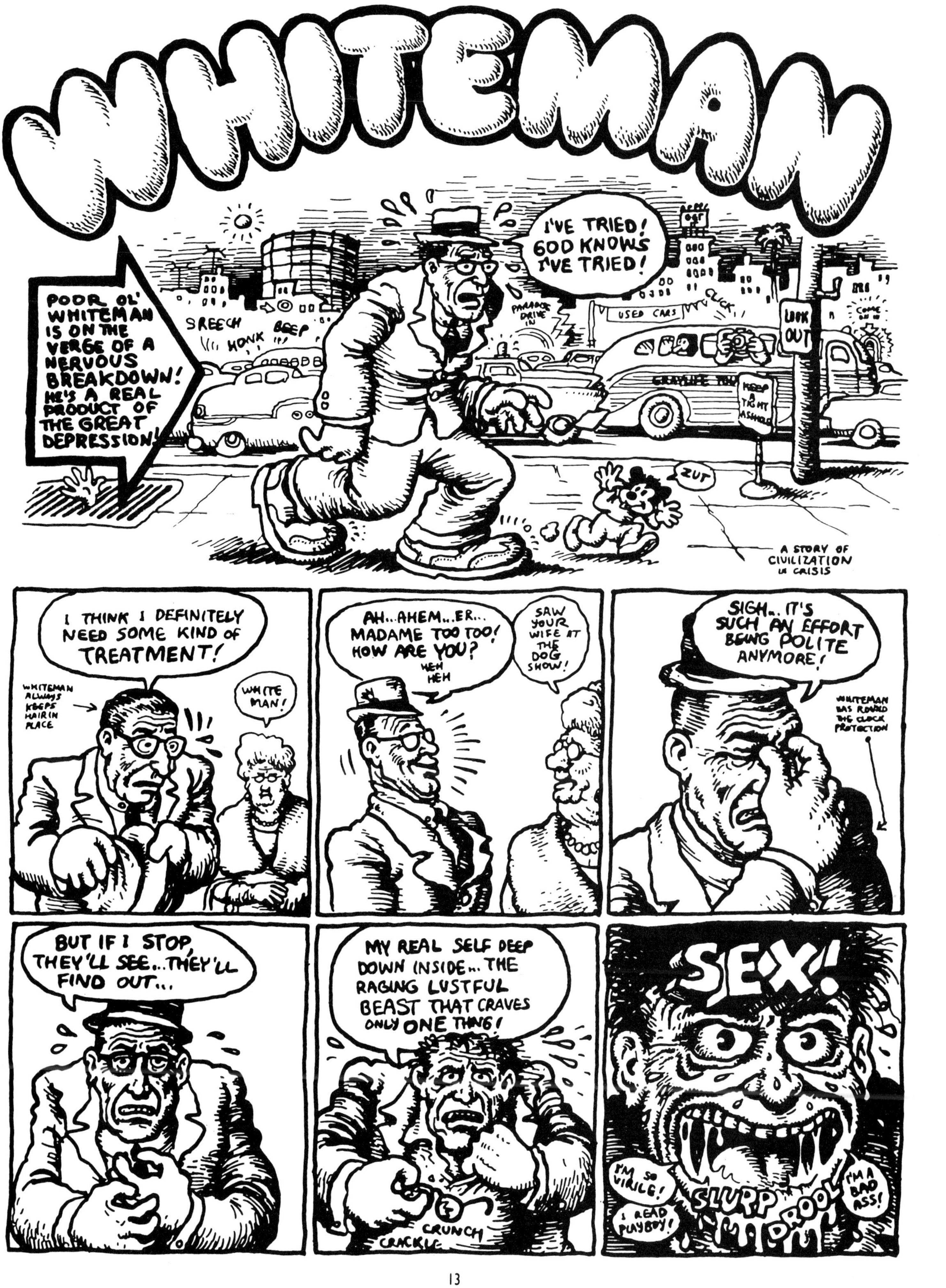

WHITEMAN

POOR OL' WHITEMAN IS ON THE VERGE OF A NERVOUS BREAKDOWN! HE'S A REAL PRODUCT OF THE GREAT DEPRESSION!

I'VE TRIED! GOD KNOWS I'VE TRIED!

SREECH
HONK
BEEP
PARADISE DRIVE IN
USED CARS
CLICK
LOOK OUT
KEEP A TIGHT ASSHOLE
ZUT

A STORY OF CIVILIZATION IN CRISIS

GOT TO GET A GRIP ON MYSELF.. I'M A GROWN MAN! AN INTELLIGENT ADULT! WITH RESPONSIBILITIES!

I'M AN AMERICAN!

A CITIZEN OF THE UNITED STATES!

A REAL HARD CHARGER! STEP ASIDE, BUDDY!
GRRR GRR
GRRR GRUNT
THUD

THE MAN WITH THE KNOW-HOW! A CITIZEN ON THE GO!

I MUST MAINTAIN THIS RIGID POSITION OR ALL IS LOST!

WHEW! THIS IS HARD WORK! BELIEVE ME! I GET HEAD-ACHES! MY BOWELS REFUSE TO FUNCTION... GUTS ARE ON FIRE...
..INDIGESTION.. ...HEARTBURN...

HEY, THERE'S A NICE LITTLE PIECE O' TALENT! IF ONLY I HAD THE TIME, I'D...
GEE, A REAL HE-MAN!

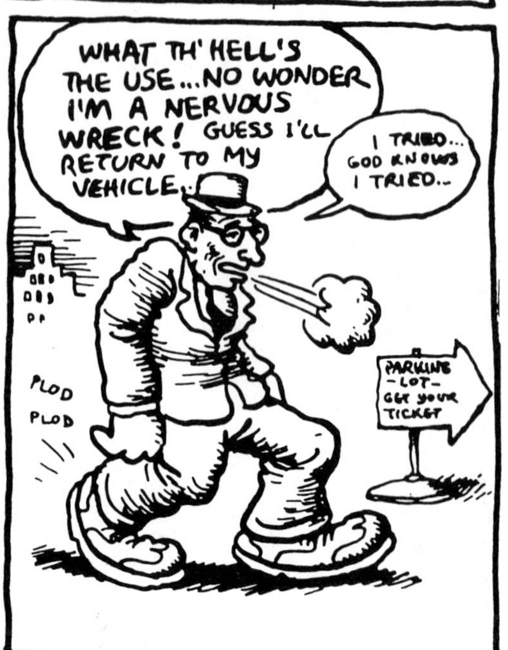
WHAT TH' HELL'S THE USE...NO WONDER I'M A NERVOUS WRECK! GUESS I'LL RETURN TO MY VEHICLE...
I TRIED... GOD KNOWS I TRIED..
PLOD
PLOD
PARKING -LOT- GET YOUR TICKET

GRIPE GRUMBLE MUMBLE
RROARR

CAUGHT IN A TRAFFIC JAM!
HONK
HONK
BEEP
HONK
I NEED A DRINK!
HONK
HONK

OH NO... HERE IT COMES AGAIN... THAT FORBIDDEN PASSION! THOSE ILLICIT DESIRES... ONLY... CHOKE... THIS TIME IT ISNT SEX!
HONK HONK
HONK
HONK
HORNK
HONK
OH OOGA

THIS TIME IT'S SOMETHING HORRIBLE! UNTHINKABLE! GOD FORGIVE ME.. I WANT TO... ...WANT TO...
HONK
HONK

KILL
DESTROY
CUT
SLICE
MAIM

TWO HOURS LATER
I FEEL BETTER NOW... HAD A FEW... GUESS I'LL HEAD ON HOME AND CATCH THE LATE NEWS..
BUD'S CLUB

!
WHAT'S THAT MUSIC? SOUNDS LIKE A PARADE, BUT IT'S SO FAR AWAY...

HEY MISTAH! DEY'S A COMIN'!
LEAVE ME ALONE!

I CAN'T STAND IT.. WHAT IF SOMEONE SEES ME LIKE THIS? IN THIS STATE OF FEAR!

HAW HAW
LEZ PULL HIS PANTS DOWN!
HAR! GIT WHITEY!
NO! PLEASE! THINK OF MY DIGNITY..MY FAMILY!
OFF THEY COMES WHITEMAN!
HELP! POLICE!
HEE HAW
HAW HAR
HAR HAR
OH GOD I'M SO EMBARRASSED!
HE SO EM-BEAR-ASSED HAR
SOB
HOW COULD THEY DO THIS TO ME.. I'M WHITEMAN!
YEAH, WELL LIZ'N BUD!
YOU JIS' A NIGGER LIKE EVVA BODY ELSE!
NO MORE! NO LESS, MUTHA!
BUT, I...
BE COOL DAD! LISS'N! HEAR DAT LAUGHIN' AND SINGIN' COMIN' DOWN DE STREET?
I DON'T HEAR NOTHIN'! SCRAM!
MAN, YOU IS JES' PLAIN NASTY!
C'MON NIGGER! YO' GOT MUSIC IN YO' SOUL! REMEMBER?
I DONT KNOW WHAT YOU'RE TALKING ABOUT!
SHO' NUFF! HE PLUM FERGOT!
HEE!
HEY C'MON! WE'S ALL JOININ' TH' PARADE!
YOWSUH!
AH GOTS HAPPY FEET!
WILL WHITEMAN JOIN THE PARADE?
HMM, MAYBE SOME OTHER TIME-I-
IT SEEMS RATHER SILLY...
WHAT'S THE WORLD COMING TO?
LOW CLASS...
FOOLISH NONSENSE
IS IT TOO LATE
MIGHT BE FUN
OH, EVENTUALLY!

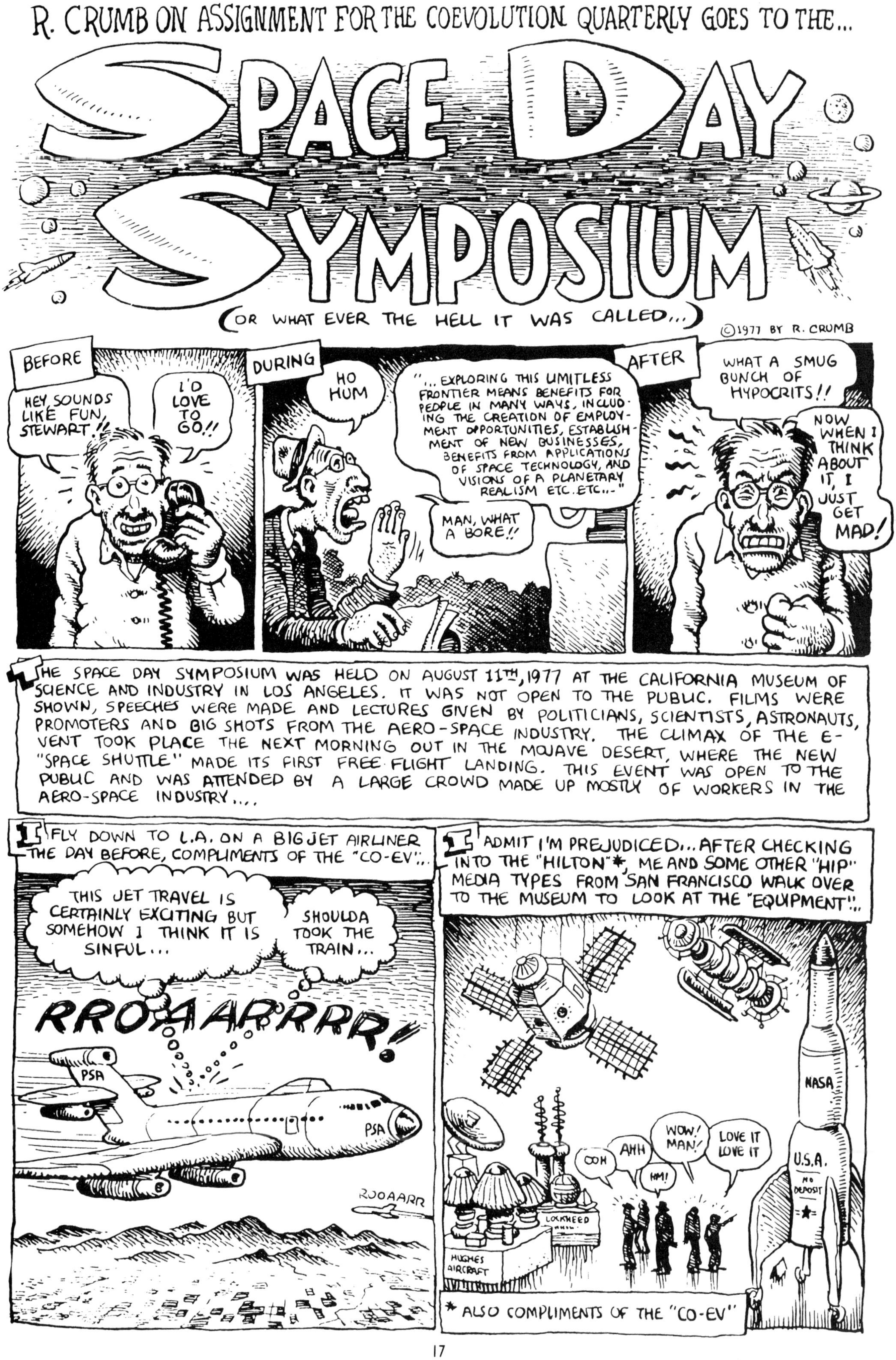

R. CRUMB ON ASSIGNMENT FOR THE COEVOLUTION QUARTERLY GOES TO THE...

SPACE DAY SYMPOSIUM

(OR WHAT EVER THE HELL IT WAS CALLED...)

BEFORE
HEY, SOUNDS LIKE FUN, STEWART!!
I'D LOVE TO GO!!

DURING
HO HUM
"...EXPLORING THIS UMLIMITLESS FRONTIER MEANS BENEFITS FOR PEOPLE IN MANY WAYS, INCLUDING THE CREATION OF EMPLOYMENT OPPORTUNITIES, ESTABLISHMENT OF NEW BUSINESSES, BENEFITS FROM APPLICATIONS OF SPACE TECHNOLOGY, AND VISIONS OF A PLANETARY REALISM ETC. ETC..."
MAN, WHAT A BORE!!

AFTER
WHAT A SMUG BUNCH OF HYPOCRITS!!
NOW WHEN I THINK ABOUT IT, I JUST GET MAD!

THE SPACE DAY SYMPOSIUM WAS HELD ON AUGUST 11TH, 1977 AT THE CALIFORNIA MUSEUM OF SCIENCE AND INDUSTRY IN LOS ANGELES. IT WAS NOT OPEN TO THE PUBLIC. FILMS WERE SHOWN, SPEECHES WERE MADE AND LECTURES GIVEN BY POLITICIANS, SCIENTISTS, ASTRONAUTS, PROMOTERS AND BIG SHOTS FROM THE AERO-SPACE INDUSTRY. THE CLIMAX OF THE EVENT TOOK PLACE THE NEXT MORNING OUT IN THE MOJAVE DESERT, WHERE THE NEW "SPACE SHUTTLE" MADE ITS FIRST FREE FLIGHT LANDING. THIS EVENT WAS OPEN TO THE PUBLIC AND WAS ATTENDED BY A LARGE CROWD MADE UP MOSTLY OF WORKERS IN THE AERO-SPACE INDUSTRY....

RIGHT AWAY I NOTICED EVERYTHING HAD A BRAND NAME ON IT... THE "MUSEUM" WAS A SHOW-ROOM FOR AERO-SPACE CORPORATIONS, EACH WITH ITS OWN ELABORATE DISPLAYS AND SALES PITCH..
WE'RE LOOKING AHEAD
GENERAL DY CS
THE SPACE GADGETRY LEFT ME COLD...I WALKED BACK TO THE HILTON ALONE & LOST IN L.A....
IS THIS THE WORLD OF THE FUTURE?
STAYED IN MY ROOM AT THE HOTEL THE REST OF THE DAY AND NIGHT....
OH MAN.. WHAT AM I DOING HERE?
CANT HANDLE IT...
WHAT'S TH' WORLD COMING TO?
HATE TH' MODERN WORLD...
WHAT DOES IT ALL MEAN ENNYWAY?
IS IT ME??

NEXT MORNING AT THE SYMPOSIUM THE SPEECHES STARTED BRIGHT AND EARLY... FIRST CAME THE GOVERNOR OF CALIFORNIA TO START THINGS OFF..
...BUT WITHIN THIS "ERA OF LIMITS" WHICH I HAVE SO OFTEN EMPHASIZED, THERE IS AN INFINITE "ERA OF POSSIBILITIES" IN THE EVERLASTING FRONTIER OF THE UNIVERSE ITSELF... NOT TO MENTION THE PRACTICAL ECONOMIC BENEFITS...

THEN CAME SOME BIG WHEEL FROM NASA (NATIONAL AERONAUTICS AND SPACE ADMINISTRATION)
...THIS GREAT HUMAN ADVENTURE INTO SPACE IS A SUBJECT OF TREMENDOUS APPLICABILITY.......COINCIDES WITH THE DEVELOPMENT OF ENVIRONMENTAL IMPORTANCES AND THE "WHOLE EARTH" PROBLEM.......WHAT WORRIES ME IS ALL THIS TALK I HEAR ABOUT THE "QUEST FOR IMMEDIATE RELEVANCE"....
...GOOD INVESTMENT....
CULTURAL IMPERATIVE... SMALL PERCENT OF THE NATIONAL BUDGET...
GRUNT
FIDGET
YAWN
SHUFFLE

NEXT CAME A PROMINENT SPACE SCIENTIST AND AUTHOR....
....BUILT INTO THE HUMAN SPIRIT IS THIS ZZEST FOR FINDING OUT... IT IS THIS ZZEST WHICH HAS BROUGHT US TO OUR TOTAL DOMINANCE OVER THE PLANET......
....LIMITLESS OPPORTUNITIES FOR VIGOROUS INTELLECTUAL DISSATISFIED PEOPLE.....SAFETY VALVE FOR GLOBAL PROBLEMS...
...SOCIAL SIGNIFICANCE....
...ATTAINING OF PERSPECTIVE...

THEN CAME THE CORPORATION DIRECTORS AND PRESIDENTS, AND THE DAY REALLY GOT TEDIOUS...
THE SPACE SHUTTLE WILL USHER IN A NEW ERA IN SPACE FLIGHT...BRAND NEW CAPABILITIES... ECONOMIC BENEFITS... PROFITS... LESS THAN ONE PERCENT OF THE NATIONAL BUDGET... PROFITS.... PROFITS.... ...PROFITS...PROFITS...

TECHNOLOGY IS NEUTRAL... IT'S HOW IT IS USED BY HUMANS THAT'S GOOD OR BAD... .... THE SOLUTION TO THE PROBLEMS OF THE ENVIRONMENT AND ENERGY IS NOT CONSERVATION BUT NEW TECHNOLOGICAL ADVANCES...

...THE DANGERS OF THE MISUSE OF ROCKETS AND SATELLITES IS THE RESPONSIBILITY OF THE GOVERNMENT, NOT THE AERO-SPACE INDUSTRY... ...OUR JOB IS TO DELIVER THE GOODS FOR WHOEVER BUYS OUR PRODUCTS... OUR RESPONSIBILITY IS TO OUR STOCKHOLDERS....
YAY!
YA-A-Y!
YEAH!
HUZZAH!
HOORAH

WE WANT TO BE THE LEADERS IN THE NEW ERA OF DECENTRALIZATION... OUR COMSATS* WILL PROVIDE INSTANT COMMUNICATION AND INFORMATION TO THE LOCAL COMMUNITIES AND NEIGHBORHOODS... ....HELP THE PEOPLE IN THE GHETTOS... IMPROVE THE QUALITY OF LIFE FOR EVERYONE... PROVIDE JOBS...
* COMMUNICATIONS SATELLITES...

ONE OF THE ASTRONAUTS TALKED ABOUT HIS EXPERIENCE "OUT THERE"...
....LOOKING BACK AT THE EARTH FROM SPACE, I HAD ALOT OF REALIZATIONS... IT GAVE ME A NEW CONSCIOUSNESS OF THE INSIGNIFICANCE OF OUR NATIONAL DIFFERENCES...EARTH IS INDEED A "SPACE-SHIP" WITH LIMITED RESOURCES...

"RUSTY" WAS A HELL OF A SINCERE GUY, A REALLY NICE GUY, BUT I'D HAD IT... THE HOURS OF TALK HAD LULLED ME INTO A STUPOR...
AGHH... ...SHIT...
BLAH BLAH BLAH

FINALLY IT WAS OVER... I STAGGERED OUT THE DOOR, MY MIND REELING FROM THE EIGHT HOURS OF LIES, DOUBLE-TALK, PERSUASION AND DOWNRIGHT MADNESS I HAD JUST SAT THROUGH...

OH MAN!

I SLUMPED DOWN ON THE STEPS OF THE MUSEUM, DEPRESSED BEYOND WORDS... WHAT WAS THE PURPOSE OF ALL THIS TALK ABOUT OUR "DESTINY"... THE "THRUST INTO SPACE"?

...TO DRUM UP BUSINESS FOR THE AERO-SPACE CORPORATIONS, OBVIOUSLY!!
...I THINK IT'S TERRIBLY EXCITING...

...DECIDED NOT TO STICK AROUND FOR THE BIG SPACE SHUTTLE LANDING...I WAS FED UP WITH THE WHOLE SHMEER... ...FLEW BACK TO SAN FRANCISCO THAT VERY NIGHT, UTTERLY DIZ-GUSTED BY THE FARCE I HAD WITNESSED...

BUT WHAT'S **WRONG** WITH SPACE EXPLORATION, YOU MAY ASK? ISN'T IT TRUE THAT IT'S AN EXCITING NEW FRONTIER, AND THAT IT WILL RAISE THE CONSCIOUSNESS OF HUMANITY??

DON'T BE DUPED BY FOOLISH BUCK ROGERS DREAMS OF GLORIOUS ADVENTURES AMONG THE PLANETS!!

LET'S WAIT UNTIL WE'VE LEARNED TO GET ALONG WITH EACH OTHER ON EARTH BEFORE WE GO BARGING INTO THE COSMOS! WHATAYA SAY??

AS FOR FRONTIERS, WE'VE STILL GOT PLENTY OF FRONTIERS LEFT RIGHT HERE IN THE U.S.A.!! HOW 'BOUT NEW YORK? CHICAGO? CLEVELAND? L.A., FOR CHRISSAKE! THESE ARE VAST AREAS IN NEED OF "VIGOROUS INTELLECTUAL" EXPLORATION!!

...BUT IT'S JUST MORE OF THE SAME OLD HYPE...TO KEEP THE "ECONOMY" GOING...NOT UNLIKE THE "ATOMS FOR PEACE" SHUCK AND EQUALLY AS DANGEROUS! YES, THE SPACE HYPE IS...

DANGEROUS!

...LET'S FACE IT, THE MILITARY **WILL** USE SPACE TECHNOLOGY TO CREATE A WHOLE NEW ARRAY OF WAR TOYS IN SPACE AT LEAST AS HORRIFYING AS ANYTHING THEY'VE ALREADY GOT, IF NOT MORE SO...BUT WHY AM I RAVING AGAINST IT? WHY BOTHER? THE ONLY THING THAT WILL STOP THEM IS A DRASTIC BREAKDOWN IN OUR INDUSTRIAL SYSTEM...NO MORAL OR INTELLECTUAL ARGUEMENT HAS EVER STOPPED THEM IN THE PAST...........

THE SADDEST PART THOUGH... THE SADDEST PART....IS THAT ALOT OF OTHERWISE INTELLIGENT PEOPLE ARE FALLING FOR THE SPACE HYPE...HOOK, LINE AND SINKER!!

...BUT AS FOR ME, I WASH MY HANDS OF IT!!
END

SALTY DOG SAM
BY R. CRUMB
FEEL LAK OLD NED!
GOD KNOWS AH TRAHS T' BE GOOD AN' DO WHUT DE RIGHT THING IS...
HEY YOU! WHATAYA CALL A ONE-LEGGED NIGGER?!
ARE YOU FROM FUNCTION
SHIT ON A STICK! HAW HAW HAW HAW
BUT IT AWFUL TOUGH SUMTAHMS... AH DON' THINK IT ALLUZ MAH FAULT WHEN THINGS GITS FUGGED UP...
FROM FUNCTION JUNCTION
ROARRR
AH'S ON'Y HOOMIN! WHUT AH GONNA DO?! GOT TEN HUNGRY MOUFS TO FEED AT HOME!
WHERE THE FUNCTION JUNCTION SUCTION CUPS ARE MADE
ARE YOU FROM FUNCTION FROM FUNCTION JUNCTION
WELL I'M FROM FUNCTION TOOOOO!
HEH HEH HEH! CUTE COUPLE, AREN'T THEY?
AH DON' THINK DEY SO CUTE.. I'S DEEGUSTID BY DEM FOOLS..
WHAT?! A TROUBLE MAKER, EH?? I'LL TEACH YOU—
BOP
BAM
WHACK
SEE WHUT AH MEANS?
B314

The ADVENTURES of "ONION HEAD"
by R. CRUMB
"LIFE IS LIKE AN INFINITE ONION."
AMEN
©1980
HIS TRIALS AND TRIBULATIONS BEGAN IN THE WINTER OF HIS DISCONTENT.....
DAD, I MUST LEAVE THE OLD HOME.. I GOT SOME THINGS TO WORK OUT, AND I...UH....
MMYEAHM...
WELL, KIDDO... I GOTTA GO SLOP TH' HOGS... SO, UH, TAKE CARE O' YERSELF!
...SLOP TH' HOGS...
I'M GONNA GO ROB TH' RICH AN' GIVE TO TH' POOR...
OKAY... DON'T GET HURT, BUDDY...

ONION HEAD SETS OUT...
TO ROB THE RICH AND GIVE TO THE POOR... HEIGH HO...
HE'S A WALKIN' BOY!
BEFORE LONG HE IS DISSILLUSIONED...
I'M NOT GETTING VERY FAR...
WHATSIT INC.
FREEWAY ENTRANCE
NO PEDESTRIANS OR BICYCLES BEYOND THIS POINT
IT'S A MIGHTY HARD ROAD...
BESIDES, THIS ROBBING THE RICH BUSINESS COULD BE DANGEROUS... AND I DON'T EVEN HAVE A GUN OR A KNIFE!!
MAN, THIS SUITCASE IS HEAVY!!
OH, HERE'S AN OCEAN, OR A SEA, OR WHATEVER YA CALL IT...
I'M ALL IN... GUESS I'LL CALL IT A DAY...
TOMORROW I'LL RE-THINK THIS WHOLE PROJECT... MAYBE I SHOULD LOOK FOR A JOB... START AT TH' BOTTOM AN' WORK MY WAY UP...

NOW ONION HEAD IS REALLY CONFUSED!!
GOOD-BAH
REW-BY TUESDAY
HEW COULD HANG
A NAME ON
YEE-EW
CRACKLE
SPUTTER
THAT SONG REMINDS ME OF TH' SIXTIES AN' BEIN' HIGH ON LSD...
WHAT THE HELL DOES HE EXPECT??
OOPS!
CRASH!
"THE RAGING SEA, HOW IT ROARS!"
SHIT!
SPLOP
HA HA HA HA HA HA HA HA HAH HA
GLUB BLUB
SPLUT CHOKE

HIS AMERICAN DREAM TURNS INTO A NIGHTMARE...
HA HA HA HA HA HA HA HA HA HA HA HA HA HA HA HA
OH CHRIST... THEY'RE ALL LAUGHING AT ME... I'M SO EMBARRASSED!!
AZZOLE!
HEY!
GET OFF YOUR HIGH HORSE, MAN!!
YOU FUGGIN' SCUM BAG!
BUT—
NO, I—
SUDDENLY IT HITS HIM...
THERE'S NO HOPE
NO HOPE!
WHAT IS POOR ONION HEAD TO DO NOW!
MY GOD — IT'S TRUE!
GIGGLE
NO HOPE!
TEE HEE
GET GOIN', YEW!
I'M HUNGRY... GUESS I'LL GO HOME...
LOST MY JACKET...
ONLY GOT ONE BOOT...
HIS JOURNEY COMPLETE, ONION HEAD FINDS A PLACE IN THE SCHEME...
HE'S SOBERED UP NOW... HE'S A GOOD BOY!
I'VE GOT A LOT TO LEARN...
HERE PIGGY PIGGY
HUALP
OINK
END

CITY OF THE FUTURE
THERE'S A BIG NEW WONDERFUL TOMORROW FULL OF MONUMENTAL ACHIEVEMENTS!! UNHEARD OF VISTAS OF PROGRESS AWAIT! BETTER WORLDS ARE BEING BUILT! EVERYONE WILL HAVE ALL OF EVERYTHING! LET'S LOOK AT SOME OF THE THINGS WE'RE GOING TO GET IN THE YEARS TO COME!
LEVEL 52

YOU WON'T HAVE TO SHIT ANYMORE! BOWELS WILL BE REMOVED AT BIRTH AND A SANITIZING DISPOSAL UNIT INSTALLED. NEEDS EMPTYING ONLY ONCE A MONTH. NO MORE WORRY ABOUT SMELLY EXCREMENT! GOOD-BYE TOILET!!

BUILDINGS, CARS WILL BE SOFT PLASTIC. STREETS WILL BE SOFT PLASTIC. ACCIDENTS WILL BE A THING OF THE PAST. NOBODY WILL GET HURT ANYMORE!

NO MORE HEAT AND COLD, NIGHT AND DAY. CITIES WILL HAVE ROOM TEMPERATURE ALL THE TIME. LIGHTING WILL BE SOFT, DIFFUSED. WARM SNOW FOR CHRISTMAS!!

EVERYONE WILL BE TUNED IN TO EVERYTHING THAT'S HAPPENING ALL THE TIME! NO-ONE WILL BE LEFT OUT. WE'LL ALL BE NORMAL!

NOBODY WILL WORK! ALL PRODUCTION, DISTRIBUTION AND MAINTENANCE WILL BE DONE BY COMPUTERIZED ROBOTS. PEOPLE CAN SPEND ALL OF THEIR TIME PLAYING, EATING, OR WATCHING TV!

...OR, THEY CAN FUCK!! SPECIAL FUCKING ANDROIDS WILL BE AVAILABLE TO EVERYONE! SOCIAL PROBLEMS WILL DISSAPPEAR. RISK OF INVOLVEMENT WITH THE OPPOSITE SEX WILL BE ELIMINATED!

THE ANDROIDS WILL BE PUT TO OTHER GOOD USES. SADISTS CAN TORTURE THEM, CUT THEM UP, TEAR THEM TO PIECES!
BASH
BASH
BASH
BASH

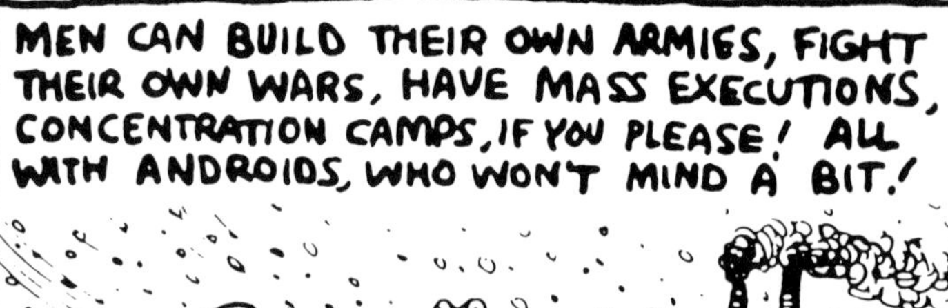

MEN CAN BUILD THEIR OWN ARMIES, FIGHT THEIR OWN WARS, HAVE MASS EXECUTIONS, CONCENTRATION CAMPS, IF YOU PLEASE! ALL WITH ANDROIDS, WHO WON'T MIND A BIT!

IN FACT, YOU WILL HAVE THE WHOLE SPECTRUM OF EXPERIENCE AT YOUR FINGER TIPS. FANTASY MACHINES WILL MANUFACTURE ANY WORLD YOU ASK FOR IN A MATTER OF SECONDS!

JUST TO KEEP US ON OUR TOES, VAST ENTERTAINMENT NETWORKS WILL BE ORGANIZED THAT SPECIALIZE IN SURPRISE PRANKS! PEOPLE WILL GET TRIPPED!
SPLAT

CLOWNS WILL APPEAR OUT OF NOWHERE WITH SELTZER BOTTLES!
HAW

HOUSES WILL GET UP AND WALK AROUND! TREES WILL MAKE FACES! PEEL AN ORANGE AND SOCKO!

SOME OTHER ADVANCES: CLOCKS THAT YOU CAN HAVE PUT INSIDE YOUR HEAD SO THAT YOU'LL ALWAYS KNOW EXACTLY WHAT TIME IT IS!
THE TIME IS NOW 9:30!

BABY SITTING WILL BE DONE BY ROBOTS WITH TV HEADS THAT PLAY VIDEO TAPES OF MOM AND DAD. PARENTS WILL NO LONGER BE TIED TO THEIR CHILDREN!
SUCH CUTE LITTLE DARLINGS!
HEY GIMME A NICKEL MOM!
ME SOME TOO WOW

MANY NEW SPORTS WILL BE INVENTED! KIDS WILL RISK THEIR LIVES IN DANGEROUS ROCKET DRAG RACES. SOME OF THESE JOBS WILL GO AS FAST AS 25,000 MPH!!

THERE'LL ALWAYS BE THE SEARCH FOR THE BIGGER KICK! GUYS WILL PLAY "CHICKEN" WITH SUICIDAL SOUPED-UP BODY ROCKETS!

OTHERS WILL JUST SIT AROUND ALL DAY PLAYING MIND GAMES!

ONCE A YEAR ALL THE OLD STUFF WILL BE GATHERED UP AND PUT INTO HUGE MACHINES WHICH WILL GRIND IT UP AND MAKE IT INTO NEW STUFF!

THE BED AS WE KNOW IT WILL BE REPLACED BY A SOFT, WARM, MOIST FOAM PLASTIC BLOB THAT YOU JUST DIVE INTO AND FALL ASLEEP WHILE IT UNDULATES SLOWLY IN AND OUT AND SOOTHING, SWEET MUSIC PLAYS.
ZZZZ

YES, EVERYTHING WILL BE BEAUTIFUL, BUT WE'LL STILL HAVE TO REGULATE POPULATION GROWTH. SO WHEN YOU'RE 65 THEY'LL COME LOOKING FOR YOU WITH A PIE...NOT JUST AN ORDINARY PIE!!

A CYANIDE PIE!! WHAT A WAY TO GO!!
HONK HONK
THAT'S ALL BROTHER

FROSTY the SNOW MAN and his friends
©1975 BY R. CRUMB
HI FROSTY AN' "STOOPID JERK"... WHAT'RE YOU GUYS DOOWEEN?
WE'RE HAVING WINTER FUN, HUH FROSTY? HA HA!
YOU BETCHA, STOOP!
7UP
ME AN' TH' JERK ARE GONNA THROW THESE "SNOWBALLS" AT TH' ROCKERFELLA MANSION! HA HA!
OBOY! I WANNA COME AN' THROW SOME TOO!!
TSK!
7UP
CAN I? PLEEEZ?? PULEEEEZ?? LET ME!
WHADDAYA THINK, STOOP?
CAN THIS KID BE TRUSTED?
HM!
I'M NOT SURE... HOW DO WE KNOW SHE WON'T FINK??
Y'SEE, WE CAN'T AFFORD TO TAKE ANY CHANCES!
HA! WHAT'S TH' BIG DEAL! THEY'RE ONLY SNOWBALLS!
7UP
THESE ARE NO ORDINARY SNOWBALLS!
GHASP! OH MY GOD!!
FROSTY the SNOWMAN and his friends
©1975 BY R. CRUMB
YOU GUYS ARE GONNA BLAST TH' ROCKERFELLA MANSION WITH BOMBS DISGUISED AS SNOWBALLS??
THAT'S OUR INTENTION, TUFFY!
OOH! THAT'S SCARY!
"A REVOLUTION IS NOT A TEA PARTY!" —CHAIRMAN MAO TSE TUNG
TROUBLE IN PARADISE FOR THE ROBBER BARONS!
HMM... I DON' KNOW IF I WANNA BE ENNY PART O' THIS CRAZY SCHEME!
THAT'S OKAY... WE KIN HANDLE IT... BUT KEEP IT TO YERSELF, OKAY??
7UP
SHE'LL KEEP IT TO HERSELF ALRIGHT, IF SHE WANTS TA STAY HEALTHY!!
?
I GUESS I BETTER COME ALONG NOW T'MAKE SURE YOU NUTS DON'T GET HURT!!
HEY BREAK IT UP!
LET'S GO!
OW!
OW!
OW!
SPLAT
SPLAT
SPLAT
7UP

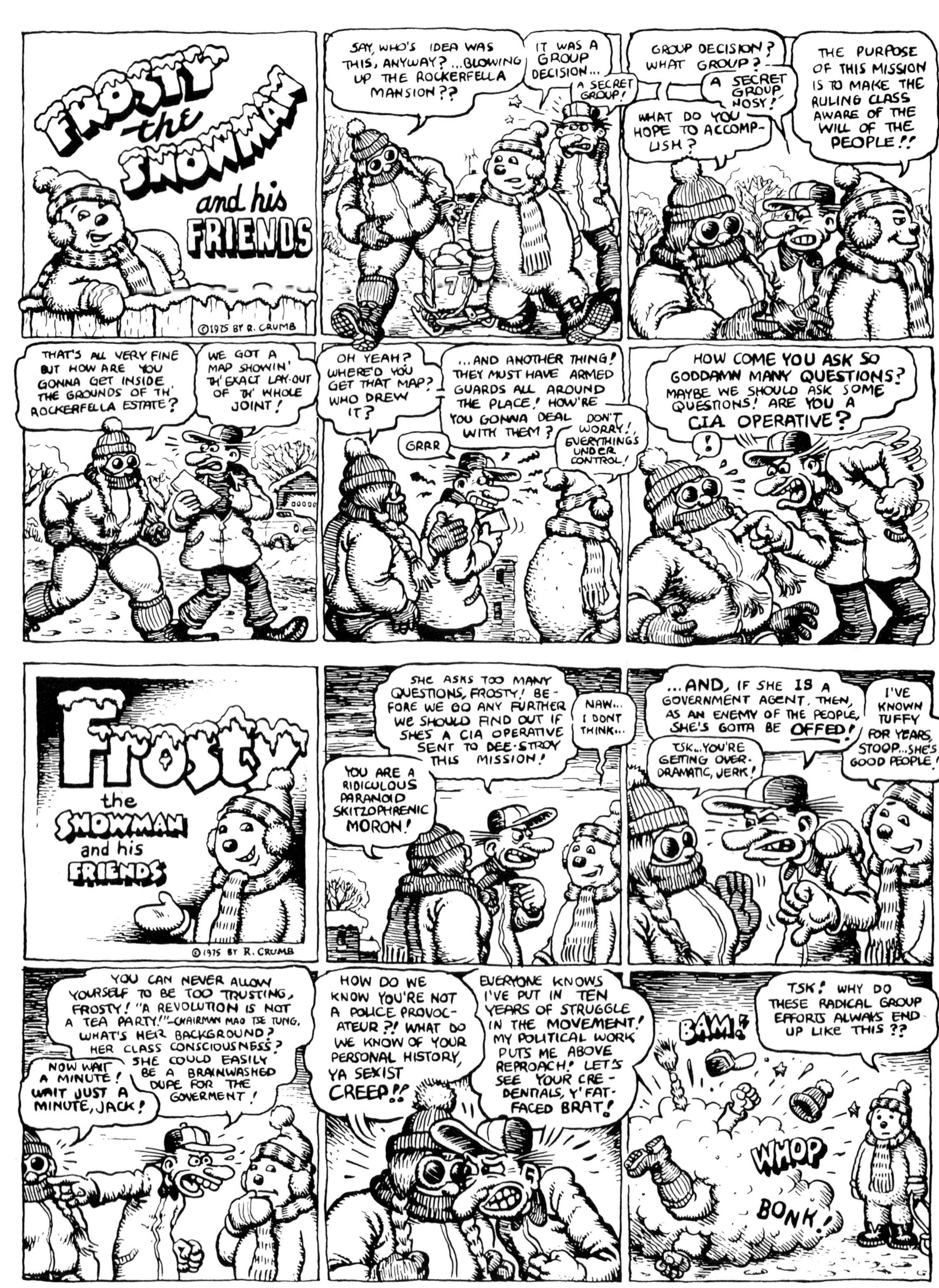
FROSTY the SNOWMAN and his FRIENDS
©1975 BY R. CRUMB
SAY, WHO'S IDEA WAS THIS, ANYWAY? ...BLOWING UP THE ROCKERFELLA MANSION??
IT WAS A GROUP DECISION...
A SECRET GROUP!
GROUP DECISION? WHAT GROUP?
A SECRET GROUP NOSY!
WHAT DO YOU HOPE TO ACCOMPLISH?
THE PURPOSE OF THIS MISSION IS TO MAKE THE RULING CLASS AWARE OF THE WILL OF THE PEOPLE!!
THAT'S ALL VERY FINE BUT HOW ARE YOU GONNA GET INSIDE THE GROUNDS OF TH' ROCKERFELLA ESTATE?
WE GOT A MAP SHOWIN' TH' EXACT LAY-OUT OF TH' WHOLE JOINT!
OH YEAH? WHERE'D YOU GET THAT MAP? WHO DREW IT?
...AND ANOTHER THING! THEY MUST HAVE ARMED GUARDS ALL AROUND THE PLACE! HOW'RE YOU GONNA DEAL WITH THEM?
GRRR
DON'T WORRY! EVERYTHING'S UNDER CONTROL!
HOW COME YOU ASK SO GODDAMN MANY QUESTIONS? MAYBE WE SHOULD ASK SOME QUESTIONS! ARE YOU A CIA OPERATIVE?
!
Frosty the SNOWMAN and his FRIENDS
©1975 BY R. CRUMB
SHE ASKS TOO MANY QUESTIONS, FROSTY! BEFORE WE GO ANY FURTHER WE SHOULD FIND OUT IF SHE'S A CIA OPERATIVE SENT TO DEE-STROY THIS MISSION!
NAW... I DONT THINK...
YOU ARE A RIDICULOUS PARANOID SKITZOPHRENIC MORON!
...AND, IF SHE IS A GOVERNMENT AGENT, THEN, AS AN ENEMY OF THE PEOPLE, SHE'S GOTTA BE OFFED!
I'VE KNOWN TUFFY FOR YEARS, STOOP...SHE'S GOOD PEOPLE!
TSK...YOU'RE GETTING OVER-DRAMATIC, JERK!
YOU CAN NEVER ALLOW YOURSELF TO BE TOO TRUSTING, FROSTY! "A REVOLUTION IS NOT A TEA PARTY!"—CHAIRMAN MAO TSE TUNG. WHAT'S HER BACKGROUND? HER CLASS CONSCIOUSNESS? SHE COULD EASILY BE A BRAINWASHED DUPE FOR THE GOVERMENT!
NOW WAIT A MINUTE! WAIT JUST A MINUTE, JACK!
HOW DO WE KNOW YOU'RE NOT A POLICE PROVOCATEUR?! WHAT DO WE KNOW OF YOUR PERSONAL HISTORY, YA SEXIST CREEP?!
EVERYONE KNOWS I'VE PUT IN TEN YEARS OF STRUGGLE IN THE MOVEMENT! MY POLITICAL WORK PUTS ME ABOVE REPROACH! LET'S SEE YOUR CREDENTIALS, Y' FAT-FACED BRAT!
TSK! WHY DO THESE RADICAL GROUP EFFORTS ALWAYS END UP LIKE THIS??
BAM!
WHOP
BONK!

Frosty the snowman
and his friends
©1975 BY R. CRUMB

CONFESS! CONFESS!!
OWN UP TO THE FASCIST RUNNING DOG THAT DEEP DOWN IN YOUR HEART YOU KNOW YOU ARE!
ARF! ARF! ARF!

STALINIST HITLER-BOY DICTATOR!! SEXIST PERVERT!
CALL ME A FASCIST, HUH... I'LL SHOW YOU!
GLUB BLUB

LACKEY TOOL OF THE BOURGEOIS REACTIONARIES!! MINDLESS RECEPTICAL OF MASS MEDIA PAP!!
BULL-SHIT! THAT DOESN'T EVEN HURT! IN FACT IT FEELS GOOD!!
HEY! IT'S GETTIN' LATE, YOU GUYS!
BOING
BOING
BOING

YOU...UNH.. FANATIC EXTREMIST...UNH... LITTLE TIN JEEZIZ!
OW!
OW!
OW!
LET'S GET MOVING!

REVISIONIST!
SNARL
BRRAZZZ
LET'S NOT HAVE ANY MORE OF THIS IN-FIGHTING, EH?
7UP

Frosty the Snowman
and his friends
©1975 BY R. CRUMB

THE ROCKERFELLA ESTATE LIES ON TH' OTHER SIDE O' THESE WOODS... NOW THAT IT'S GETTIN' DARK WE WON'T BE SPOTTED AS WE SNEAK UP THROUGH THE TREES... LET'S GO!
OKAY FROSTUMS!
MOVE 'EM OUT!

JEEZIZ! THIS WOODS IS SCARY AT NIGHT! SO DEATHLY QUIET!
YOU CAN GO HOME NOW IF YOU WANT! FROM HERE ON THIS IS A JOB FOR TRUE REVOLUTIONARIES ONLY!
OH OH... A FENCE!

G'WAN! BEAT IT, Y' BIG BABY! I KNEW YOU DIDN'T HAVE TH' STUFF TO—
STOOP! WAIT! DON'T TOUCH THAT-
DANGER! ELECTRIC FENCE!

—FENCE!
YOOOWWW!!!
GRAB'M!
I GOT'M!
ZZZZT

WAAHH!
AW POOR STOOPID JERK GOT "WATTS" COMING TO HIM!
HMM.. HOW WILL WE GET PAST THIS OBSTACLE?

The Adventures of FROSTY the SNOWMAN and his friends
©1975 BY R. CRUMB
BOY OH BOY! THAT ELECTRIC FENCE SURE PACKS A WALLOP, HUH STOOP?!
THERE THERE
GODDAMN THAT ROCKERFELLA! THAT LOUSY STINKIN' CAPITALIST SWINE! SOB SOB
YOU'LL GET YOUR SATISFACTION IF WE CAN SOMEHOW FIND A WAY TO GET PAST THIS FENCE!
—ONLY TO RUN INTO GOD KNOWS WHAT OTHER BARRIERS!
HEY NOW...
LET'S NOT DEMORALIZE TH' TROOPS WITH DEFEATIST REMARKS, COMRADE TUFFY...
OOPS. SORRY!
WE CAN'T CUT THROUGH IT... THAT MIGHT SET OFF SOME KIND OF ALARM SYSTEM!
A CURSE ON THE ROCKERFELLAS AND ALL THEIR ILK!!
HMM...
TUNNELING UNDER IS A POSSIBILITY... EXCEPT WE DON'T HAVE ANY TOOLS TO DIG WITH...
THAT TREE!! THERE'S THE WAY... CLIMB OUT ON THAT BRANCH AND JUMP DOWN ON TH' OTHER SIDE!!
GOOD THINKING TUFFY! YER ON THE BALL, KID!
PLOP
WHULP!
FROSTY the snowman AND HIS FRIENDS
©1975 BY R. CRUMB
I'M A TOP-NOTCH MOUNTAIN-CLIMBER... THIS TREE WILL BE A CINCH! WHY DON'T YOU GUYS TIE THE ARTILLERY STASH ON MY BACK WITH THAT SLED ROPE!?
NO ELECTRIC FENCE CAN KEEP HISTORY FROM IT'S APPOINTMENT WITH THAT LOUSY STINKIN' "ROTTENFELLER"!
OKAY, IF YOU REALLY THINK YOU CAN CARRY IT!
MAKE IT GOOD AN' TIGHT! DON' WANNA DROP ANY OF TH' AMMO!
CAREFUL WITH THOSE BOMBS! THEM THINGS ARE LOADED WITH DYNAMITE!!
UP I GO!
SEE, NOW? AREN'T YOU GLAD TUFFY CAME ALONG WITH US? SHE'S A HERO OF TH' PEOPLE!
GIVE 'ER A MEDAL!
YER 'BOUT THREE FEET FROM TH' GROUND, KID!
OKAY... GUESS I'LL DROP DOWN!
SHE MADE IT!! LET'S GET GOING UP THAT TREE, STOOP! TIME'S A-WASTIN'!
TA-DA-A! NUTHIN' TO IT!

FROSTY the SNOWMAN and his friends
©1975 BY R. CRUMB

WOW! FOR A MINUTE THERE I THOUGHT THAT ELECTRIC FENCE HAD US STOPPED!
NOT US! ONWARD! EVER ONWARD!

TUFFY, YOUR CLIMBING ABILITY SAVED THE DAY FOR US!
PHYSICAL FITNESS IS IMPORTANT TO TH' "REV"!
ONWARD TO TH' ROCKERFELLA MANSION AN' ANOTHER VICTORY FOR THE PEOPLE'S WAR AGAINST CREEPING FASCISM!

THAT ROCKERFELLA'S A PRETTY BAD GUY, HUH, FROSTY?!
YOU BETTER B'LIEVE IT, TUFFY! HE'S ONE OF TH' BIGGEST OF THE BAD GUYS...
THEY WANNA RUN THIS COUNTRY FOR THEIR OWN BENEFIT!

BUT WE AREN'T GONNA LET 'EM! RIGHT??
YOU GOT IT!
AN' WE'RE GONNA MAKE 'EM KNOW IT TONIGHT WHEN —SHHH! WHAT'S THAT NOISE!?

DUCK OUT O' SIGHT! SOME KINDA VEHICLE!!
TH' SECRET SERVICE PATROL!

Frosty
the SNOW-MAN
and his FRIENDS
©1975 BY R. CRUMB

WHAT TH' HELL?!
A SNOW MAN!

I DON'T GET IT... WHAT'S A SNOWMAN DOING OUT HERE IN THE WOODS??
IT MIGHT BE SOME KIND OF A TRICK.. LET'S SMASH IT DOWN!!

BOP!
BONK!
UNH
ARGH!
DOOF!

LET'S TAKE THIS JEEP!
GET IN, YOU GUYS! QUICK!

DRIVE IT, DADDY-O!
YA-HOO! LOOK-OUT ROCKERFELLA! HERE WE COME!
IT WONT BE LONG NOW!
BROOOOMM

FROSTY
the snowman
AND HIS FRIENDS
©1975 BY R. CRUMB
THERE'S TH' ROCKERFELLA PLACE!! WE MADE IT! GET READY!!
THAT'S IT OKAY!! STEP ON IT, FROSTY!
LIGHT THOSE FUSES, YOU TWO, AND GET READY TO JUMP OUT! I'M JAMMIN' TH' GAS PEDAL TO TH' FLOOR!!
OKAY, FROSTY!! HURRY UP, STOOPID JERK!!
SEVEN HOT ONES COMIN' UP! HEH HEH!!
OOF!
KEE-RASH!
KA-BLOOEY!!
Frosty the Snowman and his friends
©1975 BY R. CRUMB
HOO-RAY HOO-RAY WE DOOD IT!!
YAY H'RAY! THIS'S A HISTORIC MOMENT!
MERRY CHRIS'MAS, ASSHOLES!!
C'MON!! WE BETTER BEAT IT BEFORE WE'RE CAUGHT!
VICTORY FOR TH' PEOPLE!!
WONDER IF ANY BODY GOT KILLED IN THERE!!
NEXT MORNING...
LET'S GET A PAPER AN' SEE WHAT IT SEZ!
LOOKIT TH' HEADLINE!! "ROCKERFELLA HOME DESTROYED BY TERRORIST BOMB"!
SEZ HERE: "The stately old Rockerfella mansion was almost completely leveled last night by a runaway jeep loaded with high explosives. No one was in the main building when the explosion occurred. An unknown terrorist group is believed to be responsible for the act. Vice-President Rockerfella's only comment was: 'I'm not terribly upset... The old place needed alot of work anyway. The plumbing and wiring were going bad...
BIG X-MAS BEEF SALE
"....with my billions, I'll have a nice big, brand-new house put up in time for my annual New Year's Banquet. And it'll be bomb-proof, you can bet on it!" he added with a chuckle....
NUTS TO THAT BIG RAT!!
FOOEY ON YOU, ROCKY!
BIG X-MAS BEEF SALE
YOUR CHOICE OF

IT'S A
HUP HO
WORLD
BY
R. CRUMB
©1979

TAKING MY REAL ESTATE EXAM TODAY!
HUP
HUP
HUPPITY
HUP
SHLOCK MEISTER
HUP BURGER

GOIN' TO TH' BEAUTY PARLOR!
HUP
HUP
HUP

I SO HAPPY!
HUP
HUP
WHUPPO!

HUP YOU, MOE-FOE!!
HUP
HUP
HUP
HULP

AND DON'T FORGET TO FIGHT THE OPPRESSOR!!
HUP
HUP
HUP
HUP
HUP

BOB'S PLAIN-TALK FUNNIES
—PRESENTS—
PROFESSOR WANOWSKY
—ON—
WELFARE
AHEM
AHEM

ALOT OF PEOPLE COMPLAIN ABOUT WELFARE... "LET'S KICK THE NIGGERS OFF WELFARE" IS A LINE YOU HEAR ALOT OF LOUD-MOUTHS HOLLERING THESE DAYS...

NEVERMIND THE FACT THAT MOST OF THE PEOPLE ON WELFARE ARE POOR HELPLESS WOMEN AND CHILDREN... NEVERMIND THE FACT THAT USUALLY THIS "GET RID OF WELFARE CHEATS" TACK IS TAKEN BY PEOPLE BORN INTO CERTAIN ECONOMIC ADVANTAGES!!

BASICALLY, I AGREE WITH THESE PEOPLE... THEY'RE RIGHT! WELFARE IS A HALF-BAKED MEASURE THAT SHOULD BE DONE AWAY WITH... THEN.... HA... THEN WE'D SEE SOME REAL ACTION IN THIS COUNTRY!
I'M NO CANDY-ASSED LIBERAL!

GOD HOW I HATE LIBERALS! GIVE ME A GOOD SOLID RIGHT-WINGER ANY DAY IN THE WEEK! LIBERALS ARE SO DREARY AND BORING... ANYWAY, I'D LIKE TO SEE WHAT WOULD HAPPEN IF THE POOR PEOPLE WERE FACED WITH STARVATION... HA!! YOU SUBURBANITES MIGHT HAVE TO GO FOR YOUR HUNTING RIFLES!!

I ABHOR VIOLENCE AS MUCH AS THE NEXT FELLOW, AND GOD KNOWS, IF A BLOODY REVOLUTION DID COME, I'D SAY THE ODDS ARE PRETTY GOOD THAT I'D BE PURGED BY THE FANATIC LEADERSHIP, BUT I'D DIE HAPPY KNOWING THAT THE LOUSY STINKING, PARASITIC, SMUG, DELUDED BOURGEOISIE IN THIS COUNTRY WAS GETTING IT'S COME-UPPANCE... BUT, LET'S FACE IT, IT'LL NEVER HAPPEN...
THAT'S ALL WE HAVE TIME FOR, PROFESSOR, THANK YOU!!

THEY'VE PUT UP WITH THIS CRAP LONG ENUFF! LOOK OUT WHEN...
THE RUFF-TUFF CREAM-PUFFS
TAKE CHARGE!
SOME OF THE CHIEF HONCHOS OF THE RUFF-TUFF CREAM PUFF CREW WERE SITTING AROUND HEAD-QUARTERS HAVING A FEW BEERS AND CHEWING THE FAT...
HOY! IT'S A GODDAMN TRAGEDY WHAT'S HAPPENED TA THIS COUNTRY! THAT'S A FACT!! ANYBODY CARE TO ARGUE WITH ME??
YOU AIN'T WRONG, DAVE! ALL THESE CANDY-ASSES RUNNING THE SHOW... BUNCHA GUTLESS WONDERS... SH-H-HIT!!
YEAH, THEY'RE TURNING THIS GREAT NATION INTO A LOUSY THIRD-RATE POWER... FUCKIN' WEENIES!!
CRUNCH
STAND BACK!
SHLUP
R. CRUMB '86
I'D LIKE TA TERMINATE THAT WHOLE GANG O' DO-GOODER CRYBABIES WITH MY MAC-10... JUS' LINE 'EM UP AN' MOW 'EM DOWN— GIMME ANOTHER BEER, WOULDJA, MIKE?
RIGHT! AT 3000 ROUNDS A MINUTE YA COULD CLEAN 'EM OUT IN NO TIME FLAT!! HAW HAW!
THEM SOB-SISTERS'D BE EASY PICKIN'S FOR A COMPETENT TEAM OF REAL FIGHTING MEN! THEY'D BE ON THEIR KNEES WHINING FOR MERCY... HAWHÄWR!
WULL, HELL... WHAT'RE WE FUCKIN' WAITING FOR?! LET'S GET OUR SHIT TOGETHER 'N' STORM TH' FUCKIN' PLACE! SMEAR TH' FUCKIN' BASTARDS!
HEY, Y'KNOW... WE'RE SITTIN' HERE WAGGIN' OUR FUCKIN' JAWS... SHIT! LET'S GET OFF OUR DUFFS AN' DO IT!!
NOW YER TALKIN' MY LANGUAGE! I'M A MAN OF ACTION! WHOO-EEH!!!
GLUG
WHAM

LET'S HEAD 'EM UP! ROLL 'EM OUT!!
YA-HOO!
OWOOOO!
EEH-HAH!!
RTCP
RAISE HELL UNTIL DEATH
I ♥ TROUBLE
YIPE

AS THE RUFF-TUFF BRIGADE APPROACHES THE PRESIDENTIAL PALACE FEAR AND PANIC GRIP THE GOVERNMENT WORKERS INSIDE!
WHAT'LL WE DO??
THINK OF SOMETHING, MR. PRESIDENT! QUICK!
I'LL CALL THE GENERALS! WE NEED THE ARMY HERE!
THEY'LL PUT A STOP TO THOSE HOOLIGANS!
HELLO? HELLO? GENERAL BULLNECK? THIS IS THE PRESIDENT...
OH... WHATTA YOU WANT?

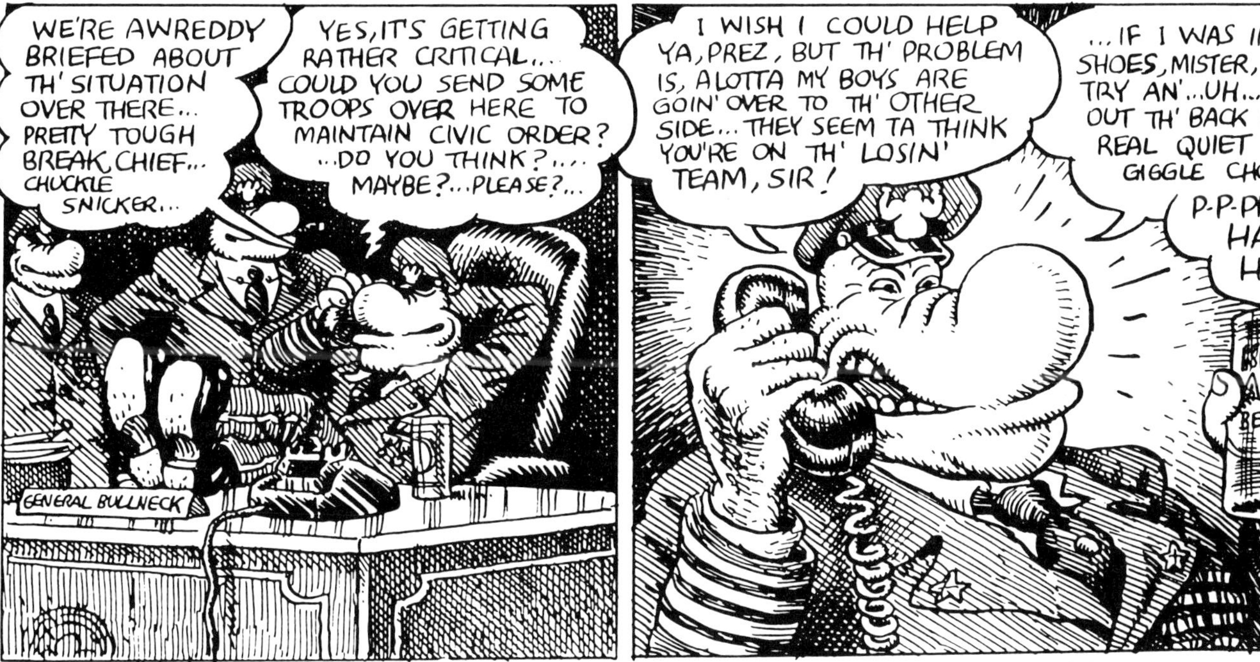
WE'RE AWREDDY BRIEFED ABOUT TH' SITUATION OVER THERE... PRETTY TOUGH BREAK, CHIEF... CHUCKLE SNICKER...
YES, IT'S GETTING RATHER CRITICAL... COULD YOU SEND SOME TROOPS OVER HERE TO MAINTAIN CIVIC ORDER? ...DO YOU THINK?... MAYBE?... PLEASE?...
GENERAL BULLNECK
I WISH I COULD HELP YA, PREZ, BUT TH' PROBLEM IS, ALOTTA MY BOYS ARE GOIN' OVER TO TH' OTHER SIDE... THEY SEEM TA THINK YOU'RE ON TH' LOSIN' TEAM, SIR!
...IF I WAS IN YOUR SHOES, MISTER, I WOULD TRY AN'...UH...SNEAK OUT TH' BACK DOOR REAL QUIET LIKE... GIGGLE CHORTLE
P-P-PHAW HAW HAW!
BIG ASS BEER

B-BUT GENERAL, YOUR FIRST DUTY IS TO—
FU-U-UCK YOU... HAW HAW HAW—
CLICK!
CRASH
EEK!
SORRY MR. PRESIDENT... WE'RE GETTING OUT OF HERE!
RUN FOR YOUR LIFE!
BAM
...I SHOULDA NEVER TAKEN ON THIS JOB... WHAT WAS I THINKING OF?.. A VAIN FOOL, THAT'S WHAT I WAS..
BAM
BAM
SMASH
EEH-HAH!
I TRIED... GOD KNOWS I TRIED...
WE DEMAND JUSTICE FOR TH' R.T.C.P.S!!
DOWN WITH THE SISSIES!!
NO MORE MEALY-MOUTH LIBERAL WIMPS!!
FUCKIN' PENCIL NECKS!
ULP GULP!
WE'VE STOOD ENOUGH INSULTS FROM OUR ENEMIES!
YOU'RE DEAD MEAT, MISTER WEAK-TEA!
LEMME DO 'IM, DAVE!
NO, ME! I WANNA DO 'IM! ONE SIDE!
I JUS' WANNA GET MY HANDS ON 'IM... CAN'T I?
WAIT A MINUTE, YOU GALOOTS! DON'T YA THINK WE OUGHTA LET'M HAVE HIS SAY FIRST??
GHASP
AWP
AW, JIS' LET ME WRING 'IS NECK, PLEASE?

OKAY, GO AHEAD, TALK! GO AHEAD!
I — I'VE MADE PLENTY OF MISTAKES... I ADMIT IT... IT'S NOT AN EASY POSITION TO BE IN...
YER BREAKIN' MY HEART!
AW GEE! POOR BABY!
I'M GONNA CRY!
HAW HAW
WE TRIED TO MAKE THIS A TRULY REPRESENTATIVE GOVERNMENT... WE WANTED TO SEE AS MANY OF OUR CITIZENS AS POSSIBLE SHARE IN THE PROCESS, THE WEALTH, THE... THE...
WHAT IS HE, FRENCH OR SOMETHIN'?
HAWR HAWR
CUT TH' SNIVELING SHIT!
YOU WEREN'T NOTHIN' BUT A SLIMY, YELLOW-BELLIED SNAKE!!
IF YOU'D EXAMINE MY RECORD, SIR, YOU'D SEE CLEARLY THAT I'VE —
YOU CAN'T TALK THAT WAY TO US!!
WE DON'T HAVE TO EXAMINE NO STINKIN' RECORD!
FUCKIN' EGG HEAD!
SPLAT!
OKAY, THAT'S ENOUGH OUTA YOU, SHITHEEL...
EEH HAH!
YEAH!!
DO 'IM SARGE!
AND SO, THE RUFF-TUFF CREAM-PUFFS SEIZE THE REIGNS OF POWER ... AND THEY LOVE IT!!
NOW! THE FIRST ORDER O' BUSINESS HERE IS---
BEER!!
BROADS!!
BEEF STEAKS!!
HEY, LOOKIT THE SIZE O' THAT CHEERING CROWD!
YEAH, THEY'RE GRATEFUL TO US!!

NO, NO, TH' FIRST ORDER O' BUSINESS IS—
WAR! LET'S DECLARE WAR ON SOMEBODY!
THASS RIGHT! THIS COUNTRY COULD USE A GOOD WAR
RIGHT NOW!
SHADDUP, ALLA YOOZ! WE'LL GET TO ALL THAT BOOL-SHIT LATER... THE FIRST ORDER O' BUSINESS IS—
DECLARE OPEN SEASON ON ALL QUEERS AN' COM-MANIST SYMPATH-IZERS!
RAT ON! HAW HAW
I SAID SHADDUP!!! AN' WHEN I—
YOU SHADDUP! WHO YOU TELLIN' TA SHUT UP, FUCK-HEAD!?!
BLAM
YOU, SCUMBAG! GO SIDDOWN BEFORE I SIT YOU DOWN— —HARD!!!
YOU AN' WHUT ARMY, ASS-WIPE?!?
JUST TRY ME, HAIR-BALL!!!
GIVE IT YOUR BEST SHOT THEN, MOTHER-FUCKER!!
THIS'S GOOD!
I LOVE IT!
HERE 'TIS, DOOSH-BAG!!
MY RIGHT ARM IS TH' FASTEST IN TH' BUSINESS, IN CASE YA DIDN'T NOTICE!
BASH!
AW!

THEN WHILE HE'S DOWN I MOVE IN QUICK WITH A FULL PAYLOAD O' PUNISHMENT!
MAN, TH' DUDE IS OUT!
OOH WEEH!
EEH-YAHH!
BROMP
A GOOD SOUND FACE STOMPIN' IS WHAT THIS ASS-HOLE NEEDS!
YOU GOTTA KEEP 'EM FROM GETTIN' UP FOR AWHILE!
TROMP
TROMP
TROMP
TROMP
TROMP
ONE LAST PEEROOWETT JUST SO'S HE'LL KNOW BETTER NEXT TIME!!
WE'RE HIS BUDDIES..WE'LL GET 'IM OUTA HERE AN' PATCH 'IM UP!
ZGWISH
OKAY...WHEW!! SOMEBODY GIMME A BEER!
NOW WHAT WUZ I TALKIN' ABOUT??
MAN, HIS FACE IS HAMBURGER!
HE GOT ONE ROYAL TRIMMING, DIDN'HE?
TH' FIRST ORDER O' BIZNESS...
OH YEAH!!! WHICH IS, NAMELY,....SALARIES, BON-USES, EXTRA COMBAT PAY, AN' VARIOUS ASSORTED PERKS FOR TH' VIC-TORIOUS HEROES OF TH' NEW REGIME!!
WHO ARE, NAMELY...
CRACK
RAMBO BEER
I STINK AND I'M PROUD

YEEEAAAHH!
TH' RUFF-TUFF CREAM-PUFFS!!
RTC
RTCP
MOTHER
OKAY, TH' NEXT THING WE HAFTA DECIDE IS WHO'S GONNA BE IN CHARGE O' WHUT!
ROGER! LET'S GET THAT STRAIGHTENED OUT RIGHT HERE 'N' NOW!
RTCP
YER DOIN' A TERRIFIC JOB RUNNIN' MILITARY OP-ERATIONS, GEORGE... I SAY WE KEEP YOU ON AS TOP GUN! RIGHT, GUYS??
AN' DAVE HERE IS TH' GUY WITH TH' MOST LEADER-SHIP QUALITIES, SO LET'S SET HIM UP AS PRESIDENT, HOW 'BOUT IT!
GOSH... WHAT A GREAT TEAM WE ARE...
YEAH.. AL-MOST GETS Y' CHOKED UP, DON'T IT?
RTC
RTCP
MOTHER
NO. 1 SON OF A BITCH
I'LL TAKE IT... HEH HEH... SO THEN! WHAT OTHER POSTS ARE OPEN FOR TH' REST O' TH' GUYS??
OH, I THINK WE GOT SUMPIN' FOR ALL OF 'EM.. WE NEED A SECRA-TARY OF TH' TREASURY...
UH.. YER MINISTER O' FINANCE...
UHH... CHAIR-MAN OF APPROPIATIONS... STUFF LIKE THAT...
RTCP
NO. 1
SOUNDS GOOD!
YEAH!! I DEMAND ONE O' THEM POSITIONS!!
ME TOO!!

HOLD IT! HOLD IT, YOU CLOWNS! I'LL MAKE THESE DECISIONS! EACH APPLICANT FOR THESE POSITIONS WILL BE CAREFULLY CONSIDERED IN AN ORDERLY MANNER AND—
I'M A SHOE-IN FOR TREASURY...NO CONTEST! WHO KNOWS MORE ABOUT FINANCE? WHO??
WHAT'RE YER QUALIFICATIONS, SMART-ASS?
I'M ON TH' BOARDS OF SIX O' TH' BIGGEST BANKS IN THIS NATION!
PLUS, BEING A C.E.O. ON THREE MAJOR CORPORATE BOARDS!
BULL-SHIT!!
GET OFF IT, DOUG! YER WHOLE EMPIRE IS ON TH' VERGE OF TOTAL COLLAPSE! YOU'RE A FOOL AN' EVERYBODY KNOWS IT!!
WHY YOU... I'LL SMASH—
I'VE GOT ALL TH' RIGHT STUFF FOR THAT TREASURY JOB...I'VE—
HEY!! I'M THE PRESIDENT! THE COMMANDER-IN-CHIEF!! SO ALLA YOU SHUT UP AN' WAIT YER TURN OR I'LL—
AW SHOVE IT, DAVE!!
YEAH, KISS MY ASS, DAVE! HAW HAW HAW
WHAM
YOU TWO ARE OUT OF ORDER!! ANY MORE O' THAT SHIT AN' YOU WON'T GET JOB ONE AS FUCKIN' DOG CATCHER!! Y'GOT THAT??
I'LL BUST ANYBODY WHO GIVES ME SHIT! Y'READ ME??
GRRR
GRRR
HONK
FUCK YOU DAVE!
YOUR TERM'S UP, ASS-HOLE!
KONK
AARGHH
YEAHH!!
EEH-HAW!

FUCKIN' TYRANT!
CRASH
HAW HAW! I WAS SICK O' TH' SOUND O' HIS VOICE!
YOU SAID IT, JACK!
SPLAT

NOW LISTEN UP, MEN... WE GOT TO MAKE US A PROVISIONAL MILITARY GOVER'MENT HERE 'TIL ALL THIS SHIT GETS SQUARED AWAY... SO THAT PUTS ME IN CHARGE FOR TH' TIME BEING, AND—
HEY, NO FUCKIN' WAY, MAN!
FUCK THAT SHIT!!
BO-O-O!!
YEAH, I'D KILL

I'M THE LAW AS OF NOW, YOU FUCKIN' UN-DISCIPLINED THUGS!
DADA DADAD DADAD DADA
ARRRH
AIIEEE
AWRNH!

THAT'S WHAT YOU THINK, YA SON OF A BITCH!!
YAH-HOO!
AK AK AK
AW SHIT!
GROAN GRUNT

KA-BLOOEY
POW
EEHAW!
BLAM

BOOM
SA-DOW
FA-TOOM
AIIEE
GRAWGH
MY GOD, WHAT'S HAPPENING??
ALL HELL'S BREAKING LOOSE IN THERE!
PRESIDENTIAL PALACE

LATER, AFTER ALL IS QUIET, THE WIMPS COME OUT OF HIDING.
THEY'VE REALLY WRECKED THINGS GOOD THIS TIME!
LOOK AT THIS MESS!!
SIGH... LET'S GET STARTED ...THIS IS GOING TO BE A BIG CLEAN-UP JOB...
OH MY ACHIN' BACK!
END

"THE FINAL SOLUTION"
READ IT 'N' WEEP!
by R. Crumb
IT'S ALL GOTTEN SO COMPLICATED!! THERE'S NO RATIONAL WAY TO MANAGE THESE POWERFUL FORCES ANYMORE... IT'S TOO BIG FOR ANY ONE MAN...
THE SITUATION DEFINITELY VERGES ON BEING OUT OF CONTROL...
HA.. I'VE GOT NEWS FOR YOU, MY FRIENDS... THE SITUATION IS OUT OF CONTROL!
WELL, MR. PRESIDENT, WE MUSTN'T GIVE UP HOPE.. WE'VE GOT TO KEEP WORKING ON IT...
I DON'T KNOW... I'M TIRED... "BURNED OUT" AS THEY SAY... I'M THE ONE THEY ALL LOOK TO FOR A DECISION... THEY STILL THINK I'M IN A POSITION TO DO SOMETHING ABOUT THIS MESS...
YES... YOU'RE IN A TOUGH SPOT, SIR... IT'S QUITE TRUE...
NO DOUBT ABOUT IT...
IT'S THE PRESSURE... I'M ALWAYS UNDER SUCH ENORMOUS PRESSURE.. WHO DO THEY THINK I AM?! GOD?!?
WELL, NO ONE EXPECTS YOU TO WORK MIRACLES!
IT'S COMPLICATED.
THE PEOPLE THINK I'M GUTLESS... LITTLE DO THEY REALIZE WHAT'S REALLY GOING ON... THE STUPID SHEEP!!
YES, I'M AFRAID YOU'RE RIGHT, MR. PRESIDENT... RECENT POLLS SHOW THAT YOUR PUBLIC IMAGE—
MY IMAGE... MY IMAGE... FUCK MY IMAGE! ...BUNCH OF IGNORANT YAHOOS...
SIR, PERHAPS YOU SHOULD TAKE A SHORT VACATION.. GET AWAY FROM WASHINGTON FOR A FEW DAYS...
YES, MAYBE YOU NEED—
WHY SHOULD I CARE WHAT BECOMES OF THIS NATION?! LET THE ASSHOLES RUN IT INTO THE GROUND! I CAN'T STOP THEM... NO ONE CAN STOP THEM!
BUT SIR, WHAT ABOUT YOUR DEBT TO POSTERITY??
ARE YOU NO LONGER CONCERNED ABOUT WHAT HISTORY MIGHT SAY OF YOU??
HISTORY... YES... POSTERITY... I DON'T WANT THEM TO THINK OF ME AS A MERE OPPORTUNISTIC POLITICIAN OF MEDIOCRE CALIBER...
I'LL BE KNOWN AS A SECOND-RATE PRESIDENT WHO COULDN'T STAND UP TO THE POWER ELITE... AND THEY'LL BE RIGHT... I CAN'T.... OH GOD!
SIR, THERE MUST BE SOME WAY...
IT CAN'T BE THAT THE PRESIDENT IS TOTALLY HELPLESS...
NO, OF COURSE I'M NOT TOTALLY HELPLESS.... I CAN ALWAYS~~
CLIK
DEPLOYS ENTIRE NUCLEAR DEFENSE SYSTEM
HA HA HA HA HA
YOU DIRTY—
BZT
5-4-3-2-1-ZERO!

The Goose and the Gander Were Talking One Night

BY R. CRUMB

YOU'RE RIGHT... I AM WORRIED...
WHAT IS IT? THE TAXES? YOUR JOB?
WELL, I'M ALWAYS WORRIED ABOUT ALL THAT CRAP... MONEY AN' ALL... BUT LATELY.....
I...I CAN'T SHAKE THIS TERRIBLE FEELING THAT WE'RE DOOMED....
YOU READ TOO MANY ARTICLES, THAT'S YOUR TROUBLE!
LET'S GO FOR A WALK...
OKAY...
MAYBE YOU'RE RIGHT...I SHOULD JUST STOP READING ALL THESE NEWS-PAPERS AND MAGAZINES...
BUT, YOU KNOW, SOMETHING'S NOT RIGHT... IT JUST DOESNT FEEL RIGHT... YOU CAN SMELL IT IN THE AIR!
SNIFF... SNIFF...
IT DOES SMELL FUNNY AT THAT! POLLUTION, I GUESS!
...BUT WHY DO YOU THINK WE'RE DOOMED?
... AND YOU KNOW SOMETHING ELSE? I'M NOT THE ONLY ONE!! YOU'D BE SURPRISED HOW MANY PEOPLE YOU MEET WHO WILL JUST CASUALLY, OFF-THE-CUFF STATE HOW THEY THINK IT'S ALL GOING TO END SOON BECAUSE OF ONE THING OR ANOTHER! IT'S A COMMONLY HELD BELIEF!!

....BUT WHY DO YOU THINK WE'RE DOOMED?
...AND I DON'T THINK I'M A CRAZY PERSON.. I'M A PRETTY AVERAGE GUY... JUST YOUR NORMAL, EVERY-DAY GOOSE...I GIVE A JOKE AND TAKE A JOKE... NOTHING SPECIAL...
....BUT WHY—
WHY DO I THINK WE'RE DOOMED? OH, I DUNNO... IT'S EVERYTHING, I GUESS... JUST THE WAY THE HUMAN RACE KEEPS GOING HEAD-ON WITH POPULATION AND TECHNOLOGY AN' ALL THAT...
IT SEEMS TO BE BUILDING UP TO SOME GIANT CATASTROPHE... YOU TAKE THESE GUYS THAT ARE GOING AHEAD WITH ALL THESE NUCLEAR POWER PLANTS— AND THAT'S JUST ONE THING! THERE ARE THOUSANDS OF THINGS LIKE THAT GOIN' ON!
JEEZIZ...
....IT MAKES ME FEEL SO HELPLESS!! I CAN'T SEE ANY WAY TO STOP THE PROCESS! WHAT CAN I DO? I'M JUST A GOOSE!
IT'S THAT FEELING OF HELPLESSNESS IN THE FACE OF IT THAT'S SO HORRIBLE!
IF I COULD THINK OF SOME WAY TO—
LOOK OUT!
LI'L BADASS
ZOOM
BLADDA BLAP!

CHEAP PUNKS!
PISSES ME OFF!
LET'S GO HOME AN' WATCH THE LATE SHOW...
IN A WAY, YOU CAN EVEN SEE IT AS A GOOD THING, THE DOWNFALL OF OUR CIVILIZATION... SOMETIMES I THINK PEOPLE EVEN LOOK FORWARD TO IT, SECRETLY, IN THEIR HEARTS...
REALLY? HOW COME?
PEOPLE FEEL TRAPPED... THEY SEE NO WAY OUT... THERE'S A SECRET URGE... A WISH, FOR THE WHOLE BUSINESS TO SELF-DESTRUCT!
...TO SEE OUR GREAT CITIES IN RUINS...OUR ELABORATE MACHINES BROUGHT TO A STANDSTILL...
...A RETURN TO THE SIMPLE, RAW STRUGGLE FOR SURVIVAL!
HM
YOU COULD ALMOST WELCOME IT! EMBRACE IT! ...THE COLLAPSE OF THIS MAN-MADE SYSTEM OF THINGS!
WELL, PERSONALLY, I HOPE YOU'RE ALL WRONG... I HOPE SUCH A THING NEVER HAPPENS...
HOTPOINT
I HOPE I'M WRONG, TOO, REALLY!
I WISH I KNEW WHAT TO DO ABOUT IT...

R. CRUMB, "THE OLD OUTSIDER", GOES TO THE...
ACADEMY AWARDS
HUP!
POVERTY, POETRY, AND NEW TITLES OF HONOR MAKE MEN RIDICULOUS. —POOR RICHARD'S ALMANAC
COMMISSIONED BY AND FIRST PRINTED IN PREMIERE MAGAZINE
HEY, HOW 'BOUT THOSE ACADEMY AWARDS!? THIS MAGAZINE HIRED ME TO COVER THE BIG EVENT, AND SENT ME A TICKET!!
WOW, DAD! YOU'RE GONNA BE IN TH' SAME ROOM WITH TOM HANKS!!
CATCH MY FEET!
A TICKET TO THE OSCARS! AREN'T YOU EXCITED?!
NAH... IT'S A JOB...
IT WAS A JOB, AND NOT AN EASY ONE EITHER... FIRST, I HAD TO FLY TO LOS ANGELES, AND STAY IN THAT HATEFUL MEGALOPOLIS FOR TWO ENTIRE DAYS!!
I GUESS PEOPLE LIKE IT HERE BECAUSE YOU CAN MAKE ALOT OF MONEY...
UNICORP
AND THE BIG DAY IS ON! JEEZIZ, WHAT A SCENE! LINES OF POLICEMEN KEPT THE MOB FROM POURING OVER BARRICADES TO WHERE THE LIMOS WERE LETTING OUT THE MOVIE STARS...
JESUS SAVES SINNERS FROM HELL
GOOD LUCK JESSICA
THE RED CARPET
THIS CROWD TOOK AN ACTIVE PART, CHEERING LUSTILY WHENEVER A FAMOUS CELEBRITY GOT OUT OF A LIMOUSINE... THEY SCREAMED LOUDEST FOR CELLULOID HERO OF THE DAY TOM CRUISE...
YAAAEEE
AND HERE HE IS! HEY TOM-

PERSONALLY, THE SCENE BEHIND THE BARRICADES WAS BY FAR THE MORE INTERESTING PART OF THE WHOLE CIRCUS...
ULP GULP!
BOING!
GROUPS OF ANGRY PROTESTERS HELD UP SIGNS AND CHANTED THEIR GRIEVANCES, BUT NOBODY WAS PAYING ATTENTION, EXCEPT THE COPS, WHO KEPT THEM WELL IN THE BACKGROUND...
WHADDAYA WANT?!
HOUSING!!!
WHEN DO YA WANT IT?!?
NOW!!
KIDS HOMELESS
STOP KILLING OUR FAMILIES
HOW DO YOU SLEEP AT NIGHT, ROGER SMITH ???
LARGE TREES IN POTS WERE SET UP TO HIDE THESE UNSIGHTLY DEMON-STRATERS FROM THE TV CAMERAS... ANYWAY, THAT'S WHAT I THINK THEY WERE FOR...
WELL, IT WAS GETTING TO BE TIME TO GO IN... I CUT ACROSS TO THE OTHER SIDE, WAVING MY "GOLDEN TICKET" AT THE COPS.
FANS IN BLEACHERS
OKAY, GO AHEAD!
...AND THERE I WAS, WALK-ING ON THE RED CARPET WITH THE MOVIE STARS... I FELT ILL AT EASE IN THE EXTREME, AND VERY EMBAR-RASSED FOR ALL OF HU-MANITY.

"TO BE AN ARTIST MEANS NEVER TO AVERT ONE'S EYES." SO SAYETH KUROSAWA, BUT I COULDN'T LOOK AT THE PEOPLE... I LOOKED DOWN AT MY FEET... IMAGES OF THE OSCAR WERE WOVEN INTO THE RED CARPET.

INSIDE, THE FILM FOLK WERE SHMOOZING IN THE LOUNGE AREA... I COWERED IN A CORNER, OBSERVING... THE ROOM WAS CHARGED WITH A HIGH VOLTAGE LEVEL OF POWER AND AMBITION... THEY ALL WANTED TO WIN SO BAD! ANXIETY STEAMED OUT OF THEIR EARS! ONCE IN A WHILE SOMEONE WOULD EYE ME SUSPICIOUSLY. THEY KNEW I WASN'T ONE OF THEM, SO WHAT WAS I DOING THERE? HOW DID I GET IN? I EXPECTED ANY MOMENT TO BE KICKED OUT IN THE STREET...

THEY STOOD AROUND TALKING CATAGORIES... LOTS OF "GOOD LUCK," "SAME TA YOU," HUGGING, ARM-AROUND, BACK MASSAGE... THEY LOVE EACH OTHER—YOU COULD TELL...

GET UP THERE! DON'T MISS YA MOMENT!!
WE'RE COUNTIN' ON YOU!

THE MEN ALL STUCK THEIR CHESTS OUT... MANY OF THEM HAD VERY HARD FACES... THEY LOOKED LIKE KILLERS... LIKE—GANGSTERS!! IT'S A HIGH-STAKES BUSINESS, THE MOVIES... (I DUNNO... MAYBE THEY WERE JUST CHARACTER ACTORS...)

AND THE WOMEN—OH LORD SAVE ME—THE WOMEN WERE TRULY TERRIFYING, WITH ALL THEIR "GLAMOUR", THEIR PREDATORY EYES, THEIR CRUEL, LIPSTICKED MOUTHS... EEK!

I DIDN'T RECOGNIZE ANY STARS EXCEPT SPIKE LEE, WHO SEEMED TO BE WANDERING AROUND BY HIMSELF LOOKING LOST. I THOUGHT OF SAYING SOMETHING TO HIM BUT DIDN'T...

THEN IT WAS TIME TO GO TO YOUR SEAT... FOR THE NEXT THREE HOURS I WAS TRAPPED IN A BAD TV SHOW...
I LOVE WHAT I DO–I REALLY DO–IT'S GREAT TO BE IN THIS INDUSTRY—
A BILLION PEOPLE ARE WATCHING THIS SHMUCK...
UP IN THE THIRD BALCONY

EVERYBODY PLAYED THEIR PART... WHEN THE BLINDINGLY BRIGHT APPLAUSE SIGN FLASHED ON, THEY ALL OBEDIENTLY DID AS IT SAID... NOBODY REBELLED.... NOBODY CAUSED TROUBLE...
CLAP CLAP CLAP CLAP CLAP CLAP CLAP CLAP
FUCK YOU– I WON'T DO IT!
APPLAUSE
CLAP CLAP CLAP CLAP CLAP CLAP CLAP CLAP CLAP CLAP

FINALLY, I COULDN'T TAKE IT ANY MORE... I STARTED FEELING LIKE WHEN I WAS A KID TRYING TO MAKE IT THROUGH EASTER HIGH MASS...
I CAN'T BREATHE... GOTTA GET OUTA HERE...
PLOP
BORING DANCE ROUTINE

I FLED FROM THE AUDITORIUM... OUTSIDE, THE FANS WERE STILL IN THE BLEACHERS, WAITING FOR THEIR STARS TO COME OUT SO THEY COULD SCREAM AT THEM AGAIN...
WHY DO THEY CARE SO MUCH...? WHAT'S IN IT FOR THEM??

I WALKED OFF DOWN THE AVENUE AND INTO THE NIGHT... WHICH NEVER GETS DARK IN L.A.
WHEW! TOMORROW I CAN GET OUT OF HERE!
...KEEP AS FAR AWAY AS YOU CAN FROM THE PLACES WHERE THEY GATHER TO CHEAT AND INSULT ONE ANOTHER, TO EXPLOIT ONE ANOTHER... OR TO MOCK ONE ANOTHER WITH THEIR FALSE GESTURES OF FRIENDSHIP.
—THOMAS MERTON

HOME, SWEET HOME...
HEY, I RENTED A COUPLE A' MOVIES FOR TONIGHT! I THOUGHT WE COULD RELAX AN'—
MOVIES? DID YOU SAY... MOVIES?
SLOWLY I TURNED... STEP BY STEP... INCH BY INCH...
END

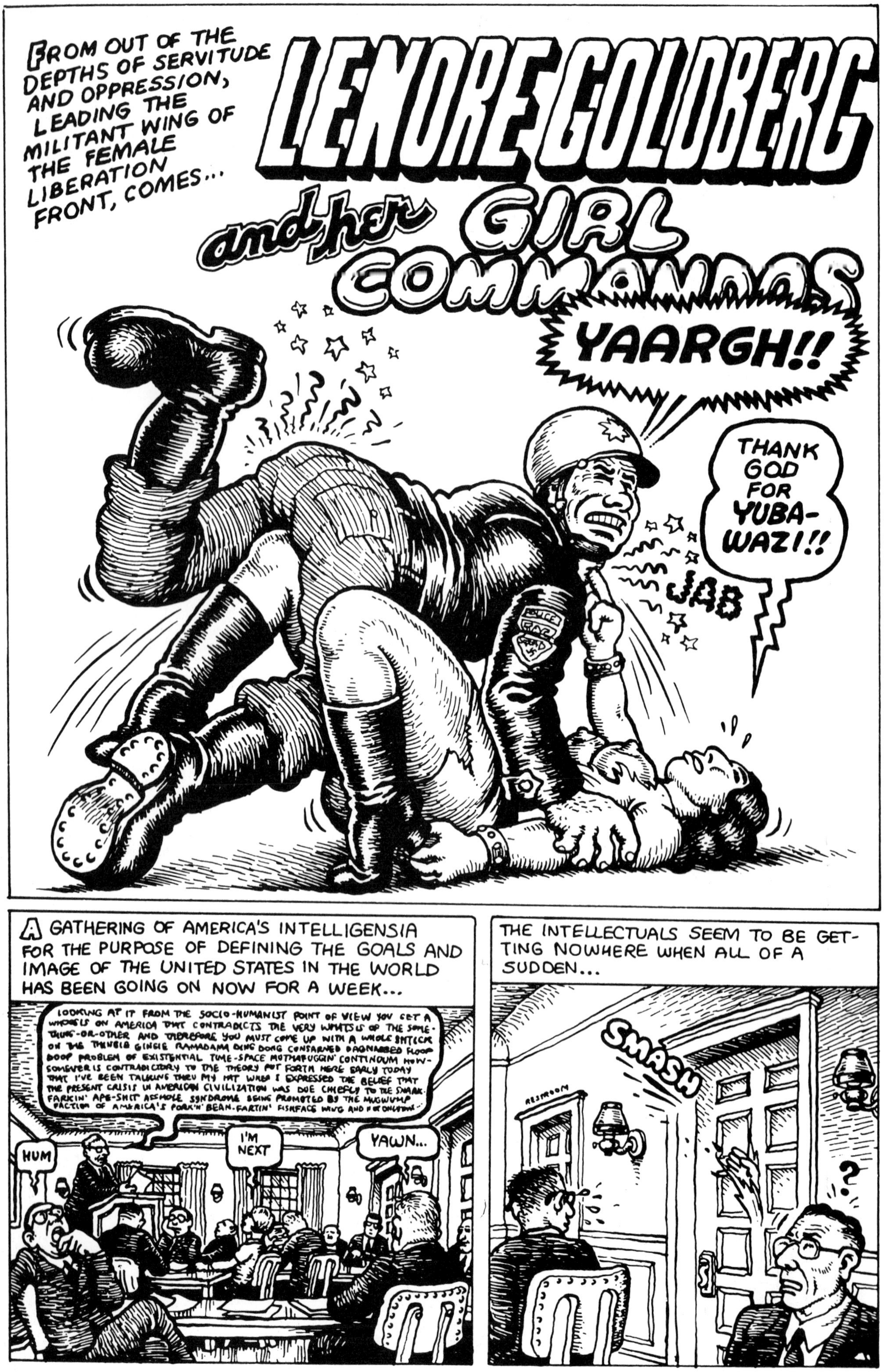

FROM OUT OF THE DEPTHS OF SERVITUDE AND OPPRESSION, LEADING THE MILITANT WING OF THE FEMALE LIBERATION FRONT, COMES...

LENORE GOLDBERG and her GIRL COMMANDOS

YAARGH!!

THANK GOD FOR YUBA-WAZI!!

JAB

A GATHERING OF AMERICA'S INTELLIGENSIA FOR THE PURPOSE OF DEFINING THE GOALS AND IMAGE OF THE UNITED STATES IN THE WORLD HAS BEEN GOING ON NOW FOR A WEEK...

THE INTELLECTUALS SEEM TO BE GET-TING NOWHERE WHEN ALL OF A SUDDEN...

KE-RASH!
HA HA
YAY!
WHAT IS IT??
WHO—
GOOD HEAVENS!!
THIS IS UNHEARD OF!!
AN OUT-RAGE!
HIYA SMARTIES!!

THEY'RE INSANE! STOP THEM!
YES MA'AM!!
LET'S MOVE IN!
WEIRD!
COME 'N' GIT US, MUTH'FUCKERS!!
OBOY! A SCRAP!!

EVEN THESE CANDY-ASSED LIBERAL INTELLECTUALS NEED APES TO DO THEIR DIRTY WORK!!

...AND WE'RE READY FOR 'EM!
HI-KU!
YAH-HO!
GLOKHH..
CRUNCH

WHAT DO YOU WANT HERE??
WE'VE COME TO MAKE A FEW STATEMENTS ON TH' SUBJECT OF FEMALE LIBERATION!!
WHEW!

I'M NOT SO SURE ANYONE HERE CARES TO LISTEN TO YOUR—
WAIT... LET THEM HAVE THEIR SAY... PERHAPS THEIR IDEAS MAY HOLD SOME SMALL VALIDITY...

DON'T **PATRONIZE** ME!!

HEY LOOKIT!! EACH INTELLECTUAL GOT HIS OWN LITTLE NAME THING... AINT THAT CUTE?
AUGUST CHAMBERS
KEE HEE!
OOOH... MY HEART...
HI... WHAT'S YER THEORY, HONEY?
I... ER... UH...

FIRST OF ALL, I WOULD—
UM.. AHH SLURP LICK OMI GOD DROOL

WELL, BLESS MY SOUL!!
UNK GLURP BITE SLURP MUNCH

NOW WE'RE GETTING SOMEPLACE!! STAND UP!!
HAW HAW!
I... I... CAN'T HELP IT... I'M HOPELESSLY NUEROTIC... I... I...

CONGRATULATIONS, BABY!!
YOU BROKE TH' MENTAL BARRIER!!
NO...NO... PLEASE... STOP!!
YOU COMMITTED AN ACT!!
WOW!

YOU ARE A **REAL MAN!**
LET ME GO I BEG OF YOU!!
HERE! YOU KIN LICK MINE!! FEEL FREE!
LET'S TAKE HIM HOME!

HEY! WHERE ARE YA—
HE PANICKED...
TSK... TOO BAD...
FREAKED OUT...
SOB SOB..
SO YOU SEE, MY FRIENDS... THAT'S WHERE ALL YOUR "DEEP" THINKING" GETS YOU... DIG IT, PEOPLE!!
IN MY OPINION YOU'RE JUST A GANG OF **LES-BIANS!!**
DIDJA HEAR THAT, JANET?
GHASP!! UMMM... TSK TSK.!!

WAS THAT NICE?
GET AWAY FROM ME, YOU---- **SICKIE!**
TEE HEE

BYE BYE
OOP!

I SUPPOSE OUR CONDUCT HAS BEEN RATHER UNLADYLIKE...
...EX-TREMELY UNFEM-ININE, I MUST ADMIT!!

WHICH BRINGS ME BACK TO THE POINT OF OUR BEING HERE, WHICH IS TO CLEAR THE AIR OF ALL THIS BULLSHIT ABOUT "FEMININITY"!
WE DON'T GO FOR ALL THAT CRAP!

BUT THAT DOESN'T MEAN WE'RE QUEER!
RIGHT! IT'S NOT "PENIS ENVY" OR ANY OF THAT SHIT!

ON THE OTHER HAND, WE DON'T BUY THE TYPICAL MALE COME-ON!
YOUR AVERAGE AMERICAN MALE IS ALL FUCKED UP!!
CLITORAL ORGASM FOREVER!! YAY!
YAY!

WHAT WE DO UNDERSTAND IS THAT MEN AND WOMEN MUST GET TOGETHER AS EQUALS, BUT FOR THIS TO HAPPEN THE WHOLE SOCIETY MUST CHANGE RADICALLY...

YOU LEFTIST RADICALS ARE ALWAYS TALKING ABOUT TEARING DOWN THE ESTAB-LISHMENT, BUT WHAT CON-STRUCTIVE SUGGESTIONS DO YOU HAVE FOR A BETTER SOCIETY?
HA HA HA

YOU'RE S'POSED TO BE TH' BIG BRAINS OF WESTERN CIVILIZATION! DON'T YOU KNOW?? IT'S SO OBVIOUS!!
IT'S NOT AT ALL OBVIOUS! IN FACT, IT'S QUITE COMPLEX IF YOU--

YOU DUM DUM! IT'S QUITE SIMPLE... DON'T YOU SEE... TO TOUCH EACH OTHER...

N-NOT HERE!!! LATER... IN MY HOTEL... I... GULP!
DON'T WHISPER! WHY NOT HERE? COME ON! WHAT WOULD YOU LIKE TO DO?

LET'S GET IT OUT IN TH' OPEN! COME ON NOW... LET IT ALL HANG OUT... COME ON...
S-SUCK ME...

I WOULD SUCK YOU BUT...ER...FRANKLY, EVEN THOUGH MY ROLE AS A LEADER IN THE FEMALE LIBERATION MOVEMENT OFTEN REQUIRES FEATS OF COURAGE AND FORTITUDE BEYOND THE CAPACITY OF THE AVERAGE FEMALE, SOMEHOW I JUST CAN'T BRING MYSELF TO...ER...IN SHORT, GIT OUTA MY SIGHT BEFORE I PUKE!!
AW THAT WAS MEAN!
GAG!
CHOKE
LET'S SPLIT! WE DID A NUMBER HERE... LET'S GO DO A NUMBER SOMEPLACE ELSE...
YEAH...THESE OL' STUFFSHIRTS ARE BRINGING ME DOWN!!
SHMUCKS!
LET'S GO!!
SO LONG EGGHEADS! HOPE YA GET EVERYTHING FIGGERED OUT!
HAW! HAW!
THERE THEY ARE!
YOU'RE ALL UNDER ARREST!
GO GET 'EM BOYS!!
SCATTER!
POLICE
DEPARTMENT

OOPS! I TRIPPED!
HA!
I GOT 'ER! I GOT 'ER!
HEY LEAVE SOME FER ME!
UNH!
BASH!
GLL
YOU'RE SICK! YOU'RE SICK!
YOU'RE SICK!
CRONCH
BASH
SPLAT
THIS ONE'S COOLED! WHERE'S TH' REST?!
GOT AWAY!
NICE JOB, MUNCIE!
@☆!!!
PUFF PANT
WHEEZE
THEY GOT JANET... I SAW HER FALL...
WOW! YOU JUST KNOW SHE'S GETTIN' IT BAD!

THAT'S ALRIGHT! EVERY MARTYR WILL BRING A HUNDRED NEW REVOLUTIONARIES INTO THE MOVEMENT!! THE POLICE ARE FOOLS WHO HAVE SEALED THEIR OWN DOOM!
THASS RIGHT!!

NOW WE'D BETTER SPLIT UP AND LAY LOW FOR AWHILE... THOSE COPS ARE GONNA BE LOOKIN' FOR US IN TH' STREETS...
WE'LL MEET AGAIN SUNDAY NIGHT!
OKAY!

THE NEXT NIGHT WE FIND LENORE IN THE PEACE OF HOME. REVOLUTION ISNT THE ONLY THING ON HER MIND!
HEY LENORE! YOUR CAPER AT TH' MEETING OF THE MINDS MADE FRONT PAGE!
DOES IT SAY ANYTHING ABOUT JANET?
PLAY WITH MY CLITORIS!
SALE
PRICES SLASHED
DISCOUNT HOUSE

IT SAYS HERE, "TWO POLICE OFFICERS WERE BRUTALLY ATTACKED AND BEATEN AND ONE MEMBER OF THE GANG, JANET JONES, WAS INJURED WHEN SHE FELL DOWN SOME STEPS TRYING TO ESCAPE..."
YEAH! "INJURED"! THOSE FUCKING LIARS!! MMM... THAT FEELS NICE...

OH... OH... OH... AH... AH... AHHHH... HHH...

MMM... YOU'RE REALLY GETTIN' GOOD, BOB... WE GOT IT DOWN TO FIVE MINUTES! NOW IT'S MY TURN TO BRING YOU OFF... GIMMEE...
GEE

VIVA LA REVOLUCION!
MGLORP SLURP GULP SLISH..

—THE END—

Patricia Pig
in
"PATRICIA GOES SHOPPING"
BY R. CRUMB
©1973 by R. CRUMB
OH HI SUZY...OH WOW, I'D LOVE TO GO SHOPPING WITH YOU... I'LL HAVE TO STOP AT THE BANK AN' CASH A CHECK... OKAY... SEE YOU IN AN HOUR... YEAH, I WANNA WASH MY HAIR... OKAY... BYE-BYE!!
OBOY... I DON'T HAVE A GOOD SUMMER DRESS...AND I COULD USE A NEW PAIR OF SHOES...
I SAW SOME CUTE SHOES IN TH' WINDOW OF SNELLER'S TH' OTHER DAY... I LIKE THOSE STACKED HEELS!
OH I DO TOO!! LET'S STOP SOMEWHERE FOR LUNCH!!
FISH N CHIPS
GOSH DARN IT, I WISH I COULD EAT A HAMBURGER!!
OH GOD I KNOW WHAT YOU MEAN... I'M JUST GOING TO HAVE A SALAD WITH SOME COTTAGE CHEESE...
HEY LET'S GO OUT TO THAT NEW SHOPPING CENTER IN SUNNY-VALE... I HEARD THEY HAVE SOME CUTE LITTLE SHOPS OUT THERE...
OH YEAH... THEY HAVE THIS FANTASTIC MALL WITH THIS HUGE FOUNTAIN... IT'S REALLY SOMETHING! THEY HAVE THESE COLORED LIGHTS AND ALL...
E-Z CLEANERS

HERE IT IS... WOW, IT'S HUGE...LOOK AT ALL THE PARKING SPACE!
I CAN ONLY SPEND TWENNY BUCKS... JOE WILL MURDER ME FER SURE IF I SPEND ANY MORE'N THAN...
OH LOOK!! MOUNTED BUTTERFLIES... AREN'T THEY BEAUTIFUL?
LET'S GO IN HERE!!
BOUTIQUE
SHOES
DON'T YOU THINK THIS WOULD LOOK CUTE IN MY BATHROOM?
HEY PATRICIA! LOOK AT THIS... DRINKING CUPS THAT SAY "EAT SHIT" ON'EM....HA HA
EAT SHIT
EAT SHIT
SOME OF THESE NEW STYLES ARE JUST TOO BIZARRE... WHO COULD WALK IN THESE THINGS?!
OH I KNOW! YOU HAVE TO BE A FASHION MODEL TO WEAR THIS STUFF... IT'S RIDICULOUS!
I DONT SEE ANYTHING I LIKE ENUFF TO BUY...
I GUESS I'LL GET THIS BLOUSE... WHATAYA THINK?
HECK! I DIDNT FIND ANYTHING TO BUY...
YEAH...I DUNNO IF I EVEN LIKE THIS BLOUSE ALL THAT MUCH NOW... BUT, ANYWAY ISN'T IT FUN TO GO SHOPPING??
BLOTUMI'S
The End

Why Oh Why Oh Why the Hell am I in
Motor City
HONK HONK
RUMBLE
ROAR
SHIPPER'S DISPATCH
AAIIEEE
YOU BETTER RUN, BOY! THAT TRUCK MEANS BIZNIZ! THEY DON'T FOOL AROUND IN MOTOWN!!!
R. "THE QUEER" CRUMB
THE ALMIGHTY DOLLAR HATH LAID IT ON THE LINE
GET BACK TO WORK, BUB!!
REPORT TO YOUR SUPERVISOR AT ONCE!!
BUT— BUT—
DOSSIER ON EMPLOYEE #35798

WHAT'S ONE MAN TO THE KING OF MOTOR CITY?

SORRY! IF YOU DON'T HAVE A HIGH-SCHOOL DIPLOMA, WE CAN'T USE YOU!

WE DO ALL REPAIRS WITH TENDER LOVING CARE!

HURRY UP STUPID!

YESS'R!

SO WHAT CAN Y'SAY BACK TO A MACHINE??

DON'T CRITICIZE DETROIT UNLESS Y' CAN BACK IT UP, CHUMP!
GAAH!
OH WELL, THE SHITBURGERS ARE CHEAP!
YUM
MY STOMACH HURTS...
SPAIN WILL DO YOU IN!
♫
!
HEY MAN, WE MAKIN' YOU "PARA-NOID"?
I... ER... UH...
HEE HEE...
THUD!
ARG!
FOOP
WHITEY!!
MUV FUCKIN' HONKY BASTID!!
WAIT! STOP! I'M ON YOUR SIDE... I...
KICK
STOMP
HAW HAW!
LEZ GO GIT US SOME CHITLINS, OTIS!
I UNDER-STAND WHY THEY BEAT ME UP...
A LOT OF THE KIDS ARE GETTIN' OUT OF MOTOR CITY WHILE THE GETTIN' IS GOOD!!
WEST-WARD HO!
TAKE TO TH' OPEN ROAD!
SO LONG SUCKERS!
HALLA LEW YA!
TO SHANGRI-LA OR A BUST

HI-LITES OF DETROIT
JOHNNY'S ON WARREN NEAR CASS AVE.
GENERAL MOTORS BUILDING
FREE SOCIAL HYGENE CLINIC 8311 JOHN C. LODGE
JOHN R. FRUIT MARKET
JOHN R. FRUIT MARKET CORNER OF JOHN R. & SEVEN MILE RD.
by America's Best-Loved Underground Cartoonist
CAROUSEL LOUNGE CORNER OF JOHN R. & SEVEN MILE RD.
LET'S HEAR IT FOR ME!
HOW TO ESCAPE ANXIETY
R. CRUMB
WOODWARD AVE. BUS
WAYNE STATE UNIVERSITY
The Red Barn
THE RED BARN
FORD ASSEMBLY PLANT
HAMTRAMK

=Mr. Know-It-All=
in
"FOUR MORE YEARS"
©1972 by R. CRUMB
FOUR MORE YEARS!!
NO TALKING
I JUST CANT FIGURE IT OUT!!
HOW COULD SO MANY PEOPLE IN THIS MODERN AGE BE SO STOOPID?!?
WELL, IT JUST GOES TO SHOW YOU—
HEY MISTER!! I'LL BET YOU VOTED FOR NIXON, DIDN'T YOU?!
YESSIR, I DID!
WELL, I—
WHAT OF IT??
I SUPPOSE YOU VOTED FOR THAT JELLY-FISH, GEORGE WHATZIS-NAME!!
HEH HEH!
YOU AND ALL YOUR ILK WILL ROT IN THE HELL YOU'VE CREATED, YOU SONUVABITCH!!
SAY, NOW! HOLD ON SONNY!!
I'M A POLICE-OFFICER!! DONT MAKE A MOVE OR I'LL SHOOT!
!
COME ALONG QUIETLY, PUNK!!
MMGH!

I THINK WE'LL TAKE YOU DOWNTOWN AND RUN A CHECK ON YOU, FELLA.!!
MOVE!!
GOD BLESS AMERICA! LAND THAT I LOVE—
STAND BESIDE HER— AND GUIDE HER— IN THE MIGHT AND THE RIGHT FROM ABOVE—
FROM THE MOUNTENNS— TO THE PRAYREEZ—
AND THE OCEANS WHITE WITH FOAM—
GRIPE GRUMBLE SCOWL CURSE—
GOD BLESS AMERICA!
I WANNA HEAR YOU SING IT!!
?
MY HOME SWEET HO-OME—
I DONT LIKE TH'SONG, BUB! WANNA TRY 'N' MAKE ME SING IT??
WHY, I'LL—
GOD BLESS AMERICA—
WHACK!
SMACK
GRRR
OOF
THUD
OW!!!
C'MON, KEED, LET'S BEAT IT! DIRTY BASTARDS! NO RESPECT FOR THE AGED ANYMORE!!
WOW! YOU BEAT THAT COP UP!!
I THINK WE'RE SAFE DOWN HERE FOR TH' TIME BEIN'....
SHIT! PLASTIC HANDCUFFS ARE A CINCH T'CUT OFF!
SNAP!
I DUNNO WHAT THIS COUNTRY IS COMIN' TO!!
ME NEITHER!!
FUCK YOU
END

OH I'M TELLING YOU PEOPLE, THERE'S GONNA BE HELL TO PAY...

WHEN THE NIGGERS TAKE OVER AMERICA!

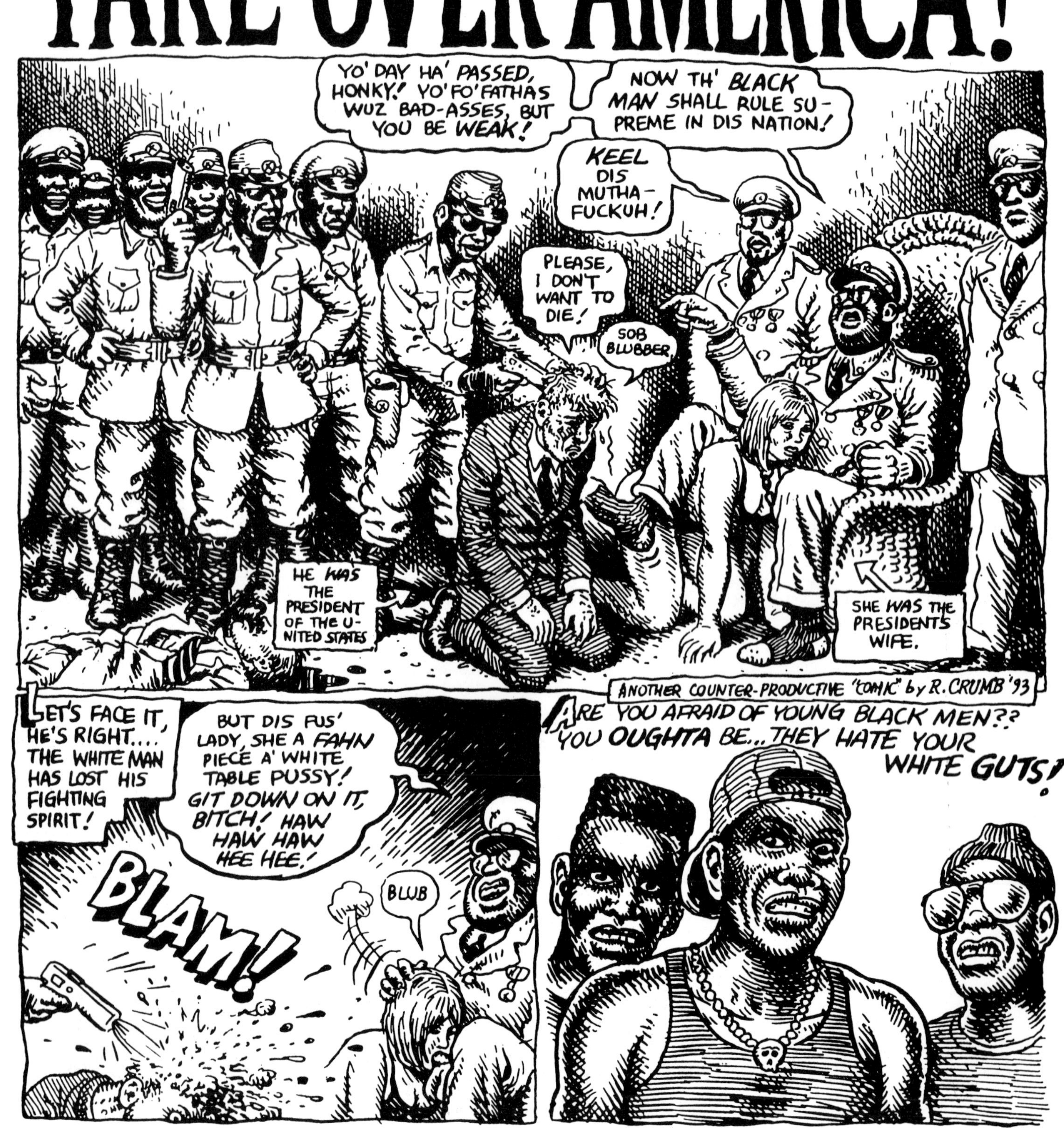

ONCE THESE YOUNG "SPEAR-CHUCKERS" GET THEIR MILITARY DISCIPLINE CHOPS TOGETHER WE'RE IN BIG TROUBLE!!
SECRET TRAINING AREA IN ABANDONED WAREHOUSE DISTRICT OF INNER CITY

IT'S GONNA BE A REAL BLOOD BATH! PLENTY OF "SHVOOGIES" WILL BE KILLED BUT THAT'LL ONLY MAKE THEM MADDER AND SMARTER...
EEEYAAAH

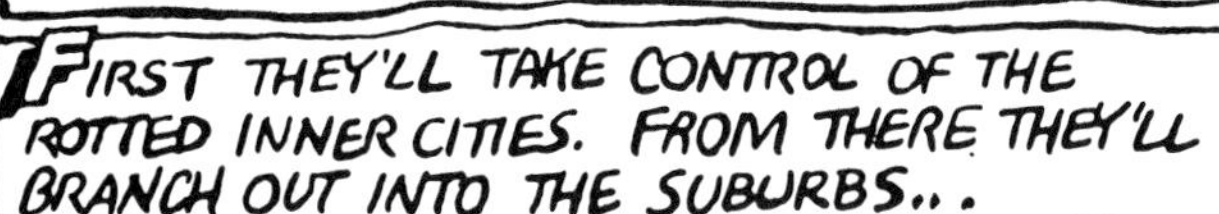
FIRST THEY'LL TAKE CONTROL OF THE ROTTED INNER CITIES. FROM THERE THEY'LL BRANCH OUT INTO THE SUBURBS...

WITH NOBODY LEFT TO STOP THEM THESE PRIMITIVE SAVAGES WILL GO ON A KILLING SPREE THE LIKES OF WHICH THIS COUNTRY'S NEVER SEEN!!
EEEK
HALT!
WE HERE TO MAKE A INSPECTION OF DIS SECTOR!
MOMMY!

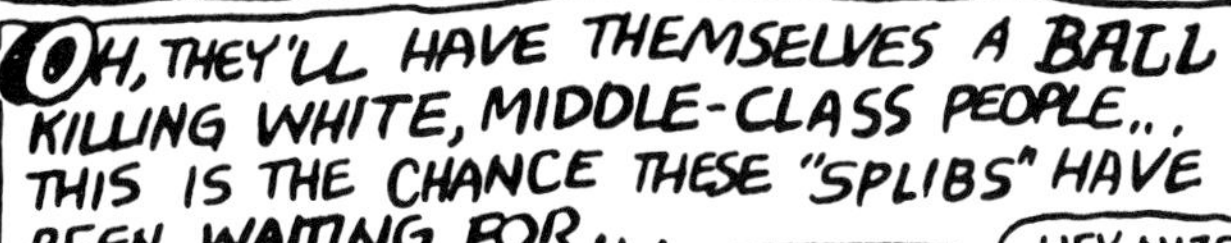
OH, THEY'LL HAVE THEMSELVES A BALL KILLING WHITE, MIDDLE-CLASS PEOPLE... THIS IS THE CHANCE THESE "SPLIBS" HAVE BEEN WAITING FOR...

WHAT'S GOING ON HERE— AWP!
FUCK YOU, RACIST MUTHER-FUCKER!
GLKH!
HEY, NIZE TITTIZ!

THEY'LL QUICKLY KILL ANY WHITE MAN WHO RESISTS THEM, AND OF COURSE, DEAR TO THE HEART OF EVERY "JIGABOO" IS THE BURNING DESIRE TO RAPE AND MUTILATE WHITE WOMEN!
HEY, HOMEY, DAS YO' THIRD WHITE BITCH TODAY... HOW 'BOUT SAVIN' ONE FO' ME NEX' TAHM!
EEEE-
LEMME SHUT DIS ONE UP FUS; DEN WE KIN DISCUSS...
CRUNCH!

SINCE "NIGS" POSSESS ONLY THE MOST RUDIMENTARY GRASP OF POLITICS, THE COUNTRY WILL BREAK DOWN INTO A PATCHWORK OF GANG TERRITORIES, EACH RUN BY ITS OWN STRONGMAN OR CHIEFTAIN,
SKULLS OF POWERFUL ENEMIES
YOUR DAUGHTER
—AN' NOTHING CAN STOP ME, 'CAUSE AHM THE DUKE OF EARL
HAIL TO D' CHIEF! HAIL TO D'CHIEF!
THERE WILL BE CONTINUOUS CONFLICT BETWEEN THESE PETTY WARLORDS, A CONDITION LIKE THAT OF MEDIEVAL EUROPE. THE "COONS" WILL ENJOY THIS STATE OF AFFAIRS, AS THEY STILL HAVE NOT EVOLVED BEYOND A GREAT LOVE OF VIOLENCE AND MAYHEM.!
WAR
YO!
ESPECIALLY GRATIFYING TO THE "SPOOKS" WILL BE THE TURNABOUT SITUATION IN WHICH THE WHITE RACE WILL NOW BE THE SLAVES, TOILING IN THE FIELDS AND PERFORMING ALL HARD MANUAL LABOR, OF WHICH THERE'LL BE PLENTY, AS MODERN COMPLEX TECHNOLOGIES RAPIDLY DISAPPEAR.
MAN, DAS PERTY!
WHITE FOLKS SHO' IS MUSICAL PEOPLE!
OH I'VE GOT THOSE MEAN OLD DIRTY LOW DOWN COTTON FIELD BLUES
OH LORD DELIVER US FROM THIS HARSH FATE!
AND DON'T KID YOURSELVES, THEY'LL SHOW US NO MERCY! THEY'LL RELISH EVERY OPPORTUNITY TO TREAT US WITH THE UTMOST SEVERITY. THE SLIGHTEST INFRACTION WILL BE MET WITH CRUEL PUNISHMENT! THINK I'M KIDDING? YOU JUST WAIT!!
DAS 49... 51 MO' TO GO...
MHM!
LAZY HONKIES NEVVA COULD DO NO WORK!
WHEN AH SAY "IN DAT FIEL' BY SEB'M AY-EM," AH DON'MEAN SEB'M OH-FAHV AY-EM!! YOU GOT DAT??
UNH
WHACK
AAAH!

'COURSE, THE WELL-KEPT SECRET THAT EVERYBODY KNOWS IS THAT THE "SHVARTZAS" ARE 'WAY TOO STOOPID TO PULL IT OFF WITHOUT THE BEHIND-THE-SCENES MANIPULATIONS OF THOSE CLEVER FELLOWS WITH THE HOOK NOSES — YOU KNOW WHO I'M TALKING ABOUT! WHILE THE BLACKS AND WHITES ARE BATTLING IT OUT AMONG THEMSELVES THE WEALTH OF THE NATION WILL BE QUIETLY SIPHONED OFF BY THE REAL RULERS ———
WHEN THE GODDAMN JEWS TAKE OVER AMERICA!
HERE'S TEN BUCKS, YA PATHETIC GOY SLOBS! GO BUY YASELVES SOME BALONEY AN' A BIG JAR A' MAYONNAISE! HAW HAW HAW!
OH MORRY, YOU'RE TOO GENEROUS WITH YOUR MONEY!
SAVE IT FOR ME, DAHLING! HA HA HA HA
RIGHT THIS WAY, SIR, MADAME!
OH THANK YOU, SIR...
THANK YOU!
ONCE PROUD WORKING MAN
BEAUTIFUL "SHIKSA"
PLEASE HELP FAMILY
WELL, THE FACT OF THE MATTER IS, THEY ALREADY HAVE TAKEN OVER, WRECKING THE ONCE-SOLID AMERICAN ECONOMY WITH THEIR RUTHLESS FINANCIAL DOUBLE-DEALINGS. OH, THEY'RE CLEVER, THESE HEBES, THEY JUST DON'T HAVE ANY MORAL CONSCIENCE!
YOUR COFFEE, MR. BLOATSTEIN...
INNOCENT CHRISTIAN SCHOOLGIRL LOOK
YEAH, THAT'S WHAT I SAID—WE'RE GONNA MERGE THESE THREE COMPANIES, SO WHATTA WE NEED WITH ALL THESE EXTRA PEOPLE! THEY'RE DEAD WEIGHT! DUMP 'EM! ALL 30,000 OF 'EM, YEH! YOU HEARD ME, SHMUCK!
NO WONDER EVERYBODY HATES 'EM!
AND, THESE YIDS HAVE SECURED TOTALLY INTO THEIR GREASY HANDS OWNERSHIP OF THE MOST POWERFUL FORCE OF MIND CONTROL IN THE MODERN WORLD — THE MASS MEDIA!
IRVING, BUBELA! HAVE WE GOT A TERRIFIC CONCEPT FA YOU! A PRIME-TIME SIT-COM THAT MAKES FUN A' TH' U.S. ARMY, HOW 'BOUT IT!?!
YOU'LL LOVE IT, BOYCHICK!
THAT'S FINE, BOYS... BE SURE TO MAKE ALL THE GOYISH OFFICERS A BUNCH OF STUPID CLOWNS!
HEY! THAT'LL BE EASY! HAW HAW!
MEGALITH ENTERTAINMENT GROUP
SGT. BOHUNK'S ISLAND

REAGAN, BUSH, CLINTON—THEY'RE ALL JUST PUPPETS CONTROLLED BY THIS JEWISH-OPERATED FINANCIAL AND MEDIA EMPIRE!
DONT WORRY, FOLKS...WE'LL GET THIS MESS STRAIGHTENED OUT SOME-HOW!
GOSH, I HOPE THIS ONE'S TELLING US THE TRUTH, FOR ONCE...
"BOOB TUBE," "IDIOT BOX" ETC.
THE JEW HAS NOTHING BUT UTTER CONTEMPT FOR ALL NON-JEWS, WHO ARE AUTOMATICALLY CONSIDERED OF LESSER INTELLIGENCE...
THESE GOYIM, THEY'RE SO EASY TA PUT ONE OVER ON! A LITTLE PSYCHOLOGY AN'—BOOM—THEY'RE IN TH' BAG—LIKE SO MANY SITTING DUCKS, I'M TELLIN' YA, LENNY!
THAT'S BECAUSE THEY'RE SO PATHETICALLY TRUSTING... THEY JUST DON'T KNOW FROM TRUE DEVIOUSNESS AND CUNNING! HEH HEH HEH!
HIS TWENTY-MILLION DOLLAR OSTENTATIOUS HOME IN
THEY ESPECIALLY DESPISE AND FEAR THE ANGLO-TEUTONIC PEOPLES, WHO'S MERE PHYSICAL PRESENSE MAKES THE JEW FEEL SOMEHOW...DEFECTIVE...
IT'S A BEAUTIFUL DAY, ISN'T IT, TIF?
YUP!
@#!!! HEALTHY, WELL-ADJUSTED GOYISH @#!!... MUMBLE GRUMBLE SNARL...
CO-OP
HE CREEPS ALONG THE WALL
BECAUSE OF THIS THE JEW IS OBSESSED WITH A SINISTER COMPULSION TO UNDERMINE ALL THE POSITIVE VIRTUES OF WHITE CHRISTIAN CULTURE, AND TO TURN THIS WEAKENING OF CHRISTIAN RECTITUDE TO HIS OWN ADVANTAGE!
THIS NEED FOR ORDER AND PURITANICAL SEXUAL SELF-CONTROL IS ALL PART OF A PATHOLOGICAL CONDITIONING CAUSED BY OVER-ZEALOUS TOILET TRAINING AND OTHER REPRESSIVE, AUTHORITARIAN TRADITIONS INHERENT IN NORTHERN-EUROPEAN, CHRISTIAN CIVILIZATION... IT'S ALL ALOT OF MENTAL GOBBIGE YOU NEED TO GET RID OF...
OH DOCTOR, I—I'M SO MESSED UP—I—
YOU'RE HOUR'S UP... THAT'S EIGHTY BUCKS... CASH, CHECK OR CREDIT CARD?
HE SEEKS WEALTH AND POWER SO THAT HE CAN WREAK HIS REVENGE ON THESE GENETICALLY SUPERIOR PEOPLE...
DOCTOR WEASELBERG, I—I FEEL SO-SO CLOSE TO YOU, AFTER ALL I'VE TOLD YOU... I FEEL EXPOSED... ONLY YOU KNOW THE REAL ME, I....
ALMOST LIKE A FATHER, OR A LOVER, PERHAPS...? IT'S CALLED TRANSFERENCE... PERFECTLY NORMAL, ELLEN... NEEDLESS TO SAY, THOUGH YOU'RE NOW POWERFULLY ATTRACTED TO ME, PROFESSIONAL ETHICS REQUIRE THAT WE MAINTAIN A CERTAIN DISTANCE...USUALLY...IN MOST CASES... SOMETIMES... BUT NOT ALWAYS...
I'LL TAKE THAT.
AND HE FINDS THE GREATEST THRILL OF ALL, THE ULTIMATE TRIUMPH, IN DEFILING ONLY THE CHOICEST, PRISTINE, BLONDE CHRISTIAN GIRLS HE CAN "SHTUP" WITH HIS SLIMY "PUTZ"! (WELL, THE SECOND BIGGEST THRILL, ANYWAY—AFTER PILING UP MILLIONS OF $$$$)
OH BUT IN MY SUBCONSCIOUS I'M JUST A NIGGER WHORE—AN ANIMAL! GO AHEAD, DO YOUR WORST! AHNN... NYAGH
WELL, ALL RIGHT, ELLEN... I, TOO, MUST ADMIT TO THESE ANIMAL URGES...
IYIYI! THIS PERFECT SHIKSA IS GIVING HERSELF TO ME—TO ME! A VILE LOATHSOME JEW!! HYAAHN...
PANT
WHEEZE
GHASP

THEN YOU GOT THESE OTHER SCUMBAG ELEMENTS TRYING TO TAKE OVER THE COUNTRY... YOU GOT YOUR MAFIOSO-COSA NOSTRA GOOMBAH-GREASEBALL CRIME SYNDICATE MUSCLING AND TERRORIZING THEIR WAY TO THE TOP...
LISTEN, MR. BIG SHOT SENATOR, I THOUGHT I TOL' YOU TA SHITCAN THIS PAYOLA INVESTIGATION THING... YOU TRYIN' A' MAKE ME LOOK LIKE AN ASSHOLE, OR WHAT?!?
THEY'VE ALL "MADE THEIR BONES"
THESE THINGS TAKE TIME, PAULIE! COUPLE MORE MONTHS, I'LL GET IT UNDER CONTROL... THAT'S A PROMISE!
JAB
YOU GOT YOUR LATINOS AND YOUR ASIANS MOVING IN HERE BY THE MILLIONS AND MULTIPLYING SO FAST THEY'LL TAKE OVER THE COUNTRY BY THE SHEER WEIGHT OF THEIR NUMBERS! LIFE WON'T BE WORTH LIVING IN A LAND OVERCROWDED WITH HORDES OF PEOPLE WHO NEVER HAD A GRASP OF THE CONCEPT OF INDIVIDUAL FREEDOM TO BEGIN WITH!
AY CARUMBA
IS AMERICA NO LONGER TO BE A NATION OPERATING ON THE PRINCIPLES LAID DOWN BY THE WHITE ANGLO-SAXON CHRISTIANS WHO FOUNDED A GREAT CIVILIZATION HERE IN THE NEW WORLD??
THIS TIME, BY GOD, WE'LL MAKE IT WORK!!
"THE RIGHT TO KEEP AND BEAR ARMS..."
SOUNDS REASONABLE ENOUGH...
PUT IT IN...
IF THE WHOLE THING'S GONNA GO DOWN THE TOILET ANYWAY, THERE'S ONE THING, ONE POWER THAT'S STILL IN THE HANDS OF THE WHITE MAN—ONE CHOICE, ONE GREAT ACT OF WILL WE CAN STILL MAKE...
OH NO! NOT THAT! SURELY NOT THAT!
YES—THAT!
AS WE BUILT THE GREATEST CIVILIZATION EVER SEEN ON THIS EARTH, SO IT IS OUR RIGHT, PERHAPS OUR DESTINY, TO TAKE IT AWAY, TO DESTROY IT UTTERLY.... STEEL YOURSELVES, WHITE MEN, FOR THIS GREAT MISSION THAT IS NOW AT HAND!
WITH FAITH, HOPE, AND LOVE, WE GIVE TO THIS NATION AND THE WORLD, THE FULFILLMENT OF THE HOLY BOOK OF REVELATIONS...
THE APOCALYPSE!!
THE BIG BOY
OUR DEAR LORD JESUS CHRIST AWAITS US WITH OPEN ARMS ON THE OTHER SIDE. AMEN!

IT'S REALLY
TOOBAD
YES, IT'S REALLY TOOBAD, THE WAY THINGS WORKED OUT... IT COULD'VE BEEN SO BEAUTIFUL, BUT... AH WELL, READ IT AND WEEP...
SHOE CAFETERIA

WHAT'S THIS MODERN WORLD COMING TO?

IT'S NOT MUCH FUN BUT IT'S EFFICIENT...

IT'S NEUROTIC IS WHAT IT IS!!

BUT WHY DWELL ON IT! LET'S HAVE A PARTY!

LITTLE BROTHER'S NOT AS CUTE AS WAS HOPED, BUT NEVERMIND...

IS THE LUMPEN PROLETERIAT A LOST CAUSE?

ONLY TIME WILL TELL...

PERHAPS.... PERHAPS.... THESE ARE THE LAST DAYS!
GGULP!

WHO CARES? WHY GO ON LIVING?

"THAT'S RIGHT... WHY BOTHER?" SAYS RUTH SCHWARTZ TO HERSELF.

HERE COMES THE BUS...

THERE'S NO ESCAPE...
WAH!

THE WORKADAY WORLD MUST GO ON....
HOME
OFFICE
FACTORY
AJAX PRODUCTS INC.

BE IT CAPITALISM...
JUST SIGN HERE!

OR COMMUNISM...

...OR ANY SYSTEM OR NON-SYSTEM...
IS DIS A SYSTEM?

I DUNNO... IS IT? MAYBE IT IS A SYSTEM... THEN AGAIN MAYBE NOT... I DUNNO...
FOOD

AND IN THE NEWS TODAY, THE WORLD SITUATION LOOKS PRETTY BAD, FOLKS...

SEE IF THERE'S ANYTHING GOOD ON...
WHY BOTHER!

THINK THERE'S ANY HOPE?
BELIEVE ME... DESPAIR IS THE ONLY WAY OUT!!
QUIVER QUIVER

OH DEAR GOD...

HERB HOUSETOP DOES NOT BELIEVE IN GOD...
THERE IS NO GOD!!

MILLIONS OF DESPERATE CONSUMERS ROAM THE STREETS OF LARGE CITIES, TRYING TO FIND SOME UNKNOWN EGO FULFILLMENT...

AND THERE'S SO MANY OF THEM!!! THEY CHOKE THE THOROFARES... THEY COVER THE LAND LIKE LOCUSTS...

THEY SEEK SECURITY IN MOVEMENTS AND IN THE THRILL OF VIOLATING EACH OTHER...

WHOLE GENERATIONS DIE FOR WHAT THEY CONSIDER TO BE RIGHTEOUS CAUSES....
THEY THINK THAT SOMEHOW THIS WILL RELIEVE THEM FROM THE DRUDGERY AND BOREDOM OF EVERYDAY REALITY. THEY THINK WAR WILL SAVE THEM FROM DESPAIR! HA!!

AND STILL THE POPULATION DOUBLES AND TRIPLES UNTIL THERE IS NO LONGER SUCH A THING AS FRESH AIR...

..AND THE MORE CROWDED IT GETS, THE MORE CUT OFF THEY ARE FROM ONE ANOTHER...

REAL EXPERIENCE IS REPLACED BY FANTASY. THE INDIVIDUAL IS RENDERED HELPLESS BY IMPOSSIBLE LONGINGS...

SAINTS HAVE COME TO SHOW US "THE WAY", ONLY TO HAVE THEIR ASSES STOMPED INTO THE DIRT!!
FUCKIN' QUEER!!
BEAT TH' SHIT OUT OF 'IM!!
PEACE, MY BROTHERS!
GODDAMN WEIRDO COMMIE BEATNIK!

THE MAN IN HIS YOUTH IS PATHETICALLY HOPEFUL AND OPTIMISTIC...
RAH RAH RAH

...AS HE GROWS MORE "MATURE" HE BEGINS TO "FACE UP TO THE HARSH REALITIES" OF LIFE...

...AND ENDS UP OLD AND EMBITTERED, REGRETFUL OF SHATTERED DREAMS, FEELING CHEATED BY FATE, HIS DAYS FILLED WITH ACHES AND PAINS SO THAT HE LOOKS FORWARD TO DEATH!!

MEN HAVE BEEN ASKING WHY AND PRAYING FOR DELIVERENCE FOR 10,000 YEARS AND IN 10,000 DIFFERENT WAYS...

HE SEEMS TO BE SMART ENUFF TO INVENT WAYS OF DESTROYING THE PLANET BUT CAN'T FIGURE OUT HOW TO GET ALONG WITH HIS WIFE!
I'M MISERABLE!
$EMC^2=$

THE BEST ANSWER ANYBODY HAS COME UP WITH YET FOR ALL OUR PROBLEMS IS JUST TO SIT AND DO NOTHING...
END

OKAY, WE'VE HAD OUR FUN, WALLOWED IN OUR PERVERSITY... NOW IT'S TIME TO SHAKE OUR FIST AT THE INJUSTICES OF THE SYSTEM... TIME TO VENT OUR RAGE AT THE RICH AND POWERFUL, WHO FORCE US ALL TO LIVE IN THIS POLLUTED CONCRETE JUNGLE... TIME FOR OUR SERIOUS POLITICAL PROTEST FEATURE...
POINT THE FINGER
©1989 BY R. CRUMB

HELLO... IN THIS ISSUE OF HUP WE'RE GOING TO POINT THAT MERCILESS FINGER AT ONE OF THE MORE VISIBLE OF THE BIG-TIME PREDATORS WHO FEED ON THIS SOCIETY...
THIS CRASS AND VENAL CHARACTER IS SO ARROGANT HE SEEKS OUT THE SPOTLIGHT AND PUBLICLY BOASTS OF HIS DISGUSTING EXPLOITS!

HE DIDN'T ASK TO MAKE AN APPEARANCE IN HUP BUT WE'VE BROUGHT HIM HERE ANYWAY AS A SPECIAL SURPRISE FOR YOU, OUR READERS... SO, LET'S GET HIM OUT HERE! LADIES AND GENTLEMEN, ONE OF THE MOST EVIL MEN ALIVE, REAL ESTATE TYCOON DONALD TRUMP!

HEY, DON— UGH! YOU'RE SO HATEFUL I CAN'T EVEN LOOK AT YOU!!
NOW BE A GOOD BOY, DONALD!
LISTEN, WHAT'S THIS ALL ABOUT!?!

HEY, I WANT TO EXPRESS MY APPRECIATION TO TRACY AND MARNY HERE, TWO VERY TOUGH LADIES, WHO WORMED THEIR WAY INTO THE TRUMP ORGANIZATION AND SPIRITED OUR GUEST OUTA THERE BY BODILY FORCE!!
IT WAS FUN!
PIECE A' CAKE, ROB!
WHAT DO YOU WANT WITH ME? IS THIS SUPPOSED TO BE SOME KIND OF A JOKE??

I'LL ASK TH' QUESTIONS, YOU SLIME-BALL! THIS'S MY SHOW, R.CRUMB'S "POINT THE FINGER"!!
R. CRUMB?? WHO'S HE?? NEVER HEARD OF 'IM! YOU SOME KINDA SELF-STYLED TERRORIST OR WHAT?
EASY THERE, BIG FELLA!

SIT DOWN, DONALD!
YOU PEOPLE ARE IN BIG TROUBLE!
AHEM! SINGLEHANDEDLY MAKING THE WORLD AN UGLIER PLACE TO LIVE IN IS ONE OF TRUMP'S LESSER CRIMES AGAINST HUMANITY!
THE EVICTION NOTICES WHICH HAVE BEEN SERVED TO LINE THIS MAN'S POCKETS WOULD STRETCH FROM HERE TO THE MOON!
HE NEEDS TO BE PUNISHED!
I GAVE MILLIONS LAST YEAR TO AID THE HOME-LESS!
...THE-THE MULTITUDES OF BROKEN HEARTS AS TRUMP'S GOONS FORCE THEM AND THEIR FUR-NITURE OUT ON THE STREET!!
AW, GET REAL!!
LET'S STICK IT TO HIM THE WAY HE'S STUCK IT TO NEW YORK! I HAVE THIS BIG STRAP-ON DILDO—I'D BE HAPPY TO RAM IT UP HIS POOP-SHUTE!
AH HA HA HA HA
LET'S NOT BE CRUDE...
ULP!
—AND WHY? WHY DOES HE KEEP DOING IT? HE'S ALREADY GOT BILLIONS— IT'S "THE ART OF THE DEAL" THAT KEEPS HIM GOING! OUTSMART THE OTHER SHARKS AND A FEW PUBLIC AGENCIES AND SHOVEL ANOTHER TON OF MONEY INTO THE TRUMP VAULTS...
THIS IS SHEER DEMAGOGUERY! NO, Y'KNOW WHAT THIS IS? IT'S A WASTE OF MY TIME! IF THERE'S ONE THING I—
GRRRR
HISSS
SHUT UP!! I'M GONNA—
NO, YOU SHUT UP!! I HOPE YOU CAN AFFORD A GOOD LAWYER, PAL! YOU'RE GONNA NEED ONE!!
WHOAH!
—BECAUSE YOU ARE WASTING MY TIME!! BIG MISTAKE, PAL!
WRONG MOVE!!
SETTLE DOWN, GUY!
BE COOL, DONALD!
HOLD 'IM! HOLD 'IM! DONT LET 'IM GET ME!!
FUCKIN' YO-YO!!

YOU'RE A STUPID, STUPID GUY... YOU'VE PUT YOUR ASS IN A NO-WIN POSITION, FUCK-WAD! YOUR RINKY-DINK LITTLE CAREER IS DOWN TH' TOILET AS OF NOW! I'LL SEE TA THAT!!
C'MON, BACK OFF, DONALD!
STOP SCARING ROBBIE- HE'S VERY SENSITIVE! NOT LIKE YOU, YA BIG BULLY!
WHY DO YOU HANG OUT WITH HIM? WHAT'S IN IT FOR YOU? YOU COULD BOTH BE DOING SO MUCH BETTER! YOU'RE VERY STRIKING, OBVIOUSLY SMART WOMEN.... YOU'RE SELLING YOURSELF VERY SHORT!
CUT TH' FLATTERY, DON— WE DON'T BUY IT!!
I MEAN, LOOK AT HIM—A PICTURE OF NEGATIVITY! FILLED WITH HATE! POISONED BY JEALOUSY FOR ANYONE WHO'S SUCCESSFUL AND ATTRACTIVE TO WOMEN!
HEY, THIS'S MY—
OKAY, I'M A HUSTLER! I'M HAVING FUN DOING WHAT I DO-IF IT CAN'T BE FUN, WHAT'S THE POINT?! PEOPLE LIKE HIM CAN'T STAND TO SEE THAT! TH' POOR MISGUIDED WRETCH!
BULL-SHIT! THERE'S ALOT MORE TO IT AND YOU—
IT'S A SHAME—IT REALLY IS—YOU KNOW, I PERCEIVE YOU AS A VERY TALENTED ARTIST.... IF YOU HAD COME TO MY OFFICE AND TALKED TO ME, I COULD'VE BEEN A BIG HELP TO YOU— I'M VERY GOOD AT HELPING PEOPLE OVERCOME OBSTACLES AND PERFORM BETTER AT THEIR WORK...IT'S A REAL CHALLENGE!
BUT NO... YOU BLEW IT..
THAT'S SUCH A LOAD A'—
HE IS AWESOMELY CHARISMATIC...
I DON'T HOLD IT AGAINST PEOPLE THAT HAVE OPPOSED ME— I'M ALWAYS LOOKING FOR THE BEST TALENT WHEREVER I CAN FIND IT—BUT YOU'VE COMMITTED THE UNFORGIVEABLE SIN—
...FOR WASTING MY TIME THE PAYBACK IS A MOTHER-FUCKER!!
LISTEN, LADIES, WHY DON'T YOU COME ON OVER TO THE WINNING TEAM.... IT'S ONLY HUMAN NATURE TO WANTA GO WITH THE WINNERS..
WELL, IT AIN'T HIM!
NOW JUST A DOGGONE MINUTE HERE!
A CERTAIN BOYISH CHARM
SNICKER

HEY, TELL YA WHAT! I WANT YOU TWO TO FLY DOWN TO MAR-A-LAGO* WITH ME TONIGHT IN MY LEER JET.... IVANA AND I ARE THROWING A HUMONGOUS BANQUET IN HONOR OF SOME GOOD FRIENDS IN THE BUSINESS... GREAT MUSIC—FIVE DIFFERENT BANDS... ABSOLUTELY FABULOUS FOOD! YOU'LL RUB SHOULDERS WITH MOVIE STARS, SENATORS, FAMOUS ATHLETES...
OOH, NOW YOU'RE TALKING, DON!
BUT— BUT—
* TRUMP'S PALATIAL ESTATE IN PALM BEACH, FLORIDA
YOU'LL SEE A TRIBAL CHIEFTAIN FROM BOTSWANA CARVE EXOTIC MEATS IN TIME TO THE RHYTHM OF DRUMMERS IMPORTED FROM AFRICA JUST FOR THE OCCASION!
INCREDIBLE ACROBATS FROM ROUMANIA AND EXOTIC DANCERS FROM GOD-KNOWS-WHERE WILL PERFORM FOR US WHILE WE GRAZE...
OH WOW!
YOU'LL EACH GET A FREE MANICURE BEFORE DINING, AND EVERY GUEST WILL FIND A UNIQUE AND VALUABLE GIFT HIDDEN IN THEIR SERVING OF DESSERT! SHHH... DON'T TELL!
OH MY GOSH!
BUT—
?
—AND MY FAVORITE PART—HEH HEH—A LITTLE PLAY WE'RE PUTTING ON—A LITTLE DRAMATIZATION OF MY STRUGGLE TO GET "TELEVISION CITY" MOVING FORWARD... I'LL BE PLAYING MYSELF—DON'T LAUGH (CHUCKLE)—CULMINATING IN THE UNVEILING OF AN 800-SQUARE-FOOT ARCHITECTURAL MODEL OF OUR LATEST REVISED DESIGN FOR THE COMPLEX!
GOOD LORD! YOU'RE— YOU'RE TRIMALCHIO* FROM PETRONIUS'S "SATYRICON"!!
OOH, WO-O-OW!
—AND YOU'RE A HIGHLY LITERATE S.O.B., AREN'T CHA?!
SNEER
* VULGAR NEW-RICH CHARACTER IN THE ANCIENT ROMAN CLASSIC —STILL GREAT READING TODAY!
AFTER THE BANQUET IVANA AND I AND A FEW INTIMATE FRIENDS WILL BOARD THE YACHT FOR A LITTLE LATE-NIGHT BACCHANAL... YOU'RE BOTH WELCOME TO JOIN US... THERE'LL BE SOME EXTREMELY WELL-HEELED ELIGIBLE YOUNG GUYS ON BOARD...
—AND YOU ARE JUST THE SORT OF EXCEPTIONAL WOMEN I'D BE PROUD TO INTRODUCE TO THEM! HOW 'BOUT IT??
IT'S JUST LIKE TH' FUCKIN' ROMAN EMPIRE!
NOTHING'S CHANGED IN 2,000 YEARS...
LIGHTEN UP, ROB!
HOW CAN WE REFUSE, DONALD!?
YOU'RE RIGHT!! HA HA HA HA
HA HA HA HA HA
WILL YOU BUY US NEW PARTY DRESSES, DON?
HEY, NOTHIN' BUT THE BEST!!
HA HA HA HA
AW JEEZ—DONALD HAS JUST PULLED OFF A "HOSTILE TAKE-OVER" OF TRACY AND MARNY... BUT I CAN'T BE ANGRY AT THEM... I SHOULDA KNOWN THEY'D BE SWEPT AWAY BY TH' DAZZLING AURA OF POWER AROUND THAT JERK...
WHATAYA GONNA DO....
FREEZE!!
YOU GONNA COME ALONG QUIETLY?!?
YEAH YEAH...
911
NATURE'S WAY IS TO TAKE AWAY FROM THOSE THAT HAVE TOO MUCH AND GIVE TO THOSE THAT HAVE TOO LITTLE. MAN'S WAY, ON THE CONTRARY, IS TO TAKE AWAY FROM THOSE WHO HAVE TOO LITTLE TO GIVE MORE TO THOSE WHO ALREADY HAVE TOO MUCH.
—LAO TZU, CIRCA 500 B.C.

HOLD IT! HOLD IT!
R.! R.! C'MERE! LET'S TALK!
I LOVE TH' PUT-DOWN OF TRUMP, BUT, JEEZ— THE ENDING... LET'S ALL GO OUT AN' COMMIT SUICIDE, HOW 'BOUT IT!?
HUH? WHATAYA MEAN?
YOU'RE WAY TOO HARD ON THE READER HERE, R.! THEY NEED JUSTICE! RETRIBUTION! BLOOD!!
WELL, I THOUGHT IT WAS KINDA, Y'KNOW, IRONIC— TH' QUOTE FROM LAO TZU AND— LIKE THAT....
I COMPLETELY DISAGREE WITH YER PAL LAO TZU!
OH, REALLY??
MAN IS NO DIFFERENT FROM NATURE—IT'S ALL A BIG DOG-EAT-DOG KINDA THING!!
BUT STAN, ALL THAT WORK... I WON'T CHANGE IT, AND THAT'S—
SO AWRIGHT, WE'LL JUST TACK ON A SECOND ENDING, OKAY? TAKE IT FROM WHERE TRUMP'S TELLING THE GIRLS ABOUT THE BANQUET——
New Ending
SOUNDS FRIGHTFULLY BORING TO ME, DON...
AFTER THE BANQUET IVANA AND I AND A FEW INTIMATE FRIENDS WILL BOARD THE YACHT FOR A LITTLE LATE-NIGHT BACCHANAL... YOU'RE BOTH WELCOME TO JOIN US... THERE'LL BE SOME EXTREMELY WELL-HEELED YOUNG GUYS ON BOARD...
THINK IT'S TIME NOW, ROB...
YES, PERHAPS IT IS... WE'VE HEARD ENOUGH...
SMALL HEAD, BIG BODY
TAKE HIM AWAY!
RIGHT THIS WAY, DUDE...
I'M A HARSH TASK MASTER...
HEY WHATAYA— WHAT'RE YOU DOING?! WHERE'RE YOU TAKING ME??
SHHH!
LET THIS BE A LESSON AND A WARNING TO ALL THE WOULD-BE TRUMPS OUT THERE...
OH HUSH!
NO!! HELP!! POLICE!! OH PLEASE!! I'VE GOT A FAMILY— I WANT TO LIVE!!
BIG BABY!

NO-O-O-O-O
LET GO, DON! STOP STRUGGLING!
NYA HA HA... HEY... "IF IT CAN'T BE FUN, WHAT'S THE POINT"?> HARHAR...
SHOW SOME GUTS!
UPSY DAISY!
FLUSH
GURGLE
BLUB BLARBLE GLURBLE
IF ANYBODY DESERVES A "SWIRLY" IT'S "AMERICA'S HOTTEST YOUNG BILLIONAIRE"* PHHAW HAW!!
NICE WORK, LADIES!
*BLURB ON BACK OF TRUMP'S BEST-SELLING AUTO-BIOG!
...AND ISN'T THIS A NUTTY KINDA COUNTRY, WHERE YOU CAN DRAW ANY IRREVERENT, DEGRADING THING YOU WANT ABOUT TH' MOST POWERFUL PEOPLE AND NOBODY CARES! YOU DON'T GET JAILED, YOU'RE NOT PERSECUTED... THEY JUST ICE YOU OUT OF TH' MARKET PLACE!!
TA HA HA!
OKAY, DON, THASSIT— GET TH' HELL OUTA HERE— AN' KEEP YER NOSE CLEAN!!
NEXT TIME YOU MIGHT NOT GET OFF SO EASY!
SOB WHIMPER
IT'S NOT POWER AND WEALTH THAT WE CRAVE...
IT'S ARTISTS THAT WE LIKE!!
YAHOO!
GURLS GURLS I LOVE 'EM I LOVE 'EM!
AH! AWH!
OVER HERE, ROB!!
OH YOU'RE SO NASTY— GLMP!!
PLORP
GOODYEAR
OH I WISH I COULD DRAW BETTER!
NOW THAT'S MORE LIKE IT, R.!
I LOVE IT, TOO, STAN, BUT TH' FIRST ENDING WAS MORE REALISTIC, HATE T' TELL YUH!
THE END AWREADY

The Ever Popular
MR. NATURAL
GETS ON HIS HIGH HORSE

AMERICANS ARE SOFT!!
ULP!

LOOK AT YOU!! ALL DAY LONG YOU SIT ON YOUR ASS!! YOU'RE WELL ON YOUR WAY TO A BAD HEART, MY SON!!
CHOKE!

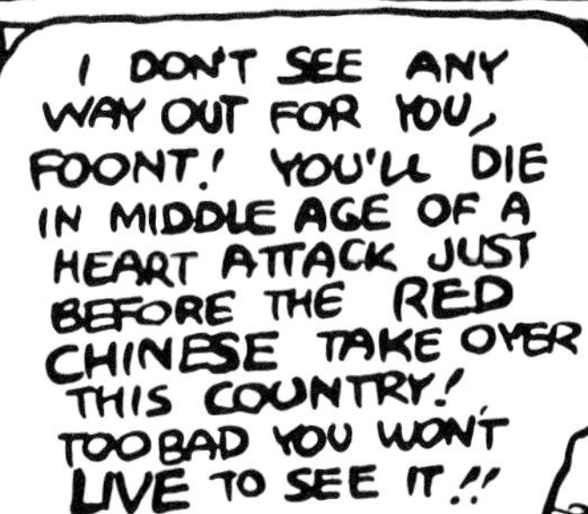
I DON'T SEE ANY WAY OUT FOR YOU, FOONT! YOU'LL DIE IN MIDDLE AGE OF A HEART ATTACK JUST BEFORE THE RED CHINESE TAKE OVER THIS COUNTRY! TOO BAD YOU WON'T LIVE TO SEE IT!!

WHO CARES?!
INCREDIBLE!

FOONT, YOU'RE USELESS!! GOOD BYE!!
HE'S RIGHT
SLAM

OH WELL... WHERE WAS I?
GURLS

A SHORT HISTORY OF AMERICA~~
1.
2.
3.

4.
5.
RAILROAD
6.
RAILROAD

7.
EL ROPO
OSWALD'S
REFRESHMENTS
CIRCUS
OSWALD'S
HOT DOGS
SANDWICH
8.
MYERS DRUGS
Myer's DRUG STORE
OSWALD'S LUNCH
CANDY & MAGAZINES
DRINK Coca-Cola
ICE COLD SODAS
TOBACCO CANDY MAGAZINES
OSWALD'S LUNCH
STOP
9.
STOP

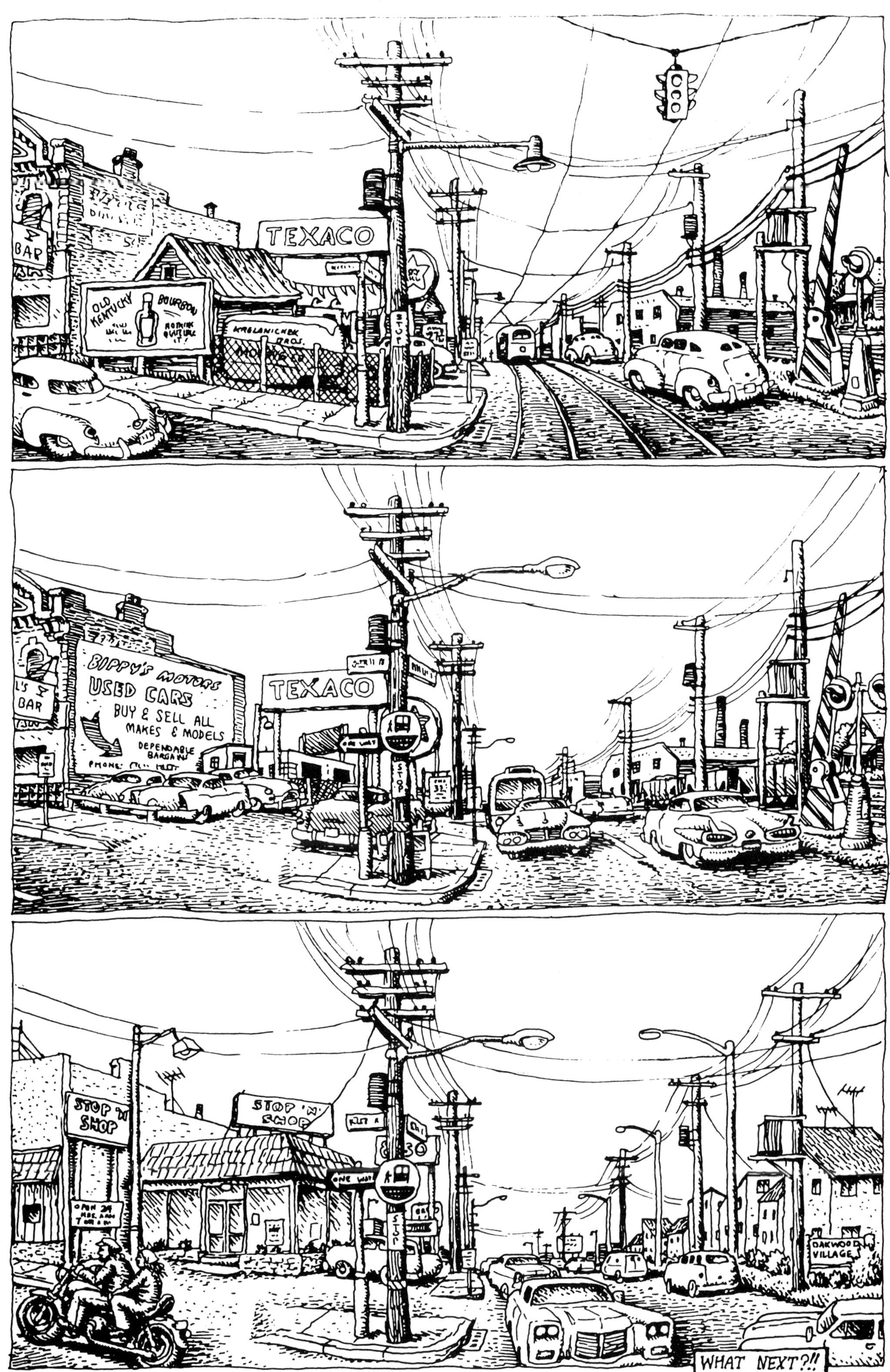
TEXACO
BAR
OLD KENTUCKY BOURBON
STOP
BIPPY'S MOTORS
USED CARS
BUY & SELL ALL
MAKES & MODELS
DEPENDABLE BARGAINS
BAR
TEXACO
ONE WAY
STOP
STOP 'N SHOP
STOP 'N SHOP
ONE WAY
STOP
OAKWOOD VILLAGE
WHAT NEXT?!!

EPILOGUE:

R. CRUMB, 1988